Chronicles

of

Donald J. Trump
An American Dilemma

GOTHIC IN POLITICS: RELIGION, THEORY AND PRACTICES.

ROBERT OSENENKO, ED.D.

Donald J. Trump An American Dilemma

Acknowledgments

This book is from new archives just released to the public and institutional reference libraries. It would not have been possible to complete such an account without researchers and investigators' hard work. Thank you for your contribution.

Library of Congress Certificate of Registration 25 February 2019

ISBN: 9798593203977

Osenenko, Robert

Donald J. Trump An American Dilemma

1. Nonfiction. 2. Political Science. 3. Crime. 4. Psychology of art and aesthetics. 5. Contemporary History 6. Identity (Culture).

Notice: Any similarity of opinion between this narrative and the United States government, Department of Defense, or any of its contractors is purely coincidental.

The author has asserted his right to be identified as the author of this work under the Copyright, Designs, and Patents Act of 1988.

"Nothing is easier than to denounce the evildoer; nothing is more difficult than to understand him." — **Fyodor Dostoevsky**

If you want to know who controls you, look at who you are not allowed to criticize. ---**Voltaire**

"And I relaxed. I *knew*. My destiny and his wound together. It was a sensation I'd never got before upon meeting a man. When I'd had it from women, the upshot ranged from disappointment to attempted murder. Understand me, Professor James Moriarty was a hateful man, the most hateful, *hateable*, a creature I have ever known, not excluding Sir Augustus and Kali's Kitten and the Abominable Bloody Snow-Bastard and the Reverend Henry James Prince. He was something man-shaped that had crawled out from under a rock and moved into the manor house. But, at that moment, I was *his*, and I remain his forever. If I am remembered, it will be because I knew *him*. From that day on, he was my father, my commanding officer, my heathen idol, my fortune and terror and rapture." — **Kim Newman, Professor Moriarty: The Hound of the D'Urbervilles**

TABLE OF CONTENTS

We are the hollow men

We are the stuffed men
Leaning together
Headpiece filled with straw. Alas!
Our dried voices, when
We whisper together
Are quiet and meaningless
As wind in dry grass
Or rats' feet over broken glass
In our dry cellar

Shape without form, shade without color,
Paralyzed force, gesture without motion;

Those who have crossed
With direct eyes, to death's other Kingdom
Remember us-if at all-not as lost
Violent souls, but only
As the hollow men
The stuffed men.

Eyes I dare not meet in dreams
In death's dream kingdom
These do not appear:
There, the eyes are
Sunlight on a broken column
There, is a tree swinging
And voices are
In the wind's singing
More distant and more solemn
Than a fading star. _____ Thomas Stearns Eliot's
THE HOLLOW MEN

A few words of introduction to readers about this work: America has involved itself in its own social, economic, and political experiment. Like an earthquake of significant proportion, its tremors and last breath are felt around the world. Some readers had perused *Donald J. Trump An American Dilemma: When the Stormer's Sang* the background and biographical accounts of his developmental history. To make it short, in the 1900s, the United States was invaded by the German representatives of the German Social Democratic Party by propaganda artists and foreign agents.

In the archives of the Republican Party, conservative members welcomed their outreach with open arms. Hoping to refresh their ranks while seeking opportunity in the *new* Germany of Adolph Hitler. Within ten years, a German Social Democratic Party was no longer replaced by the German Workers Party, then the aging National Socialist Party out of Bohemia. In another decade, by 1933, the National Socialist Party became the Nazi party.

The *Daily Stormers* were people from Germany's rural areas who believed in folklore, ritual, and superstition. The National Socialist Party was headed by professors and the German elite, some of which came from the previous expansionist German Empire's imperialist regime. The gothic past in the Nazi regime has been regenerating. Below a thin veneer, the United States' moral decadence known for has contributed to the absence of moral restraint. This has led to the regeneration of Republicans. Seeking to find their future in Russia at the expense of global security. This headline served as a warning on what was coming. Reported in the Huffington Post late on 9 September 2016, "Dec. 10, 2015, front page of the Philadelphia Daily News, which ran with the headline "The New Furor." At the time, Trump had just proposed a "complete shutdown of Muslims entering the United States."

Ultimately there was a small civil war and sabotage, espionage, and murders. The general purpose that the Weimar used to confront the United States was to push a decision about whether to include the National Socialist (Nazi) way of life in American society. A society that from that point would not enter the conflict with Germany. Seventy years after the war, on the Wannsee Conference's anniversary, and Bolshevism, the same decision has confronted America. Instead of Fritz Kuhn, the corrupt politician, and Rudolph Hess, the Deputy Führer who were doing deals with American Conservatives and the industrialist class thought they could control the dictator. Donald J. Trump and President Vladamir Putin are playing similar roles for the same outcomes.

Roughly the most accurate guess is that it took twenty years for the entire propaganda and psychographic assault by the Weimar against American values to climax in removing the German Social Democratic Party and start World War Two. In *The Stormer's Sang*, a comparison was drawn with a twist by matching the years 1900 to 2016, focusing on the above developments. Along with the biography of the Trump family.

This book critiques information and the societal trends contributing to understanding the current Republican Party Revolution and their corporate allies against democracy and its institutions. Conservatives have evolved into "something different" since President Richard Milhouse Nixon unrecognizable from their liberation model. Corporate greed and crime have been an identifiable feature of a new sort of extremist Conservatism that is more recognizable as violent, separated from the voters, and alien to traditional American standards. Conservatives have carved out an appealing message by raising extremists who bear similarity to totalitarians for their political use. In recent years this manipulation has been discovered by the far-right—a dispute on who can produce the actor to bring full-control, an extremist Conservative or far-right supremacist.

The American citizenry has watched various ways corporate raiders conduct their business. This was particularly true about MAGA audiences who witnessed Wall Street's big-capitalism and its corporate raiders who gutted out weak and obsolete industry. Often this led to lives, families, and small investors watching their retirement and future hopes being destroyed. The motto many people succumbed to was "only the strong survive," giving three cheers. That is, until real corporate raiders and their allies showed up on doorsteps of manufacturing plants from Maine to the West that shut down the manufacturing industry, leaving a wasteland of infrastructure, near-empty schools, then shipped their machinery to China. This allowed introspective moments in still landscapes among whites previously experienced by blacks after slavery and reconstruction, then began the retribution and deconstruction of what was taken. Only recently have Americans understood that coal and big oil's industrial age is over-dependence on the corporate structure to survive ended too.

The end of wasting the planet for patriotic men and women to be employed to support world wars came at the price of creating a world desert. The dramatic end of civilization, the end of the creation, might provide the last investment and profits for a hedge-fund. How Americans reached this point of environmental catastrophe has been like watching the end of the world in slow motion. For some, the last four years have been an ongoing circus, a lust film, all the contents of the way the drama of Sodom and Gomorrah must have gone. To commemorate this solemn moment, when the earth converts into a grand fireball after the upper atmosphere ignites all the gasses from industrial waste, it is noteworthy to recollect how this nationalism project came into existence through song, patriotic speech, and gothic mysticism.

To occupy our time before the flash-bang, we can extract a certain logic to our demise. Using the example of how civilizations die, the reader might spend time studying the scale of the aftermath of the Soviet Union collapse that was broadly publicized and celebrated in 1993. Coincidentally, its military and economic security picture plunged the people into despair just after Chernobyl on 26 April 1986. The two events are closely related because not only did it seem the world would be ending. It was an entirely Conservative project that began in President Ronald Wilson Reagan's administration. But, not in the way most people think and definitely not the way history has portrayed it. Let's delve into it from the perspective of underground details that are true.

It was a Conservative project, but it was an effort by Dr. Armand Hammer as Vladamir Lenin's voice. Over the years, Hammer established close ties to the Soviet Union's allies in several decades of an exchange. This entailed investment and goods to the Soviet Union and gifts of wealth to Dr. Armand Hammer. President Reagan took full advantage of Hammer's inclination toward communism in the exchange that took place. General Secretary of the Communist Party Mikhail Sergeyevich Gorbachev, reminiscent of Vladamir Lenin, found a commonality with Dr. Armand Hammer as Vladamir Lenin's operative.

President Reagan and Gorbachev were viewed as dangerous men in their own right. Both being versed in the presence of traitors when landmark decisions were being made. The new nuclear deals proved no exception. Both seemed willing to allow Dr. Armand Hammer to make his pronouncements about jewels, classical Russian art, and Fabergé eggs he pulled from Vladamir Lenin. It whetted the appetite of surrounding criminals. It also started them on a merry goose chase to obtain more from Russia. Limited by their misunderstanding of the father-son relationship between Dr. Hammer and Vladamir Lenin, the White House's operational staff imagined how they might benefit from the nuclear negotiations at hand. In a sleazy attempt to jail Dr. Armand Hammer and push him out of the way. It did not work.

Donald J. Trump was the first to take the bait, soon followed by Paul Manafort on a voyage to Ukraine to locate "wheat fields and shimmering grain like gold." Just how much President Reagan and Gorbachev fooled the traitors we may never know. Albeit Reagan knew Hammer was taking the Party for a ride portraying Russia and its people as great wealth sources. Thus, baiting capitalists who wanted to head for the jewel mines in the Urals. Notably, that administration played a significant role in the development of Donald J. Trump, who by this time did not have to announce he was from a disgraced family having been fined by Congress for fraud and being a conman under President Dwight D. Eisenhower. General Secretary Gorbachev was not going to receive a criminal family-like Trump's as he did Dr. Armand Hammer. Instead, once examining the situation, Donald J. Trump referred him to Moscow's proper authorities, namely KGB Chief Vladimir Alexandrovich Kryuchkov.

At this time, Donald J. Trump garnered the title "the most important businessman in America." Mr. Trump understood only as much he was capable of. The entourage of his friendships with President Reagan's poor staff choices and President Nixon's operatives and dirty tricksters Paul Manafort, Roger Stone, and lawyers William P. Barr, Roy Cohn. President George H.W. Bush followed suit and continued the final aspects of the nuclear agreements. To say that both President Reagan and Bush's decisions on these nuclear pacts saved the world, they also divided the Republican Party. Significantly, both presidents' idea and approval to actively allow Eastern European émigrés with ties to Nazi collaborators to diminish the perceived Communist threat into citizenship caused problems for the United States. Though in Europe, it became a standard policy. The context of the decision reinforces the extremist position of the Republican Party that had just brought Ronald Wilson Reagan into office using President Nixon's supportive pastors, the Southern Strategy.

This problem of collaboration and integration presented itself throughout Europe in a kind of reverse. The once German citizenry that was once insiders found the tables turned, now identified as outsiders, and the right of return to their home often denied. Having experienced working with Bolsheviks to destroy legacy and governments, European governments saw an investment in hiring former Nazi Party members as officials to resist Soviet forces that threatened the geopolitical boundaries of the Heartland and Rimland both the Reich and Soviet's wanted to control. A reverse occurred again in this process. Once experienced by the Nazis in exile, the outsider identity brought them back to return as insiders of a new government under Reagan's Revolution. The Nazi right of return to former Fritz Kuhn's America was handled through a sophisticated recruitment plan ostensibly was created on the myth to locate communists in the United States. Eventually, Donald J. Trump was again at the center of conflict, urging Americans to mainstream the neo-Nazis and integrate them fully into the government.

The intellectuals closely associated with knowledge about the recruitment effort was Kerry R. Bolton. His counterpart and opposite the progressive author and researcher Russ Bellant. It also included prolific writer, advocate, and New York Publisher Harold Keith Thompson, an American Schutzstaffel (SS) Officer. Jim Marrs, author of the Fourth Reich, George Sylvester Viereck, to name just a few who became associated with the Republican Party's extreme conservative positions. This is referred to as the new Republican Conservative Revolution. Presidential Candidate Donald J. Trump continued this aspect of the President Reagan legacy and received the same support beginning with his domestic Adolph Hitler speeches and terrorist threats previously documented in *When the Stormers Sang,* my previous book. Though at an early point in President Reagan's administration, it was practical to reintegrate the Nazi's collaborators as an anti-Soviet group. They had opposition to nuclear annihilation and World War III and were not violent.

While only a few would regard these efforts as entirely negative, the Reagan Revolution was also characterized according to its undercurrent. An effort displayed in two ways President Gorbachev's dismissal and Jimmy Carter's refusal to participate in what amounted to a Soviet commercial insurgency by Dr. Armand Hammer. From Edward Jay Epstein's book on Hammer, we learned that the Ronald Reagan Presidential Foundation was not naive about Hammer and had accumulated the President's own paperwork while in office enough to bill $640,000 to Armand Hammer's estate. Subsequently, the Trump gang of dirty politics became more visible over the decades during efforts they undertook to save the Trump Organization from what first appeared as the so-called Trump Empire's self-destructiveness. A closer look reveals that the limitations of understanding by Donald J. Trump became more pronounced.

In contrast, Mr. Trump garnered from crime-related friendships the wealthy elites and their billions as the Trump Organization essentially remained a limited enterprise. The end results showed Donald J. Trump was cannibalizing his own assets through overspending and over-leveraging. This aspect of his behavior pattern coincided with the Soviet Union's overextension of the Empire. Apparently, the Trump survival logic was that if President Reagan could recruit enemy collaborators, his business could recruit the banished Soviet criminals being released from the Gulag.

I should also dispel the myth that President Vladamir Vladimirovich Putin started Russians' use of Nazis to achieve their goals. KGB Chief Yuri V. Andropov and KGB Chief Vladimir Alexandrovich Kryuchkov sought to discredit François Maurice Adrien Marie Mitterrand by using Nazi organizations to create upheaval while President Ronald Reagan was in office. On some level, since President Reagan knew of these developments, he must have known the Nazi collaborators among Eastern European émigrés could also pose a threat to the Republican Party. President Reagan's declining health may have played a role in his reluctance to admit an error that President George H.W. Bush continued.

What is not a myth is that President Putin shares a similarity to neoliberalism's goals of returning the world to the social and economic status of the 1900s to the 1920s. Taking full advantage of this state of mind during President George W. Bush and the Obama administration, Mr. Putin has interjected a cast of players of that time *vis a vis* neo-Nazi who he funds to disrupt the West has been prosperous. A lesson he may wish to give Mr. Trump is a favorite epigram he is known for "be careful what you wish for. You may not have the health to enjoy it."

There is also a misunderstanding surrounding the relationship between Donald J. Trump and President Putin. Mr. Putin entered the political sphere after Mr. Trump had already engaged himself in Eastern Europe. Mr. Trump, like Dr. Armand Hammer, had coalescing interests with the Soviets. They were already five years previous married to Ivanna of the Czech Republic, a so-called model with Soviet Secret police supervision. This also indicates that before Mr. Putin's first thought to enter politics, Donald J. Trump, Armand Hammer, and Nixon's dirty tricksters already had made contact along the same timeline the Nazi collaborators entered the United States. The cycle of history surrounding the Republican Party and Conservatives certainly fits the suspicion that since the party of Abraham Lincoln allowed Confederates into the government. Then, it stood to reason they would welcome

Eastern European émigrés from World War Two Germany's collaborators into America to fulfill similar purposes.

Over the year's fascism has changed and the methods. Nidesh Lawtoo, in his book (New) Fascism, Contagion, Community, Myth (2011, Michigan Univ. Press), details how old ideas of fascism are fashioned to become compliant to present use. Other author researchers sum this up by explaining, "History is never repeated, but it borrows, steals, echoes and commandeers the past to create a hybrid, something unique out of the ingredients of past and present." — Simon Sebag Montefiore, *The Romanovs: 1613-1918*. The point is President Reagan, and Bush had no way of knowing the present circumstances of this changed fascism that Republican Party members encouraged in Donald J. Trump's speeches and policies. It doesn't seem that Donald J. Trump aspired to be a Nazi himself, probably identifying himself closer to President Reagan. Although to satisfy the Republican Party and Conservative endorsement, he did follow the path.

Taking full advantage of these deeply flawed individuals mutated into what remained of the United States and the Soviet Empire's traitors. Since elected the Republican Party reigned in 2016, it has overturned President Reagan and Gorbachev, replacing peaceful ambitions with the imagined new Russian Empire of a Third Rome consuming the Heartland and Rimland. At the center of placing the world at risk of a global disaster, the Republican Party and conservatives have put their trust in a peaceful solution in Donald J. Trump's hands.

Throwing the world into increased nuclear rearmament on medium and long-range weaponry. Mr. Aleksandr Dugin and Andranik Migranyan, Ph.D., are advising President Vladamir Putin on these matters. Their path involves interfering in Western democratic nations specializing in financing and propagandizing fringe elements such as those identified above whose birth originated from positive intentions. They are deniers of climate change, advocate for various forms of global catastrophe, and view the Earth not what they can create but a fictitious vision of destroying it.

Civil society is changing its view of the ordinary. It's no secret that I spent a good part of my life analyzing different social groups. This corresponded with the positions held in the government. From this was learned a great deal about the social and psychological aspects of deviant people and groups. One of the most useful military skills is to remove smoke screens that people put up to disguise their actions. While also revealing how the White House structurally uses its philosophy of leadership.

This book is a call to act on seven critical points that require improvement to see if the United States is evolving toward a similar government created by industrialists of the 1920s and the 1930s, an era of American "strong man theory," robber barons, and National Socialism. Not always from traditional scholarly sources, but also inquiring of fascists. It is interesting to know what it is in a society that kept populist figures in office. These studies were usually conducted on nationals outside the United States. Some would say these places were far from us and distant. The challenge presented here is whether the United States has learned the lessons it taught other societies. The 45th President is infatuated by dictator stories of the Third Reich. So, this book creates something he may like—a point-blank review of his past and future from a historical perspective.

Democratic forms of government like Germany were dissolved because they were weakened after 14 years, then defeated by the populist movement and the National Socialist/German Workers Party. It is unheard of that a long-standing intact democracy with domestic peace would be unable to fend off an extremist movement after 70 years of its arrival in the United States. Still, it does show how such extremists can harden the resolve of a portion of Americans to become outlaws. Can it be that simple to believe that a corrupt thinking leader who lies repeatedly causes a people of 300 million to become dishonest and untruthful? The new conservative vision of community life.

Or is the truth more complex so that the real problem is the structures that make up a society is too unfair and unbalanced that its policing of justice is unequal? If so, that involves not a person but a party of strong-willed partisans and, in this situation, hardened supremacists. A direct line can be drawn between the extreme Conservatism of the early Third Reich to American politics. What is yet to be shown is whether their similarity is deep enough to breed results like the 20th Century. Previously Donald J. Trump was the prominent focus in his involvement with white supremacists. Later by choice, it was as simple as having found the purpose for living, having friends, and belonging to something meaningful. Mr. Trump seemed to become entangled in his popularity and enthusiasm not only to prove he had supporters but be liked for destroying the Republic. Beginning with a series of performances, he portrayed past populists' personalities by abusing his supporters at racial rallies throughout the United States. Sleepwalking about killing someone on 5th Avenue he said, "This is crazy." Of course, it was one of his rare lucid moments that became less frequent in the future.

Previously it was learned that Trump's genealogy has always lived off the federal financial institutions. His education and intelligence, according to his vocabulary, is from 5 to 8th grade. Given this lack of qualification, his appeal to conservatives has been more like a first date. There has been a lack of conscience among conservative institutions indicating they would like to participate in the destruction of democracy. Expanding on the Stormers Sang theme, this book is a work that focuses on the broader subject of the country falling into a lull of complacency. This book opens the door to an entirely different dimension of existence most Americans only distantly recognize. It is the abrupt and subtle world of the underground replete with characters, power struggles, and crimes. Seven chapters serve as an introduction to the individual and accrued National Socialist tactics of extreme conservatives to achieve the Trump Presidency using it for its own purpose. There are minimal differences between those who supported Trump and the criminal underworld's involvement. Readers should be aware that 2020 marked the extremely important alt-right and neo-Nazi anniversaries. For them, the Wannsee Conference and Bolshevism celebration are a once-in-a-lifetime opportunity gratuitously provided by the Trump Presidency both in theatrics and actuality in wars against humanity.

Donald J. Trump's dream is not to exert power over the masses for the ideals of National Socialism nor any other cause. He seemed to only want to frighten people, at least initially. Not to become repentant for the deaths and heartache he has caused. His need is simple to figure out. Since he became President, Mr. Trump is singular in purpose. To be a satisfied man and leave office content, he would like to sustain his privilege, leave more materially complete than when he arrived, and be appreciated by those who support him. The narrative Mr. Trump has created for his family will become problematic. Despite murders and evidence of the infiltration of criminal interests into government appointments, he argues the United States has still not experienced political assassinations, terrorist-style attacks on white people, or intimidation. Even in the disadvantaged economic situation, he caused immediate tax relief to economic favorites. The Republican Party and Conservatives allege a "substantial sanity of the social fabric" is still intact.

To be a satisfied man and leave office content, he would like to sustain his privilege, leave more materially complete than when he arrived, and be appreciated by those who support him. In the process, if the entire world collapses and goes to pot, should all the globe go up in a mushroom cloud, all that is for naught so long as he can sit in the comfort that he fooled them all and lived to talk about it surrounded by his Wall Street friends. It's an easy equation. The simple reality is the system is structured to allow it. Most everyone has heard of elite immunity, privilege, the compulsion to be content by Western wealth, and mysticism in place of sincerity. From the looks of things, although people may hate this analysis, Donald J. Trump may get what he wants.

The uncanny is the psychological experience of something as strangely familiar, rather than simply mysterious. It may describe incidents where a familiar thing or event is encountered in an unsettling, eerie, or taboo context. ---derived from Sigmund Freud, MD 1919, *Das Unheimliche*

"The uncanny is a crisis of the proper: it entails a critical disturbance of what is proper (from the Latin proprium, 'own'), a disturbance of the very idea of personal or private property including the properness of proper names, one's so-called 'own' name, but also the proper names of others, of places, institutions and events. It is a crisis of the natural, touching upon everything that one might have thought was 'part of nature': one's own nature, human nature, the nature of reality and the world." ----- **Nicholas Royle,** ***The Uncanny***

1. Seven Essays on Democracy's Cynical Control

---

*"**Y**ou don't fight America…You get America's Democratic and Republican parties to fight each other… and destroy each other. Worst case scenario…the enemy can slip thru the back door while they fight like third graders. ~~High Commander Mustafa"* ----James Morris Robinson, Accelerant…The Sixth Extinction

In the United States' interior, death holds a grip on the psyche during a civil and cultural war by trying to destroy itself. Among our highest accomplishments is a compelling and intriguing story of how democracy declined from its initial stardom of just-and-noble ideals. Even for a weakened politic, one of the most disgraceful times is Democratic Party leaders' refusal to demand Congress reverse the long-standing policy of not changing the order rules. Right from the beginning of the President Trump administration, Congress could have added an enforcement procedure to the rules, and it would not require one vote from the opposition. To keep the laws allowing white-collar prosecution, a previous problematic issue it wasn't. How and why certain social activity types come to be constructed as "crime" is because the system of this democracy allowed it.

Congress was too involved in maintaining the status quo even though the public would say Congress is complicit in the President's corruption. Artificially the United States portrays itself as an inclusive society romancing its Civil Rights era. [1] That has had just minor success.

---

[1] *Romanticism* (Huckleberry Finn) was characterized by its emphasis on emotion and individualism and glorification of all the past and nature, preferring the medieval rather than the classical…. It also promoted the individual imagination as a critical authority allowed for freedom from traditional notions of form in art. *Realism* is intended to portray the lives of the common man, the ethical struggles, and the social issues of real-life situations. Credits: Britannica Encyclopedia, Mary Dorene Erickson The University of Montana.

This illustrates our subconscious myth about an imagined democracy is much more vulnerable to the hate and lies in the message than what we thought. For the common man, the economy is elite versus a financial system of "what's left." Just how far the culture has advanced is seen at night by people lining the streets with torches and 1920s-1930s chants in Charlottesville, Virginia 2017. Simultaneously like other political religions, the marches, racial rallies, and riots that have taken place have been mostly in every former enclave of National Socialism of this era. At present, there is little evidence in the media about the changes in society that led to the present authoritarianism. The spread of American National Socialism as an ideal American brand suggests citizens should see the critical questions illustrated below.

On a visit to France, Mr. Trump questioned why the United States fought against Nazi Germany and called the buried veterans' losers. The Atlantic Daily: Trump Calls Americans Who Died in War' Losers' 3 September 2020. It was reminiscent of a statement made by Germany's leader describing democracy as the "rule of stupidity, of mediocrity, of half-heartedness, of cowardice, of weakness, and of inadequacy." The Conservative extremist's future should be compared to the political architecture in the South and their monuments. [2]The predictable Democratic response appealed to the nation's intellect stating the cure-all is education and higher learning. Sir Isaac Berlin's presidential address to the Aristotelian Society explained democratically free implied knowledge and the exercise of reason. Berlin argued that education does not always liberate, which means that freedom does not always depend

---

[2] Political Architecture: "Firstly, architecture supports the system with a structural model which is used by the society to conceptualize the world which makes it connected with political power as said by Mitchell Kapor "Architecture is politics." Hence there is a structural relationship between the social and political sides, architecture reveals the power that is embodied in it and specifically the monumental architecture that is formed by the political powers." In "Relationship Between Architecture and Politics." 11 2018. All Answers Ltd. 11, 2019.

on expertise. [3]To be free, a person must first imagine and envision their part of it then act on these aspirations. Opponents of democracy also had their imaginations of creating a different system. One that maintains present corruption while on the exterior retains its image of justice. Let's recall what the Lincoln Project stands for.

A forgotten piece of Republican history, by the 1800s, Republicanism's gravitation to profits and strong-arm theology led to the preservation of slavery. In opposition, a group of Radicals far more progressive began running anti-racial platforms. Under the Radical Republicans' separate name, they tried to ban the Confederacy from serving in the government. This effort by Congressman Thaddeus Stevens and Senator Charles Sumner favored a bill abolishing ex-Confederates' possibility from entering the government. So-called moderate Republicans led to the bill's pocket veto; the chief action of defeat was performed by Abraham Lincoln, the centrist.

Today Republicans are behind all legislation to reduce voting participation and purging roles reflected in slave states' roots. Political positions from the 1800s related in some way to Congressman Thaddeus Stevens and Senator Charles Sumner. This division reemerged in 2016 under the coalition of "Never Trump." There is no longer a need to hold massive Klan rallies and Nazi campaigns. All of their demands are seen in indelible legislation. Inklings of an obsolete political party were on display during the President Richard Milhouse Nixon administration that led to his impeachment. Crime, strong man law and order, corruption, and foreign governments were exposed in hearings. Ultimately resulting in Impeachment and resignation.

President Ronald Reagan's dismantling of the government by replacing privatization and corporate state domination added public distrust. President George W. Bush led the country into what opponents

---

[3] Berlin, Isaiah and Henry Hardy. *From Hope and Fear Set Free*. Oxford Scholarship Online. Nov. 2003. Print ISBN-13: 9780199249893. In Sora, Alina. "Freedom a Way of Surviving in the Novel Everything Flows." *Linguistic and Literary Broad Research and Innovation*. Volume 5, Issue 2, 2016.

viewed as a seizure of power in Iraq. Instead of a war on terror success, it led to terrifying fatalities and casualties on Americans. Overseas the Russians stopped criticizing the U.S. based on rampant crime due to its efforts in 2012 to hack its own elections. [4]These events were primarily created by centrists. Arriving late, Steve Bannon repeated President Reagan.

Centrists believed that those of the upper class committed less than 2% of the crime. Edwin Sutherland, Ph.D., stated the system was created for purposeful neglect. "One of these neglected areas is the criminal behavior of business and professional men, which will be analyzed … The "robber barons" of the last half of the nineteenth Century were white-collar criminals, as practically everyone agrees… The present-day white-collar criminals, who are suave and more deceptive than the "robber barons," …and many other merchant princes and captains of finance and industry, and by a host of lesser followers. Their criminality has been demonstrated again and again in the investigations. Of land offices, railways, insurance, munitions, banking, public utilities, stock exchanges, the oil industry, real estate, reorganization committees, receiverships, bankruptcies, and politics." [5]The old adage is true, 'Written laws are like spiders' webs, and like them will only entangle and hold the poor and weak, while the rich and powerful will easily breakthrough.' In 2015 an expansion of President Reagan's graphic illustrations of apocryphal racial crimes took on another dimension during Donald J. Trump's Campaign. Fear campaigns were acknowledged as an intricate part of the 45th Presidency. [6] Margaret McAllister examined this kind of assault on memorization in her "Haunted: Exploring

---

[4] Polyakova, Alina. "How Russia Meddled in its Own Elections." *The Atlantic*. 18 Mar. 2018.

[5] Sutherland, Edwin H. "White-Collar Criminality." *American Sociological Review*. Volume 5 February, 1940 Number 1.

[6] Woodward, Bob. *Fear: Trump in the White House*. Simon & Schuster Audio; Unabridged edition (September 11, 2018). ISBN-13: 978-1508240099.

Representations of Mental Health Through the Lens of the Gothic."[7]The psychological inferences' and tone became a book entitled "Fire and Fury" by Michael Wolf. Mr. Wolf reported a parallel familiar to any psychiatric professional. The insane asylum's clinical environment with the male charge nurse as Lieutenant General Herbert McMaster. [8] Images were from inside the common sanitorium dayroom, where various asylum patients paced back and forth. Some would instantly, without any apparent reason, yell or shout out an obscenity. Others would merely stare, ignoring those likely held to the floor after the nurse gave them an injection of Thorazine.

In American politics, there was a lot of sharing and reuse of political graphics attaching destructive meanings with a psychological message. This psychographic language ranges from the most gothic and spectacular of World War Two into marketing efforts by political advertising. Those with racial, politically far from the center, graphics were similar to the snuff film under the President Trump administration addressed below. Privately this coincided with what the Nazis and other fascist works were shown on the internet that bordered on pornographic. In between this standard was the Vampire cults with swastikas, iron crosses designed to give subliminal messaging. Totally out of bounds were the abundant use of genocide, shootings, and war crimes. These graphic images relayed similar themes of the past in violent, racial language, and law-and-order campaigns suggesting the present White House occupants were manipulating the public and ginning up hate campaigns in communities.

---

[7] McAllister. Margaret and Donna Lee Brien. "Haunted: Exploring Representations of Mental Health Through the Lens of the Gothic." *Central Queensland Univ.* July 2015.

[8] Wolff, Michael. *Fire and Fury* Henry Holt and Co.; 1st Edition (January 5, 2018). ISBN-10: 1250158060.

Robert Osenenko, Ed.D.

Centrists and Their Violence

Republican and Democratic Parties in 2019 look compelled not to align themselves exclusively with the alternative-right or alternative-left but put all efforts to please centrists. This was a paradox, I will explain. This includes making no progressive or forward steps to improve the nation. Both parties sidestep the issue of system redevelopment. Those would-be building projects intended to bring to fruition what President Reagan named as "the shining city on the Hill" became imaginings of the distant past. That scene has been replaced by "Boot Hill," where they laid Peter Viereck's' Conservatism to rest. Centrists imposed on Mr. Trump the focus on emotional themes. Not one policy addressed rebuilding the aforementioned American carnage in Mr. Trump's inaugural speech. Just to do the will of Wall Street is all that is left. The secret in government is that many of the centrists hold similar positions as neo-Confederates. Thwarting substantial progress to alter their racial positions.

Instead, Mr. Trump's policies portrayed the end of civilization for white people. Donald J. Trump never seemed to be anything more than the nom de plume of foreign interests. Clues lead back to the 1950s in the investigative hearings of Congressman Nixon and Senator McCarthy. Edward Hunter gave a psychological analysis of the communist influence on young men that crushed their spirit. Making one ponder about Trump when he was carted off to military school, "I remember when I was a young man, every personnel department was looking for leadership qualities. What was sought was a man's capacity as an individual to achieve new things. Today that is not even considered by personnel departments in their employment policies. They ask, instead, if the man 'gets along' with everybody. They do not ask what his individuality is; they ask how he conforms. When we raise a young man to believe that he must get on with everyone at all costs. We have put him into a state of mind that almost guarantees, if he falls into the hands of an enemy such as the Communists, that he will react as he had been raised, to try 'to get on,' because he must not be 'antisocial." [9]

Undeniably centrists serve a practical function. They portray themselves as sound thinkers. They state the reasons to trust them are beneficial to societal stability. Centricity defines the sexual nature of the far-right and far-left into a midway use of women. It allows masculinity to invoke its sovereignty, offering people a safe refuge from traditionalism. All the oil-magnates are believed to be centrist. Still, due to their position in society, centrists' bastion was the first-place white-collar crime flourished. Many of the little revolts were caused by the living conditions imposed by centrists. America First Committee and the Know-Nothing parties were centrist and populist. National Socialists (Nazism) and the Bolsheviks (Communism) had always controlled centrists for their own motives. Extremists in the East and West could be unified under a centrist banner if such a collaborative person existed. All these thoughts had converted into Donald J. Trump's mind, led by evil conservatives.

David Adler points to centrism as a global movement. Adler strongly supports his research with useful sources of essential findings of the World Values Survey and European Values Survey. [10] In conclusion, centrists are not in favor of free and fair elections or liberal institutional structures on the political spectrum. Likely from what centrists say, they are most supportive of the authoritarian power structure. "In the United States, centrists' support for a strongman-type leader far surpasses that of the right and the left.", David Adler. [11]

Instead of stipulating the issues involved in racial theorist points of view, all Conservatives (Republican and Democrat) issued a new label to disguise their real preferences. In this political formula, "coming

---

[9] Hunter, Edward. Committee on Un-American Activities, House of Representatives, Eighty-Fifth Congress, Second Session, 13 Mar. 1958, Printed for the use of the Committee on Un-American Activities United States Government Printing Office, Washington 1958.

[10] Adler, David. "Centrists Are the Most Hostile to Democracy, Not Extremists." *The New York Times*. 23 May 2018.

[11] Ibid.

together" with progressive agendas seems to mean being appeased. The lies Conservatives tell their constituents of making progress have become the lies they convince themselves. Republicans and Democrats, under threat by violent societal upheaval, become more centrist. Here is how this psychological dynamic works, as Dr. Mehta explained.

"Converging lines of evidence support the threat-uncertainty model. Consider research led by Paul R. Nail of the University of Central Arkansas that illustrates how it operates. Across a series of three experiments, the investigators assessed participants' political orientation, presented them with a threat, and examined how they reacted to political issues post-threat. In so doing, they found that the presentation of risks made liberals significantly more conservative in their thinking. And demonstrated that political ideology is more malleable than we perhaps realize." [12]

When seeking an explanation, what makes a Conservative and centrist lean to the "alternative-right" because they tend to make friends with extremists when faced with political threats.   A percentage of liberal and left-wing parties have always joined extremist Conservatives. This explains some aspects of the 2016 election.

"As well, far-right parties can find ideological "neighbors" among traditional conservative parties who share the same concerns as the far-right. But who does not express their views in what many conservatives regard as a crude way by the far right? However, a simple emphasis upon a Fascist-conservative alliance as crucial can still not explain why former supporters of liberal and left-wing parties supported Fascism and Nazism in the 1920s and 1930s and why they support far-right parties today." [13] Conservative extremists are more inclined to commit violence, as reality shows in their resistance to weapon controls.

---

[12] Mehta, Vinita (Ph.D.) "Why Liberals and Conservatives Think so Differently." *Psychology Today*. 17 Feb. 2017.

[13] Rocchi, Tony. "The Myth of Fascism: misuse of a political construct." Author is librarian in the Business, Science and Technology Department of the Toronto Reference Library in Toronto, Ontario, Canada. This work was an unpublished paper. 09 Sept. 2019. Source: Academia.edu.

"Our focus was on fusion with Donald Trump, a non-traditional Republican Party presidential candidate who is "at least partially at odds with the [Republican] party." On various core conservative issues such as trade, military commitments, and immigration. All studies were conducted with White American or majority-white American samples of participants with a Republican affiliation. Although Trump has supporters among racial minority groups, White Americans constitute his leading group of supporters. Moreover, White Americans account for about half of all hate crimes annually conducted in the U.S. A type of behavior that comes close to the one we aimed to understand in the present research."[14]

Meet the extremists. The attraction for pre-radicalization and post-radicalization violence was the strongest for those with criminal histories included acts of violent crime (e.g., homicide, assault, forcible rape, etc.). Individuals with violent criminal records were 2.44 times more likely to engage in violent extremist acts once they had radicalized. [15] By far, right-wing extremists were more violent than their left-wing and Islamic extremists. The latter tend to be younger than typical Trump voters. Aggravated assault, physical harm to another person among youth (18-24) placed them at risk for becoming extreme.   This age group was the prime Trump family supporter in future elections because they were at the age for use as channels and conduits most susceptible to Trump's salacious family messaging. This was also true of Donald J. Trump radicalizing himself. This being the case, Ivanka

---

[14] Junst, Jonas R. and John F. Dovidio, Lotte Thomsen. "Fusion with political leaders predicts willingness to persecute immigrants and political opponents." 02 Sept. 2019. *Nature Human Behavior.*

[15] Research Brief. START. National Consortium for The Study of Terrorism and Responses to Terrorism. 2018. See Jensen, Michael A., Patrick A. James, Gary LaFree, Anita Atwell-Seate, Daniela Pisoiu, and John Stevenson. 2016. Empirical Assessment of Domestic Radicalization (EADR). Final Report. National Institute of Justice, Award Number 2012–ZA–BX–0005. National Consortium for the Study of Terrorism and Responses to Terrorism (START), College Park, MD.

Trump was used strategically during the campaign. More accurately, her dress was.

To put centrism into perspective, it is the primary stance of most social Conservatives. Centrism was the disguise of repression and was often used to appeal to socially progressive causes. Above are studies that prove this point. It was also contained in references Hitler made to The Big Lie because he was attracted to the fragmented truth hidden amidst them. There is a kernel of truth Nazi propagandist George Sylvester Viereck used to explain justice. "Ultimate truth, I take it, is a veiled Goddess, and it is given to no man to remove the last veil. I am content to wrest even the fragment of one veil from her face. Perhaps, after many men labor as I have done, the outline of her features will be at least faintly discernible." Writing to his son Peter, George Sylvester Viereck recounts what he saw in Germany, "A thundercloud appeared on William's brow. "Parliamentarism," he retorted to Peter, "is discredited everywhere." George Viereck implied Imperialism, on the other hand, is practical. Given the nature of man, he argues for a monarchy. [16]

"A king, being an individual, has a conscience. The mob has none. In a monarchy, one man is responsible. In the Parliamentary Republic, the government is so divided that finally, the responsibility falls upon none. "The term democracy is comparable to a decanter into which all sorts of wine may be poured and are poured. The beverage always contains a strong admixture of alcohol. The intoxicating quality of the stuff explains the enthusiasm of the consumers. Its excessive consumption leads to the unavoidable "katzenjammer."

"In two-thirds of Europe, democracy has ceased to function. Even in America, the grip of the central government tightens year after year. I agree with Mr. H. L. Mencken's paradox 'How can any man be a democrat who is sincerely a democrat?' Mencken's condemnation of

---

[16] Viereck, George Sylvester. *Kaiser on Trial.* The Greystone Press. Virginia. 1937.

the hypocritical ideology of western democracy, which in the main underlies the western parliamentarian, is vigorous and convincing. I am delighted with how he compares the soul of the mass to the soul of a child."

"The masses are an eternal child that never grows up, animated forever by child-like instincts. 'The mob,' as Mencken says, 'being composed mainly of men and women who have not gotten beyond the ideas and impressions of childhood, hovers in the mental age of puberty or even below it.' "The masses, like children, require education, guidance, care. Woe to them if they fall into the hands of unscrupulous seducers who exploit and misdirect their infantile instincts!"

"Inexperienced youth is fascinated by the form of democracy because it offers an ideal. This ideal is based on false premises. It assumes an aggregation of individuals described as 'the people.' Which does not exist, and, so far as experience permits us to judge, never will exist, a 'people' capable of reflection, devoid of egotism and possessing sound judgment! No such people live outside of Utopia! "The American opponent of democracy states a bitter truth in his remark when the city mob fights, it fights not for liberty but for ham and cabbage. Its first act is to destroy every form of freedom that is not directed wholly to that end."

Peter Viereck, George's son, whose name in the United States is not to be spoken, is regarded as the first Conservative who characterized it as the fight against National Socialism and totalitarianism. That is, the extreme Conservatism of his father warred against his confidence; Defense of Conservatism, according to critics, was defined not by what it wanted to preserve but what it tried to destroy. Mark Riebling, "George Orwell trenchantly expressed this idea in April 1940, in his famous passage about the wasp cut in half. Only when he tried to fly away did he grasp the dreadful thing that had happened to him. It is the same with modern man. The thing that has been cut away is his soul. In the same month, Viereck indicted totalitarianism. For its materialistic assault on all our non-economic values of the spirit. And called revolt against this assault conservatism. By 1952, this spiritual argument seemed so important to {Whittaker, RO} Chambers that he denied any other political idea that could be more basic. Man, without mysticism, is a monster. He wrote in Witness. The crisis of the Western world exists to the degree in which it is indifferent to God. All the politics of our time . . . will be the politics of this crisis."[17]

Conservative Defense of Hate Speech

Historians can point to Conservatism when there was a high potential of just one political party in the United States. This was at the end of President Dwight D. Eisenhower's unified administration. Having gotten out of the Great Depression's swamp, Conservatives had accomplished Eisenhower's social and construction goals defeating Dr. Joseph Goebbels' ideology from taking hold at home. And the flagrant, highly publicized Rudolph Hess's Campaign had primarily failed but was not eradicated. The harsh reality is that the culture of National Socialism is still prevalent in the U.S. today. Visitors can always go to places where American Nazis paraded in the streets and still find supporters.

In extreme Conservatism's attempt at self-defense after President Dwight D. Eisenhower, the following three administrations turned their policies to reflect Conservative racial theorists' graphic images and became overtly violent. Conservatives built an ideology of *racial appeals* that gained popular support mainly because it was masked by fiscal restraint hiding the vital unmet needs of citizens. In reaction, Conservatives began to say that, in fact, they could make racial appeals as freedom of speech and practice it. President Eisenhower's attack on National Socialism at home went into full swing, the first assault by American fascists who opposed Israeli and Soviet attempts to capture all

---

[17] Riebling, Mark. "Chomsky is a Conservative - CIA author confusion." Conservatism Turned Upside Down, Sam Steinhaus's articulate and timely critique of conservative reason. 16 Oct. 2009.

Nazi war criminals. One of President Eisenhower's first examples was Frederick Trump of Queens, New York.

Theatrics was elevated as never before in campaigns initiated by the Republican National Committee during the close of President Nixon's White House; Conservatives portrayed any free speech as a patriotic feature of democracy. The racial appeal is also expressed in social policy, voting rights, and in some places, police enforcement. This began the era of racist theatrics. It provided an opening for a legal defense on this principle that nothing could be said that was not free speech. [18] It was clear to historians that the request for free speech was recruitment for believers trafficking in racial theories. [19] Namely, it offered two attitudes, one in which Nazis openly recruited. Secondarily the Conservative call for more racial appeals also increased the likelihood of growing memberships of other extremist groups and militias. President Nixon's White House was the last bastion of liberalism and the previous that focused on services to the working classes and protection of primary education and the planet.

In 2014, and 2017 the free speech argument was incorporated into Conservative politics after having local and national debuts with Donald J. Trump. Mr. Trump used a platform of hate speech, as I documented in *Donald J. Trump, An American Dilemma May 30, 2019.* There was little difference in these flagrant speeches to Adolph Hitler's statements in content, tone, and meaning.[20] American campaign speech

---

[18] White, M. H. II, & Crandall, C. S. (2017). "Freedom of racist speech: Ego and expressive threats." *Journal of Personality and Social Psychology, 113*(3), 413-429..

[19] Scales-Trent, Judy. "Racial Purity Laws in the United States and Nazi Germany: The Targeting Process.", *23 Hum. Rts. Q.259* (2001). University at Buffalo School of Law Digital Commons @ University at Buffalo School of Law. *Human Rights Quarterly.* 23 (2001) 259-307 © 2001 by The Johns Hopkins University Press.

[20] de la Cruz Díaz-Valdés, Daniel. "A study of political manipulation in discourse: Comparing Hitler and Trump's speeches." Thesis. Degree in English Studies TFG Supervised by Dr. Elena Martínez Caro Universidad Complutense, Madrid. June 2017. In Osenenko, Robert (Ed.D.) Donald J. Trump An American Dilemma. *Independent Publisher and Amazon.* 01 June 2019. "Trump and Trumpism Their

coincided with the language of the dark speech campaigns of the Reichstag. It was so popular among Americans that it swelled Republican mailing lists and recruitment into the Party, laying the framework for future candidates. Even at the sacrifice of Conservative moral standards and threats to democracy, these concerns were secondary to the influx of new money and the revitalization the Party needed post-Sarah Palin. It was not a crime to offer an app to click and make tens of millions from Mr. Trump's speeches. This exhibition also brought Democrats back to the fold.

A warning from the past. Walter C. Langer, the MD author of *Hitler-the Man and Legacy*, posed a dilemma about the events that have led to the present situation. His analysis was that time could be wasted by examining the man and fanatic Adolph Hitler and his threat, but the enlightened path was to study why the people were enthralled with him. Particularly how they became insanely passionate and fanatical about a man they never knew. Despite the fact, he had so many deficits. Over 70 years later, larger segments of the population seem mystified over the apparent truth. The President, with distorted psychological and immoral views, is what extremists have been screaming for since the Civil War. Our leaders, the ones we loathe, and those terrifying the most are obviously the closest representations of who Americans are. As Donald J. Trump proved, conservative Americans were not requesting money, jobs, or better lives, but what they really wanted was death, murder, and terror.

Republican Nationalist affiliates knew full well of the criminal history. On his death bed, Frederick Trump was violated by Donald J. Trump, who attempted to steal his Will and tried to disinherit his siblings. Considered as the abuse of trust as a breach of fiduciary duty by a trustee. In charge of the nation, when the distribution of treasury assets among citizens becomes vital, the expectation is the President will redistribute funds to meet these needs.

Bond: How He Manifests Himself, "Then the Murders." ISBN-13: 978-1096064473.

With the impunity the system allowed him, Donald J. Trump had extensive contact with criminal networks. His connections went into the Federal Court system through his sister Maryanne Trump Barry. Although people may attribute William P. Barr, U.S. Attorney General, to personal attorney Roy Cohn Esq. President Reagan appointed Maryanne Trump Barry in the United States Court of Appeals for the Third Circuit, an appointee of President Bill Clinton. There was ample evidence that Mr. Trump was profiteering from the Asian drug cartels of David Bogatin. David Bogatin was a routine customer of the Trump Organization. [21] Maj. Derek Fitzpatrick explains the politics of organized crime and the use of violence:

"While some see the cartels as well-organized and extremely violent criminals out for financial gain, others see them as an armed insurgency, carving out territory for their own control… traditional insurgency theory, this motivational distinction argues that "to be classified as [insurgency], violence must be motivated by politics, not profit, as is the case with criminal behavior… the result of criminal enterprises competing with the state" (is-RO) in line with traditional insurgency theory. Yet, "their competition is not for traditional political participation within state structures. But rather to free themselves from state control so they can maximize profits from illicit economic circuits." [22]

The prediction for violence that Maj. Fitzpatrick speaks of is characteristic of political leaders most prone to commit violence. As the leader, they, if they have stature, solidify their position and justify

---

[21] Cay Johnston, David. "The Drug Trafficker Donald Trump Risked His Casino Empire to Protect." *The Daily Beast.* 16 Oct. 2016.

[22] Fitzpatrick, Derek Maj. "Greed and Grievance and Drug Cartels: Mexico's Commercial Insurgency." Master's Thesis. U.S. Army Command and General Staff College. 25 May 2017.

violence for their nefarious profits and politics. Jonas Kunst, "Fusion with Trump predicted Republican partisans' willingness to violently challenge elections and to persecute, with legal or authoritarian justifications, religious, immigrant, and political out-groups."[23] This was also a psychological process as extremism in Conservatism fomented how violence could be used to obtain seats in the Supreme Court as an avenue of influence. Samir Gandesha wrote, "Then as now, we see an undermining of liberal democracy; the part of Paul von Hindenburg, today, is played by Sen. Mitch McConnell. "Like Hitler's conservative allies," Browning argues, "McConnell and the Republicans have prided themselves on the early returns on their investment in Trump." [24]

Republican political positions uniformly disguise their alternative-right empathy by supporting immigrants' incarceration, dehumanization, and war crimes in some historical eras. [25] This cozy relationship with centrists exacted a deep moral cost on the avengers of white supremacy. As Ruth May reported, Congress was paid off, "How Putin's Oligarch's Funneled Millions into GOP Campaigns."[26] It could have been just as easy for a Congress controlled by Democrats to investigate who had received Russian Oligarch funds and why. Democrats were interested not by following the money but the publicity. Instead, Congress let it go by avoiding the reality they were likely as much of the

---

[23] Kunst, Jonas R. and John F. Dovidio, Lotte Thomsen. "Fusion with political leaders predicts willingness to persecute immigrants and political opponents." 02 Sept. 2019. *Nature Human Behavior.*

[24] Browning, Christopher. 2018. "The Suffocation of Democracy," *New York Review of Books.* In Gandesha, Samir. The Spectre of The 1930s. See also: Adorno, T.W. 1982. "Freudian Theory and the Pattern of Fascist Propaganda," *Essential Frankfurt School Reader*, Andrew Arato and Eike Gebhardt (eds.) (New York: Continuum): 118-137.

[25] Heller, Kevin and Gerry Simpson. *The Hidden Histories of War Crimes Trials.* Oxford University Press; 1 edition. Oxford University Press. 30 Dec. 2013. Also read *Oxford University Online* "Capitalism's Victor's Justice? The Hidden Stories Behind the Prosecution of Industrialists Post-WWII." by Grietje Baars.

[26] May, Ruth. "How Putin's Oligarch's Funneled Millions into GOP Campaigns." *The Dallas Morning News.* 08 May 2018.

problem as President Trump. Predictably the public doubted Congressional integrity. The fiasco followed.

• There is no longer a moderate Republican Conservative Party wing. The Tea Party has lapsed into a near-white neo-fascist one-leader authoritarian Trump party.

• Congress is corrupted, and though it has a Democratic Party majority, it has so much anxiety about halting the governmental deterioration. It is inescapably morally inept of shutting down or challenging the President. The Republican Senate is entirely like the Tea Party under the President's one-man rule.

• At least 10,000+ people have died as of 11 August 2019 from gun violence. Some of these are a direct result of ethnic, anti-Semitic violence.

• Militarily on at any rate two fronts, we know there is a looming probability of war because of all nuclear agreements' dropping. Army enlistment is down.

• Factions of the government Homeland Security, Border Patrol, and the U.S. Marines have been contaminated by President Trump's speech, direct orders, on the verge of committing an equivalent of "war crimes," "internment."

• Farmers are the first industry to realize no income will derive from their work unless it comes directly from the government. They no longer decide who to sell to. Have been made equivalent to Soviet farmers. All the money they receive comes from government sources while entirely cut out of the international agriculture markets.

• White supremacist attacks are increased, their membership nearly tripled.

• Climate change science has been revoked.

• Communities have become militarized.

• There were six iterations of policy documents issued by the DOJ beginning in 1999 concerning corporations' federal prosecution. The Supreme Court established the basis for corporate criminal liability in 1909, but 90 years elapsed before the DOJ issued specific guidance regarding corporate criminal prosecutions. In June 1999, the DOJ issued the Principles of Federal Prosecution of Business Organizations to delineate and standardize the factors to be considered by federal prosecutors when making charging decisions against corporations. Five additional policy memoranda followed this document during the next 16 years, culminating in the Yates Memorandum (See "Bibliography.")

• This type of welding to the underworld for profit has been under serious study for a decade regarding Russian-Émigré's. [27]

Conservatives considered criminality of critical importance in choosing Donald J. Trump for President. The Donald J. Trump Presidential campaigns showed Conservatives were more likely not to overlook his but facilitate it. This view was supported by media companies after four years; no expose to his life of crime was found in any integrated political news reporting, no reflection, and no background. A Donald J. Trump Presidency was a fertile ground for a terrorist because of poor vetting and lax media investigations. Who were the groups that supported the 45th Republican Presidency? This book's list reads like a who's who in an extremist culture centered on Wall Street.

Donald J. Trump did not have to resort to a life of crime. One has to give himself credit for attempting to gain entry into the mainstream business. With his inherent penchant for taking the easy path and not educating himself, his natural inclination was to seek a future along the societal fringes. His political interest and ability were that of a usual Washington insider. This attraction to political authority and injustice became political when Trump's relationships began with President Nixon's staff. Instead of vectoring away from crime, they were influenced by the combination of corruption and politics. With single-minded purposefulness, the Trump Organization shifted toward wrongdoing after Frederick Trump died. This was a natural extension of the family crimes of war profiteering from the Soviet Union's collapse. This development led to closer relationships with Wall Street and its white-

---

[27] State of New Jersey, "Executive Summary, The Tri-State Joint Soviet-Émigré Organized Crime Project, The Nature of Russian-Émigré Crime."

collar criminals. Mr. Trump was intensely driven to trick his way into politics. [28]

"Organized criminals find that to mobilize sufficient power to resist the state. They must move their organizations beyond pure criminalism with its limited appeal to most citizens and add political protest elements. In this way, they legitimize their activities in many people's eyes, not otherwise inclined to support them. But who are frustrated by the existing politico-economic system..."

By 2015 the Democratic Party split, and voters in the Midwest were divided more than ever existed. Inching further into the train of thought toward political Conservatism, Headquarter Democrats thought it a great deal to move Hillary Clinton to annul Bernie Sanders. Citizens know, an emerging enemy was found to lay the blame upon a verbal play on abandoned labor, conveniently called Deplorable. No other recent event made it clear that Democratic Headquarters defended Wall Street as entirely as President Obama. Due to the Obama Presidency, Bernie Sanders, the single-minded politician, exposed a logical fault in the Democratic approach. Mr. Sanders was the only candidate in the field that did not undermine his race. Everyone else set up their policies, like Clinton, that said they were progressive while simultaneously defending the centrist system. A system Bernie Sanders knew how to change before it transformed him by establishing a defense position using talented progressive millennial thinkers.

Labor Unions had succumbed to pressure by politicians they never cared to explain. When corporations, from Southern clothiers and mills to manufacturing in Ohio, began to open plants in China, there seemed to be no resistance to the United States Chamber of Commerce.

---

[28] Bunker, Robert et al. "Los Caballeros Templarios De Michoacán: Imagery, Symbolism, and Narratives." Los Caballeros Templarios de Michoacán: Imagery, Symbolism, and Narratives (2019). April 2019 *Small Wars Foundation*. Bethesda, Maryland.

Few if any protests were made that prevented corporations from abandoning their plants. No transition to other job-producing functions as they did on the coasts with Second World War restorations. Instead of resisting Wall Street, they succumbed. Wilhelm Reich, MD, in his book The Little Man, recommended workers create alliances in countries bypassing trade agreements entirely.

Neo-Liberation and Rise of Hate Campaigns

First, to describe the Democratic Congressional House, something must be understood about their recent past. They tried to work closely with President Barack Obama and VP Joe Biden. During this association, Obama became exposed to severe criticism, centered more around the President's appeasement demeanor. President prioritized making and keeping the peace as an appeasement to corporate interest. In 2009, a Democratic Party emerged for the first time officially without its labor support. It became observably more conservative and centrist, causing a general and free-ranging dissolution of the individual old guard and labor-based politics. Why labor? Because it is improvisational, able to quickly change to meet demand.

Lack of coordination between the administration and labor led to importing a deficient San Francisco-Oakland bridge from China, which President Obama considered a bookkeeping problem. President Obama shifted the Democratic Party to centrism and never won another Congressional election. These cold-blooded calculations impacted constituent identification with the Democratic Party. Still, the public determined his policies extended those of his predecessor, nothing creative nor individualistic. Sarah Palin called this "the elite structure." She was right.

Insisting on wealth immunity for Wall Street Banking as central to their confirmation as candidates, Democrats supported the corporate-insurgency model, which was an aggressive, legislatively seeking protection from government and society. It was a relatively straightforward avoidance of prosecution thru legislation during the President George W. Bush economic collapse. Wall Street Banking and its gambling culture needed some severe prosecutions, as Mr. Bush left office. After this Brumaire, the fog of misinformation cleared, tax breaks for the wealthy were being reinstated by the Obama Democrats. Such was the influential whites' aim when they did not see a credible, potential rivalry to their continuing dominance. The workings are insidious and cynical, the effects apparent. Eventually, 48% of Americans had their lifestyle impoverished, and retirement was depleted. This created a fertile ground for radicalization among those that were borderline loyal. Donald J. Trump and National Socialism's neo-Nazi counterpart appeared.

Now to Samir Gandesha, "Or, to put it the other way around, in colonialism, we see both the pre-and post-history of fascism. Fascism was, in other words, the logic by that Europe or North American (the Global North) inflicts upon itself the same forms of violence thitherto reserved for "barbarian" societies. Today, this manifests itself less through the deployment of tanks as it does through the use of banks." [29] So, it took shape in reality that President Obama and VP Joe Biden were rolled by the Wall Street Banks. By the time their error worked its way through the financial system, they had been out of office. Laying this on the next President basking in low unemployment, never changing the financial system, another round of a trillion+ in debt through tax breaks again under Donald J. Trump. President Trump, in gold fever, wanted a slice of the action, not reformation. So, all the ideas of appropriately modernizing the system, white-collar prosecutions, ended in a travesty. More fog was raised in hate campaigns, fear, and terror graphic social media manipulation.

The landslide of money for playing it safe converted the Democratic Party into one of cash. On the street, the cruel joke of a Congressman/woman going there with $50,000 and leaving there with millions like Republican Rep. Paul Ryan of Wisconsin, a centrist. Democrats, despite their protests, always wanted to pander and return to the

---

[29] Gandesha, Samir. The Spectre of The 1930s. See also: Adorno, T.W. 1982. "Freudian Theory and the Pattern of Fascist Propaganda," *Essential Frankfurt School Reader*, Andrew Arato and Eike Gebhardt (eds.) (New York: Continuum): 118-137.

territory they loved weeding out progressives in centrist states like Iowa. Iowa caucuses did what Democrats wanted. To be known for a white party similar to Republicans. [30]

Democrats saw the end coming to their constituency: the release of banking from responsibility versus the need for a brutal public hanging. Bernard Lawrence Madoff appeared to turn into the "symbol for justice victory" on Wall Street captured in 2009 tabloids. The doubt they induced by releasing all the financial culprits was ingenious. A final slap took place in one public hearing when Republicans asked Citibank's main perpetrators for advice on how they thought it was best to proceed. No legislation was enacted to cure the animosity people felt toward President Barack Obama. In an incomprehensible act, Mr. Obama was re-elected. With the re-election and how it went down, justice was ultimately denied. All the hate was a potent backlash in Donald J. Trump and Hillary Clinton's next election as the all too familiar plutocrat.

Still, despite the unrest surrounding Trump's candidacy, Republican presidents created a distinct similarity. In the *New York Times Magazine*, Ron Suskind observed, "Joe Biden was telling a story, a story about the President. 'I was in the Oval Office a few months after we swept into Baghdad,' he began, 'and I was telling the President of my many concerns.'. . . Bush, Biden recalled, just looked at him, unflappably sure that the United States was on the right course and that all was well. 'Mr. President,' I finally said, 'How can you be so sure when you know you don't know the facts?' Biden said that Bush stood up and put his hand on the senator's shoulder. 'My instincts,' he said. 'My instincts.'" Also stated in April 2006, "I hear the voices, and I read the front page, and I know the speculation. But I'm the decider, and I decide

---

[30] Cheney-Rice, Zak. "Bernie Sanders and the Lies We Tell White Voters." *Intelligencer*. New York: 11 Nov. 2018.

what is best." [31]This mentality was followed by President Barack Obama's "drone war" campaigns against children and mothers caught in the battle against the Saudis.

Neo-liberationists like to tell lies to themselves about President Barack Obama. The predominant story on the Congressional floor is that President Obama's White House's wholly-owned subsidiary was too black for America to tolerate. The people voted for any white. This is primarily a version of a hate campaign in reverse by black neo-colonialists who have profited from the Obama "victory" to increase domestic poverty. It is also a view that obfuscates and muddies the purpose of the Conservative goal of creating a political base of angry whites to carry the Republican Party for another generation. A dream that was so beyond criticism they would distance themselves from the President Reagan legacy of preventing World War III.

Political Religious-Activity

The Democratic Party never got the Republican theological apostasy. Christian neo-Protestants adopted the Trump family of unbelievers. Neo-Protestants, like evangelicals, share a political belief that includes millennialism, the one-thousand-year reign. They shared this belief with the National Socialists, who historically instituted their version as "positive Christianity." This theology of expanding the land to settle is also shared by Zionists and National Socialists as a practical, theoretical, military, and philosophical idea of Lebensraum (German for "living space"). The coalescing of these groups behind the common opinion of expansion for resource development connects and binds their interests. Though individually, they may seem opposed to one another in other ways, "realpolitik" makes the coalition strong.

---

[31] Marrs, Jim. *The Rise of the Fourth Reich: The Secret Societies That Threaten to Take Over America.* William Morrow Paperbacks; Reprint edition (June 23, 2009). ISBN -10: 0061245593. ISBN-13: 978-0061245596.

Dr. Michael A. Milton may diagram family history as an honest autopsy. This is a procedure familiar to character analysts, though with secular tools. Many of the conclusions would be similar to observe what intergenerational challenges face the crime individual, family, and nation.

"In Numbers, for instance, one notes that God's judgments, including "the sins of the father," are sometimes the observation of sin's multi-generational consequences in the "natural order" of life. "The sins of the father" represent an inherent divine judicial reality in Creation. In this sense, the phrase "sins of the father" is descriptive and pervasive. Pastors, as well as family counselors, will sometimes draw a "diagram" to better discern the "virus" of sinful behavior in a family. Then, through family memory that is spoken in honesty, one may see how vicious cycles of pain can infect successive generations. One generation's rebellious nature will have an invariable effect upon the following generation and even the age after that. Sin is like an infection that spreads throughout the whole body. It can spread throughout the family system. This can happen in a single-family unit, or it can occur in a larger family such as a nation." [32]

There was substantial power in the United States' moral majority movement, but it did not come from Christian salvation or Matthew 25. It came instead from racial prejudice, jealousy, rumor, and political dominion theory. This was a formula that bred conspiracy theories among Conservatism. A prevalent feature of neo-Protestantism they do

---

[32] Milton, Michael A. Ph.D. "What Are "Sins of the Father"? Understanding Generational Consequences." *James Ragsdale Chair of Missions at Erskine Theological Seminary. He is the President of Faith for Living and the D. James Kennedy Institute.* 17 Feb. 2020.

not publicize is that most Jews will perish in the war before the one-thousand-year reign starts leaving just approximately 144,000, including neo-Protestants. Who did the Republican Party adopt to carry forward Wall Street's coalition in the lead, the Christian evangelicals, neo-Nazis, and neo-Protestants? What kind of history did they know during the vetting process?

Donald J. Trump was not religious but gave to Jewish charities ostensibly for tax purposes and belonged to similar groups like Chabad, which ties to President Vladamir Putin. He was also implicated in an FBI investigation of Trump Tower involving elites and the thief in the law's notorious mobsters. The Republican Party background included a Trump legacy that began with Friedrich from Bavaria, Palatine, Germany, coincided with the historical Republican Party narrative. Despite this fact, Donald J. Trump sought to Araynize Friedrich, "Trump denied this German heritage altogether, instead claiming that his grandfather's roots lay further north, in Scandinavia. "[He] came here from Sweden as a child," Trump asserted in his co-written book The Art of the Deal." ---History.com Notably, the poisonous system Adolph Hitler warned of was slowly taking effect. Mr. Trump was creating a different identity as Aryan.

Friedrich's reputation came from what he did after elected as Justice for the Peace. He obtained the land's mineral rights beneath homes of more value using the office to officiate deeds. This permitted Friedrich Trump to officiate the acts of homes from unsuspecting buyers who bought the land's surface rights. Buying the mineral rights gave Friedrich Trump below surface rights invaluable for exploring minerals, silver, and gold. Friedrich Trump also owned the town's whorehouse and restaurant. Friedrich Trump was in a position to create split estates undermining the owner's full property rights. From these transactions, his practice was nicknamed "mining the miners." These prime business years for Friedrich Trump consisted of taking advantage of the less knowledgeable and vulnerable during the Alaskan Gold Rush and the World War One years.

His son Frederick Trump successfully built a reputation in New York as the "Henry Ford of Housing " that sounded exemplary. Until one realizes that Henry Ford was an early supporter of the Third Reich. Frederick Trump became involved in the publication of an event held by the Ku Klux Klan while supporting several Jewish philanthropy groups. His loyalty to the United States was questioned when he was deemed a war profiteer by Congress during the Dwight D. Eisenhower administration resulting in fines and a ban on acquiring government housing. His crime was swindling returnee combat veterans who sought housing and jobs near New York City. Several songs were attributed to Frederick Trump's fascism by Woody Guthrie, the famous folk singer that lived in his apartments.

Frederick Trump's son Donald J. Trump continued his parental legacy first by not going into the Army for what he was accused of as an erroneous claim derived from tight shoes. Donald J. Trump lived through the Vietnam War. He appeared to prosper and interacted with Republican Presidents and their staff from the notably impeached President Richard M. Nixon to Ronald Reagan and both George Bush presidencies. He attended White House and Republican functions and meetings and fundraisers with the crowd surrounding Dr. Armand Hammer. The latter hosted events for his United World College, a suspected school for the KGB. Donald J. Trump's behavior became public during each financial bankruptcy leaving the public to make up the difference in lost government revenue. Reverting to Friedrich and Frederick's activities, Donald J. Trump became comfortable and powerful in New York City politics. Publicly he revealed his rogue nature of being publicized surrounded by mob bosses, international Russian thieves enthralled with that gangster image.

In an unusual event in New York, another exhibition of character. It must not be forgotten that the cruel joke among Wall Street insiders by Steve Bannon and Dr. Robert Mercer was to use the Nazi Germany theme in Republican politics was also based on a fact. During President Ronald Reagan, extreme conservatives began recruiting Eastern European émigrés who were collaborators of the Third Reich. President Dwight D. Eisenhower and Allen W. Dulles, CIA Director, started. Donald J. Trump's involvement in the Reagan White House made him privy to all these details and history. President Reagan entered a conflict he created by visiting the SS graves at the Bitburg Cemetery. In a cruel joke, Republicans eventually never got the Adolph Hitler of Allen W. Dulles, CIA Director or the Hitler of his Eastern European émigrés, but the one of Mr. Putin. In essence, the Republican Party playing games with Donald J. Trump got two for the money. He played into Mr. Putin's hands to gain retribution for the Soviet downfall while helping Mr. Trump fulfill Mr. Putin's dream. At the same time, President Ronald Wilson Reagan was taken off his throne as the "greatest Cold War strategist."

The utility and technique of National Socialism in the United States were more like an American version of fascism. Authoritarianism does not fully explain the exercise of dominance that seeps into the waters around Donald J Trump and those that share his authority. Still, in examining the characteristics of the collapsing institutional integrity around him, one can readily witness the National Socialist way of thinking as "pretty similar." There is also a helpful outlook shared by military analysts "we know it when we see it." Though not scientific, it can relate under conditions where someone cannot get close and look in its eyes. Something that can be scrutinized through the way it projects itself on the populace. Viewing the National Socialist way of thinking, the behavior of entryism, and its use of propaganda, one will certainly get a sufficient reason not to consider it coincidental but with a plan behind its actions. In other words, a careful eye and critical mind have an excellent opportunity to see the machinery working toward a specific goal, called Führerprinzip when the Trump Presidency infiltrated and dominated institutions.

So, it is reasonable to speculate Republican Party officials found it logical and safe to continue on this slippery path without scorn and retribution for being too extreme. Mr. Trump condoned the use of his picture on the cover of a newly revised printing of My New Order, which only served to increase his popularity. Conservatives have taken advantage of this moment in history by deploying every possible agency in publicizing the present situation. Neo-liberation had its role to play in shifting time back to the 1920s and 1930s. It had the feeling of being on a drug trip. Still, despite the unrest surrounding Trump, Republican presidents created a distinct similarity. It began by encouraging a Confederate gathering in Charlottesville, Virginia, *When the Stormers Sang* "Blood and Soil."

A Witches Sabbath

"And he cried mightily with a strong voice, saying, Babylon the great is fallen, is fallen, and is become the habitation of devils, and the hold of every foul spirit and a cage of every unclean and hateful bird." ---Revelation 18:2

It cannot be ignored that once Greta Thunberg and climate change activists descended on the United Nations on 23 September 2019, things have not been the same. Ms. Thunberg's message was brief; it was about time. How much time is spent and what's left. In the United States, the Trump Presidency was in full-swing toward authoritarianism. Quick stop. The message strangely coincided with an even more bizarre coincidence. Carlo Strenger, on the state of the soul, wrote, "The current government's disconnection from the world indeed has much in common with the psychology of religious sects that become so convinced of their own truth, that they no longer care about the world at large. Theirs is a state of mind that prefers mystical vision and misguided pseudo-heroism of staring down the whole world to pragmatic politics." [33] This is a description of the spiritual Church of Laodicea in Revelation 3:14. Without defacing religion, there could never be a corruption of the mind of this magnitude without

---

[33] Strenger, Carlo. "Netanyahu and the Mystics of Safed." *Haaretz.* 17 June 2011.

corrupted religious practices such as corporatism masquerading as mysticism. [34]

In the fable of American liberalism, there is also a sub-feature of stagnation and keeping the system intact. Making the "melting pot" less of a surety and more anxiety for safety. Conservatism's view of a thriving economy is when businesses excel while placing them on a pedestal. Contrasted to the voter who considers success a fair salary who lives an existence in the rural hollow. Exploitation was built into the system legislatively using authoritative tactics. Hussain ibn Ali's website, "Fascism itself is a hard term to define. It is both a right-wing political system anchored in post-World War II European history and a far more warped world view, which is inseparable from racial superiority doctrines. The associated imagery, from swastikas to skinheads, is highly emotive."

A post-Soviet Russia believes there is a continuation of a lengthy process that bases itself on a consistent and logical path not necessarily ending in class struggles but reinterpretations of the moral, aesthetic, and religious view of societies and customs practices that prevails in power struggles. This linear interpretation is primarily used by the military, strategists, and war planners and has advantages in understanding current dilemmas. Meet the influencers historians never speak of publicly except in obscure terms. Other radicals worldwide were energized because Russia promised to save white people and dispel foreigners and the "global (Jewish) elite." [35] President Vladamir Putin has played a dangerous game a historian will examine for years to come. Doing a reverse, he plays the role of Nazi funder, stealing away the

---

[34] Riebling, Mark. "Chomsky is a Conservative - CIA author confusion." Conservatism Turned Upside Down, Sam Steinhaus's articulate and timely critique of conservative reason. 16 Oct. 2009.

[35] Picciolini, Christian. House Committee on Foreign Affairs Subcommittee on the Middle East, North Africa, and International Terrorism. House Committee on Homeland Security Subcommittee on Intelligence and Terrorism. 18 Spt. 2019.

opposite part National Socialists used to fund Vladamir Ilyich Ulyanov Lenin to begin a Russian revolt. Perhaps Mr. Putin hopes this will play well with Russians and identify the creation of Stalin with himself.

Neo-Protestants also have a measure of time that is just as explosive as Greta Thunberg. On the one hand, a message about time is measured against Christian time from Minister Louis Farrakhan. Rev. Farrakhan states that time is measured against Genesis, the ruins of Sodom, and why they explain a parallel of America's destruction. There was also a parallel by evangelicals that time may be running out, but things can still be duplicated from the Days of Noah, plenty of time to even make profits from these Last Days. Neo-Nazis also have their opinion about time in these Last Days that revolve around their global determinism ideas in conjunction with religious dominionism. Currently, there is no public forum to discuss these issues.

In 1964 Karl Hess, Barry Goldwater's anarchist speechwriter, gave this position in Arizona Senator's Republican convention acceptance speech. "I would remind you that extremism in defense of liberty is no vice!" Goldwater warned, "Mark my word, if and when these preachers get control of the [Republican] party, and they're sure trying to do so, it's going to be a damn terrible problem. Frankly, these people frighten me. Politics and governing demand compromise. But these Christians believe they are acting in the name of God, so they can't and won't compromise. I know, I've tried to deal with them."

National Socialists always had a plan for unwitting Christians. [36] Labor unions later equated Dr. Armand Hammer's ownership of a horrid low-wage meatpacking plant he used to send beef to the starving Soviet Union. Last, the Nazi propaganda program immediately saw an upsurge that was nothing incompatible between the American government and Reich radicalism. The initial success was geographically planned to first reach Midwest Germans, those in New York, and the intellectuals scattered in social clubs associated with the

---

[36] Kaplan, J. (2001) The post-war paths of occult national socialism: from Rockwell and Madole to Manson, Patterns of Prejudice, 35:3, 41-67.

Steuben Society. Dr. Hammer spent a decade in the Soviet Union as it evolved into communism. By helping Vladimir Ilyich Ulyanov Lenin solve problems of food shortage, lack of medicine, making pencils, and ruling other capitalists. [37] Donald J. Trump used these examples as evidence he could also do this by establishing his business model of "mining the Soviets" taking their money.

In Eastern Europe, Nazi surrealism and the gothic were being used in propaganda, focusing on the völkisch-rural population that acclaimed itself as the spiritual bearers of Aryan paganism. Carl G. Jung, the MD psychiatrist, met with Adolph Hitler and Benito Mussolini, relegating the movement to the ungodly. [38] Mysticism was being used in ritual by Heinrich Himmler Reichsführer Protection Squadron, SS. This was later adapted to Donald J. Trump's run for President.

"When we look back to the time before (1914), we find ourselves living in a world of events that would have been inconceivable before the war. We were even beginning to regard war between civilized nations as a fable, thinking that such an absurdity would become less and less possible in our rational, internationally organized world. And what came after the war was a veritable witches' sabbath…With such goings-on in the wide world, it is not in the least surprising that there should be equally curious manifestations on a smaller scale in other spheres. In the realm of philosophy, we shall have to wait sometime before anyone can assess the kind of age we are living. But in the sphere of religion, we can see at once that some crucial things have been happening. We feel no surprise that in Russia, the Eastern

---

[37] Hrabovsky, Serhii. "Lenin. Money. Revolution: The shady side of the Bolshevik activities." УкраїнськаРусский English. *The Day*. Ukraine. Issue: №24 (2010). 22 April 2010..

[38] Jung, G. Carl. "Essay on Wotan." Wotan, Neue Schweizer Rundschau (Zurich). n.s., III (March, 1936), 657-69. Republished in Aufsatze Zurzeitgeschichte (Zurich, 1946), 1-23. Trans. by Barbara Hannah in Essays on Contemporary Events. (London, 1947), 1-16; this version has been consulted. Motto, trans. by H.C. Roberts:].

Orthodox Church's colorful splendors have been superseded by the Godless Movement. —"

In a *Witches Sabbath*, we see both the pre-and post-Trump era fantasy, an emotional place that consists of the theatrics of fear and the Apocalypse's tragedy. Threatened by World War Three. The confluence of wealth, the thoughts, dreams, imagery, the likeness of mental illnesses, and the instability they pose to peace is a repetitious event on social media. Plus, the propensity of Congress of trying to liquidate itself. Carl G. Jung saw this before it was about to take form in the body and minds of the people writing about their attraction to the demi-gods, "[T]he gods are without doubt personifications of psychic forces..." [39]

Stitching Myth to Third Rome

The religious evangelicals that surround extremist Conservatives are easily identified. They are referred to prominently by the Saints in the Bible. Firstly, in 2020 evangelicals know they live in what is broadly referred to by all religions as the "Last Days." These times are the New Testament dispensation. Although the Old Testament Covenant is still in force for those that observe the Ten Commandments, all other things point and witness to the Cross's focus. In the trials of Lucifer, Christ identified the Great Deceiver as the father of lies that would war against nations, not be capable of knowing the truth. Other references include "the prince of this world," Lawless One, "master of death and destruction." Anything taught by people who identify themselves as Christian evangelicals but do not abide by this dispensation of time is a cult. Declaring Donald J. Trump, an Old Testament ruler, is a double-edged sword should the religious designate him anathema. He may not appreciate the meaning that he has been declared --- "In the Old Testament, an anathema was a creature or object set apart for sacrificial offering and

---

[39] Ibid.

thus removed from ordinary use and destined instead for destruction."
--- Wikipedia

President Trump has no intention to aspire to goals above his stature. Instead, he shows his purpose is in different depths. The ideas of roaming peoples may have their origins in human migrations. Mr. Trump rearranges the völkisch pagan theme by mixing the gothic into the crime and violence of refugees. Today the concern among evangelical pagan neo-Protestants does not seem to be about tribal Jews invading the West. It is distant from humanitarian assistance because, in the hardened pagan neo-Protestant calculation, "social support is merely comfort to the immigrant enemy."

Neo-Protestants seem more concerned about Jerusalem and its Shekels. In this framework, pagan neo-Protestants expanded their category of devils to include all those in poverty. Anxious to "personify psychic forces," they cleansed President Vladamir Putin from his Stalinist actions in Syria. On a recent trip to Rome, Mr. Putin went back in time as the *National Interest* reported, "The leading Russian media, either on purpose or due to ignorance, embellished the ceremony at Mount Athos. Claiming that Putin sat on the throne of the Byzantine emperors. [40] In fact, Putin spent the service in a stasidion—a monastic chair with a folding seat designed for high-ranking honored guests in the temple." Putin's symbolic visit sparked joy among those conservatives in Russia who see this as a sign of ideological revival under the slogan, "Moscow is the Third Rome. "Orthodoxy, Autocracy, Nationality" and "Communism is the brightest future of all mankind. In contrast to the West, proponents also point out that Eastern Christianity proclaims loyalty to ancient times and unchanging ideals." Noble Truth was in contrast to themselves, who believe in Ignoble Lies. [41] What I previously described also holds true here. That groups and families of

---

[40] Galstyan, Areg. "Third Rome Rising: The Ideologues Calling for a New Russian Empire: The neo-Byzantines believe Moscow will save Christendom." *The National Interest.* 27 Jun. 2016.

[41] Ibid.

power and wealth that appear atomized actually coalesce and bind their interests when pressured. Though they may seem opposed to one another in other ways, "realpolitik" makes the coalition strong.

"All that ever came before me are thieves **and robbers**: but the sheep did not hear them." –St. John 10, New Testament

The seizure of a world-popular political ideology for new uses a practice predominantly by Conservative extremists during President Reagan. In the distant past, two corresponding conspiracies were active during the 1980s. KGB Chief Yuri P. Andropov used to deal with European Nazis against France's President Mitterrand and those Americans involved in the Reagan White House responsible for Eastern European émigré recruitment. Simultaneously, in the 1980s, the Sicilian mafia also worked with the former Sicilian Reich collaborators. A group previously mastered the National Socialist Party's artistry its subliminal messaging in Gothic-inspired film. Using those foundations, in the 1980s, Sicily's organized crime families that once governed the country after being installed by the United States military were now reconstituting themselves. Dr. Anna Sergi, in *Jane's Intelligence Review*, in June 2012, noted that "…after a devastating earthquake in 1980. The group's name comes from a 1963 film 'I Basilischi' by filmmaker Lina Wertmüller, set in Matera. The Basilischi mafia a Sicilian mafia crew, number at least 2,500 Sicilian Mafia affiliates in the United States.

In this regard, most of President Putin's energy has gathered a small and influential group of wealthy metaphysical believers. Neo-Nazism was, after all, the dream of a new world order that an inner-circle wanted to choreograph into a Great Empire. President Putin was attributed as a land grabber in Crimea. Today, Prime Minister Benjamin Netanyahu is now looked upon as the prime motivator behind what Stephen Sizer calls "reordering Israeli lands." [42] With all the confusion

---

[42] Shahak, Israel and Prof. Michel Chossudovsky, "Greater Israel": The Zionist Plan for the Middle East." *Global Research*. 28 Dec. 2019.

and fog surrounding the Trump campaign, Steve Bannon alluded to the goal of stealing land through a war with Muslims as a supposed patriotic reaction to 9-11. Stephen Sizer calls this a Zionist *theology of the land that directly relates to the expansion of resources.* [43] There is also a political theory of expanding Russia called *Third Rome* (among other names to disguise the intent) that mirrors Nazi Germany's propaganda components. [44] The influx of money into Conservative holdings by marketing efforts may suggest of Maj. Gen. Flynn, who stands with Turkey in a confluence of Israeli interests. Mr. Putin has emphasized that Moscow, not Jerusalem, is the center of Christianity in a competing reality foretelling future conflict. [45]

President Putin suggests an entirely different way of viewing the world not by its strengths but by its vulnerabilities. The world had to be considered morbidly. An observer need only see a global map that readily shows his aspirational policies. In every place of military significance to Russia, there is a left-and right-wing social upheaval. When applying a morality test to Mr. Putin's motives, there requires a morality and "best intentions" overview for his position in the Third Rome.

This standard is also the key to Mr. Trump's downfall. Mr. Trump's ambitions of going to Moscow to live off the wealth of Mr. Putin's hegemonic success automatically place him in a subservient role. This motive blinds him to an unavoidable reality that leads him into a trap. Mr. Trump has no success in building a global criminal alliance from Russia's collapsed intelligence network. In short, Mr. Trump is blinded by ambition. He cannot envision he is being used to meet Mr. Putin's dreams. Senator John McCain knew an unavoidable

---

[43] Sizer, Stephen. "The Theology of the Land by Stephen Sizer." *The Balfour Project.*.

[44] Third Rome refers to the doctrine that Russia or, specifically, Moscow succeeded Rome and Byzantium Rome as the ultimate center of true Christianity and of the Roman Empire. This is the most generally misunderstood and abused of the several expressions of Russia's new place in the world resulting from domestic and international events of the 1430s and 1520s. –Encyclopedia.com.

[45] Ibid.

truth that haunts the successes of both men. Neither can discern the power of truth among all their enemies. Senator McCain was the most feared. He was able to see a change in the psychology inside Russia. From a non-Western view of history that departs from the air, history changed under President Vladamir Putin from a linear achievement to a criminal perspective that will benefit only one individual.

Senator John McCain explained President Vladamir Putin's character as the lower member of the apparatchik, "[These] people . . . are the enemies of the Russian people. They rob Russia of its wealth, its hopes, its future. They deny the God-given dignity of the people they misrule. They are thieves and murderers. They are cowards. They fear justice. They fear the truth. They fear a society in which ideals and morality are the foundation of law and order." [46] In this light, we can see John McCain and Vladamir Putin. The essence of their character, their living values test, would come to Mr. Vladamir Putin to see if he would provide the necessary food to a village entirely depending on him. [47]

"In 1992, as an elected member of the City Council, she was the first in Russia to accuse Vladimir Putin. Then the head of the Committee for External Relations of Saint-Petersburg Mayor's office of corruption. Salye collected evidence to prove that he stole 92 million dollars from the city. Via legally invalid contracts with shell firms to export raw materials to Europe in return for food supplies. Oil, timber, cotton, rare metals were duly exported, but the city never received any food. The prosecutor's office would not charge Putin, and the City Council was dissolved."

---

[46] Kara-Murza, Vladamir. "John McCain saw through Vladimir Putin better than anyone." *The Washington Post.* Opinion. 27 Aug. 2018.

[47] Volkova, Elena. "Communist Christianity as Russian Political Religion: Does Putin's Dystopia look like Trump's Dream?" *Journal of the European Society of Women in Theological Research* 27 (2019) 279-298. doi: 10.2143/ESWTR.27.0. 3286565.

Speaking of courage and character tests, we know that Marine Salye's investigation line on President Vladamir Putin was somehow insufficient to bring any charges. The apparatus wanted President Putin. [48]

"Putin was elected despite her warnings, and Salye went into hiding. She told Masha Gessen – the author and journalist who tracked her down a decade later – that someone had threatened her. (She never revealed who. This chilling encounter took place in the office of the State Duma deputy Sergei Yushenkov, murdered three years later. Gladkov, her co-investigator, also died after apparently being poisoned.) Rumors suggested that she had taken refuge in France. The story – apocryphal, it turned out – said that Putin had sent her a postcard with the message: "I wish you a Happy New Year and the health to enjoy it."

The Russian opposition politician Leonid Gozman commented on President Putin and his trustworthiness. He believed Mr. Putin was too important to ignore, "But after their handshakes, they will carefully wash their hands and count their fingers… at home, he will be forced to acknowledge his defeat. Because of the decisions he has taken, which have thrown Russia backward into the past." [49]

One of the features of Conservative extremism is that its Apocalyptic myth and occult beliefs are dissuasive motivators. Not so much based on imagery but outright religious deception often called "spiritual insurgency." The white pagan neo-Protestant Clergy considers President Trump an incarnate pagan king of the Old Testament. [50] Benjamin Netanyahu thinks of himself, Winston Churchill, following the Mystics

---

[48] Harding, Luke. "Marina Salye obituary." *The Guardian*. 28 Mar. 2012.

[49] Gozman, Leonid and Paul A. Goble. "With his changes to Russian Constitution, Putin has suffered a serious defeat, Gozman says." *Euromaiden* 22 Jan. 2020 International, Op-ed.

[50] Ibid. See also Burton, Tara Isabella. "The biblical story the Christian right uses to defend Trump." *VOX*. 05 Mar. 2018.

of Safed and Chabad Lubavitch. [51] It seems unbelievable that President Vladamir Putin's mystical conception of his greatness as 'leader of the world' came by way of the pronouncement made by his blind witch Baba Vanga. [52] Let us examine the identity of Baba Vanga and her role in understanding what is behind her popularization.

Baba Vanga (Vangeliya Pandeva Gushterova), the witch who delegated Vladamir Putin "Leader of the World," passed on in 1996 and was a prophetically catastrophic cultist who proposed different bits of knowledge comparable to those cited within the *Modern Confirmation book of Disclosure*. Her primary followers come from the folkish countryside and villages. Ms. Vanga was preceded by Helena Petrovna Blavatsky, who began the Theosophy Society, who was attributed to the "cocktail of ideas" that helped to imagine the Aryans. Her written surrealist and gothic streams ultimately became recognized as authentic writings that had appealed to the Thule Society members and eventually became a foundation for the Nazi race theory philosophy. This also sheds light on Nazi rituals involving pagan symbols that do not concern Prime Minister Benjamin Netanyahu how much this empowers the Trump family in the eyes of neo-Nazis. These universities of the occult were on the plane of thinking as *The Sandro Italico Mussolini School of Fascist Mysticism* catered to Benito Mussolini.

Thule Society was significant in the development of the Nazi mentality. Speer recalled, "Hitler had little sympathy with Himmler in his mythologizing of the SS," once stating, "What nonsense! Here we have at least reached an age that has left all mysticism behind. And now he wants to start that all over again. We might just as well have stayed with the church. At least it has tradition. To think that I may someday

---

51 Strenger, Carlo. "Netanyahu and the Mystics of Safed." *Haaretz.* 17 June 2011.

52 Lockett, Jon. "Lord of The World. Psychic Baba Vanga who predicted 9/11 terror attacks also foretold 'unstoppable' Vladimir Putin will one day rule Earth." *The Sun.* 19 March 2018.

be turned into an SS saint! Can you imagine it? I would turn over in my grave." [53]

Timothy Ryback noted in Hitler's Library *Magic: History, Theory, and Practice* (1923), a book on occultism and magic by Dr. Ernst Schertel. [54] 'Hitler's copy of Magic bears a handwritten dedication from Schertel, scrawled on the title page in pencil. A 170-page softcover in large format, the book has been thoroughly read, and its margins scored repeatedly. I found an unusually thick pencil line beside the passage, 'He who does not carry demonic seeds within him will never give birth to a new world.'

The fantasy before despotism, as Theodor Adorno stipulated, was devoid of anything to feel. It lacked love and compassion by an intense focus on male masculinity and those attracted to its homosexuality. Adorno explained fascism, "As a rebellion against civilization, racism is not simply the reoccurrence of the archaic but its reproduction in and by civilization itself... By the way, Hitler was well aware of the libidinal source of the mass foundation through surrender when he attributed specifically female, passive features to the participants of his meetings, and thus also hinted at the role of unconscious homosexuality in mass psychology." [55] Homosexuality and histrionics were Donald J. Trump's awareness in his relationship with longtime friend, business advisor, political blackmailer, and confidant Roy Cohn Esq Reagan appointee at the Dept. of Justice and Roger Stone associate. President

---

[53] Wunderlich, Sophie. "We See into the Distant Future, Because We Know What It Will Be" Destiny, Utopia, and Apocalypse in National Socialism." *Williams College.* Williamstown, Massachusetts. 16 Apr. 2018. Thomas Kohut, Advisor A thesis submitted in partial fulfillment of the requirements for the Degree of Bachelor of Arts with Honors in History.

[54] Ryback, Timothy W. "Hitler's Forgotten Library: You can tell a lot about a person from what he reads. The surviving—and largely ignored—remnants of Adolf Hitler's personal library reveal a deep but erratic interest in religion and theology." *The Atlantic.* May 2003.

[55] Adorno, Theodor. "Freudian Theory and the Pattern of Fascist Propaganda." *Political Sociology and Critique of Politics.* Essay 1951.

Reagan has been capsized, not receiving so much as a life jacket by extremist Conservatives.

Emmi Bevensee, "…The American Conservative—indicates a widespread willingness to engage in a far-reaching effort uniting ideological positions in favor of a "new detente" with the Kremlin, vis-a-vis a coalition spanning far-right and radical left. This engagement mirrors Dugin's strategic proposition that the Kremlin should propagate and spawn. Both the extreme right and left-wing politics as a means of destabilizing the US while also increasing the ground upon which larger, syncretic fascist projects, such as the Alt-Right, can be seen." [56]

This Presidential ecosphere has a disorienting effect on Mr. Trump, who seemed overwhelmed and emotionally imbalanced. In recent publications, President Barack Obama, after discussing leadership with Donald J. Trump about the world order, said: "He doesn't know anything." This underestimates Trump while insulting the American people (something President Obama did routinely), who the majority of people drop his title *President* for apparent reasons. It's not that Donald J. Trump doesn't know anything, but what he knows is "rejected knowledge." [57]

---

[56] Ibid.

[57] Rejection. This continuity over time of beliefs rejected by the mainstream is called the "underground of rejected knowledge" in his 1976 book, *The Occult Establishment*, James Webb. Those who find themselves alienated from society are likely to identify established knowledge with the established social order. Therefore, turn to "rejected knowledge" as a basis of their rejection of the mainstream. See American Council on Science and Health. 13 Sept. 2002.

2. Six Psychological Fusions to Adversaries

'When I use a word,' Humpty Dumpty said, in rather a scornful tone, 'it means just what I choose it to mean. Neither more nor less." The question is,' said Alice, 'whether you can make words mean so many different things." The problem is,' said Humpty Dumpty, 'who is the master. That Is all.' ---Lewis Carroll, *Alice in Wonderland*

In speech warfare, it's not unusual to witness people acting in their worst interests to the point they destroy themselves. Throwing themselves in the line of automatic fire, suicide missions, subservience. Massive loss of individual identity, moral compass, and personal history are necessary as preliminary prerequisites for this type of sacrifice. Putin-ism is a focused plan of destruction instead of President Trump, who has a planet earth annihilation plan. Mr. Putin's war behavior is an extreme version of no constraints, seen in World War Two. Mr. Trump's plan is apocalyptic. It depends on societal forces failing to police crime through both the breakdown of institutional mechanisms of criminal justice and informal social control mechanisms' failure.

It should be noted that internet war does have its actual combat similarity. Some techniques of this online warfare to defeat an opposing force's morale are to propagate alien ideas outside the cultural reference frame of an opposite. In the realm of ideas, internet sources want to draw in and gain the enemy's attentiveness. A favorite tactic of online enemies is to impact memory by replacing or reframing an actual event. In the realm of public speaking, it would be hard to find a more effective duo than Sarah Palin and Donald J. Trump to undermine the processing of language by merely altering the meaning of words. Changing them to refer to themselves and the directions they provide to listeners. Jim Jones' ability to convince his listeners to kill themselves is a notable example. Only because killing didn't mean what it usually does but to obey the master is all that matters.

Donald J. Trump lays his entire focus on what he determined is wrong in American society. Laying the premise of his argument on the basis that his life has not worked for him. Therefore, he claims it must be wrong for everyone else. After becoming President, Mr. Trump broadened his argument to include his admiration of heroes from his dark thoughts. History knows them well, the least of Adolph Hitler, but he doesn't end there. Mr. Trump also has to find ways to prosper, and this laid bare his history of collaborating with mafia elements. In this chapter, Mr. Trump calls on familiar methods to assist him. The speeches of ruin and the monstrous.

Nietzsche's claim that one day, "'actors,' all kinds of actors, will be the real masters." --- Friedrich Nietzsche, *The Gay Science*

A brief transcript of Sarah Palin's speech at Iowa's Freedom Summit on 26 Jan. 2017 follows.

"Another Latin word, status quo, and it stands for, 'Man, the middle-class every day Americans are really getting' taken for a ride.' That's status quo, and GOP leaders – by the way – you know, the man can only ride ya when your back is bent. So, strengthen it. Then the man can't ride ya, America won't be taken for a ride, because so much is at stake and we can't afford politicians playing games like nothing more is at stake than, oh, maybe the next standing of theirs in the next election."

Those familiar with Sarah Palin's conversations in mind know that Presidential Candidate speeches receive up to 30,000 attendees who swear he is a genius. Donald J. Trump said this, "very good, very smart — you know, if you're a conservative Republican, if I were a liberal, if, like, okay, if I ran as a liberal Democrat, they would say I'm one of the smartest people anywhere in the world — it's true! — When you're a conservative Republican, they try — oh, do they do a number —" May also recognize these words were spoken by Donald J.

Trump in South Carolina, 21 July 2015, and begin to understand the mystery and significance of the Republican Party strategy. [58]

I described the Republican Conservative approach to candidate speech borrowing from *My New Order*. Mr. Trump drew direct parallels between Adolph Hitler's content and himself. His need for acting evil is primary, and the Presidential Candidate Trump a secondary identity. There was also a deliberate series of Donald J. Trump press releases on Ishi Press's *My New Order cover*. [59] They indicated Mr. Trump was proud of his newfound role. The use of speech in this new Republican Conservative attitude draws on the fear of the unknown. In other ways, it is directed at specific audiences to also provide a shock of the past, i.e., democrats and Holocaust survivors. Perhaps this was fortuitous for those psychologically inclined as this was the first time it was possible to see his thought processes' inner workings. Every day Mr. Trump puts his new identity forward when he interacts with the world, only coping with it from behind a mask. He informed us of his uniqueness. There is actor Trump and sadist Trump.

Mr. Trump's message had an aggressive tone, including more violence and surrealism. [60] So, when we look back to the previous example of what sounded like Mr. Trump swallowing Sarah Palin's words, it was actually an exhibition of psychological manipulation; the following is an example of surrealism used in language. This reveals Mr. Trump's sophisticated preparation in linguistics. As psychologists know, its sole purpose is to gain access to an individual's subconscious, but the listener has to be willing to accept it.

---

[58] Osenenko, Robert (Ed.D.) *Donald J. Trump an American Dilemma*. Independent Publisher and Amazon. 01 June 2019. ISBN-13: 978-1096064473. p 22.

[59] Flood, Alison. "Hitler speeches published with Donald Trump as cover illustration." *The Guardian*. 03 Oct. 2016.

[60] Surrealism. The term *surrealism* indicates a specific thought and movement in literature, the arts, and theatre, which tries to integrate the confused realms of imagination and reality. The proponents of surrealism endeavor to mix up the differences of conscious and unconscious thought through writing and painting by using irrational juxtaposition of images. A 20th-century avant-garde movement in art and literature which sought to release the creative potential of the unconscious mind.

"Then an unheard-of being, unheard-of beings, will be seen to rise, their brains compressed by sonorous helmets, their temples pierced by the whistling of airwaves, their bodies naked, turned yellow by fever, pocked by deep vegetal stigmata swarming with insects and filled to the brim with the slimy juices of venom, overflowing and running down a skin tiger-striped and leopard-spotted by the gangrene of wounds and the leprosy of camouflage, their swollen bellies plugged to death by electric umbilical cords [sic] tangling with the ignominiousness of torn intestines and bits of flesh, roasting in the burning steel carapaces of the punitive tortures of gutted tanks. That is man! Backs of lead, sexual organs of fire, fears of mica, artificial hearts of the televisions of blood, hidden faces and wings — always wings, the north and south of our being!" ---*Hidden Faces* (by Salvador Dali, translated by Chevalier).

In art, literature, and plays, the entire propaganda machine was based on the gothic, including anti-Semitic posters of Jews controlling the world, which was easily adapted to include the gypsy, blacks, and enemies of the state. However, Adolph Hitler did not hide the use of "terrible tragedy" in service to him. In fact, it was assumed this trance flowed from his subconscious. When he was a boy, no one knew, of course, that he would try running an entire nation from the impulses of his subconscious.

"He was a small stature boy in Vienna May 1913, avoiding the draft being too small and weak. August Kubizek, his best friend, recounted 1904. Adolph Hitler remembered when 16 speaking with another voice in a trance. Adolph Hitler broke into a historical analysis of Germany and its people who needed a complete rebellion. After he became Führer, he reminded August Kubizek, "Yes, I've never forgotten it; because that's where it all began . . . While he spoke to August

Kubizek, Adolph held his hand. On August 03, 1914, after petitioning the government, Adolph Hitler was inducted." [61]

American Fascists--- Testimonials of Regeneration

Everyone studying the underground and its history understands the grey areas underneath a social structure's legitimate layers. Like soil, it's where all the microbes live that eat the foundations above them. It is sometimes assumed that some observers think the alternative-right movement was always synonymous with neo-Nazi because Charlottesville, Virginia *Unite the Right*. This ignores the future that requires due diligence of a closer nature than before. The alt-right movement is always expected to come through the discourse of the Republican Party and Donald J. Trump, the microbes. This confusing array of people-centered focus on Trump's family detracts from other ways extreme Conservatives busy themselves arranging the government system in their favor. In the next paragraphs, the "brains" and "central nervous system" patterns of the alternative right emerge as important fascists explain some guiding principles of the American Nazi movement and identity.

Jim Marrs, in 2008, reported on John Dean's turn from the traditional politics of preservation that went well beyond President Nixon's Southern Strategy and Dr. Armand Hammer's Soviet monetary conspiracies.   Dr. Hammer emerged after Vladamir Lenin's death, not as a socialist but as a dedicated communist with criminal ambitions. Through several presidential administrations, from Nixon to George W. Bush, Dr. Hammer was on the itinerary's advisory and dinner time. Operating as a criminal ambassador, Hammer represented the criminal as a specialist in white-collar crime in support of dictatorships, with

---

[61] Kubizek, August. *The Young Hitler I Knew: The Definitive Inside Look at the Artist Who Became a Monster*. Arcade; Reprint edition 13 July 2011. See: Murray, Henry. "Subject: Adolph Hitler" CIA File. Central Intelligence Agency. Declassified. 18 May 2000.

particular interests in the Eastern European sector. President Jimmy Carter was the only President that kicked Dr. Hammer out of the Carter White House, courtesy of Zbigniew Kazimierz Brzezinski, Ph.D. Notably, throughout this time, Donald J. Trump was repeatedly in the White House, and Washington D.C. was always working the fringes of mainstream politics.

After Dr. Hammer's death, there was an opportunity for replacement. Foreign agents (facilitators) of international Conservatives were deeply embedded in the Republican Party and activists for National Socialist causes. We know that the discussion that focuses on Donald J. Trump sometimes obscures the apparent fact that he is a surrogate for a radical but more significant (influential) global Conservatism. Describing a more self-destructive Conservatism, Kerry R. Bolton, the fascist, and Russ Bellant, anti-fascist, concluded the East European ethnic program for émigrés was a means to infiltrate the West.

As a thought system, a particular brand of conservatism is a philosophy born from extremist politics with its origins in Imperialist Germany. One of the expert resources of early Nazi philosophy and political theory is to refer to Appendix B: Reactionary, Conservative, Nazi *"Arthur Moeller van den Bruck: The Man & His Thought."* Moeller became the foundation of reactionary, conservative, and Nazi thinking in the same philosophy by distinguishing the parts. Its emphasis was never on distributing services to the people.

Instead, Conservatism in this extremist model was only interested in saving their system's integrity, an entirely mechanical accounting function. Eventually, Adolph Hitler referred to this kind of thinking as "our poisonous ideology" and "alien politics," explaining it had to be imported and digested to make it useful. It is instructive Adolph Hitler admitted he stole Karl Marx's concepts, although "people do not want to hear this."

Often spending its finances to maintain a financial structure that supports its extremism is proven in the sudden shift from German progress to war. Through the years, it has spent its time disguising this fact by creating the illusion that the ability to use critical thinking and develop an argument is based on conservatism. Strip away conservatism's social niceties by applying pressure, and there are its aggressiveness, violence, and racism that prominent displays its origin. It would do anything to seize authority. Were this not to be the case, it would not be the home to every anti-democratic cause.

The following are short descriptions of notable extremists of the past that have mainstreamed into the American consciousness. [62] Jim Marrs describes the essence of the family problem within the Republican Party establishment—it had no ideology and was weakened to the point it had a narrowing constituency shared only with the Democratic Party. In other words, just as the Republican Party is today. John W. Dean describes a new start (rebirthing) of incorporating ideas by Eastern European émigrés. Only how the Republican Party sought out a presidential candidate follows the following recipe.

"John W. Dean, former Nixon counsel, who was jailed for felonies committed at Watergate, referred to this new Republican conservatism in his 2007 book *Broken Government. How Republican Rule Destroyed the Legislative, Executive, and Judicial Branches:* "It has been new on Capitol Hill since about 1997, about three years after the GOP gained control of the House. It has been new to the White House since 2001, with the arrival of George W. Bush and Richard B. Cheney, although its roots first emerged during the Nixon presidency and began blossoming in the Reagan and Bush Senior [sic] years." Although Dean never entirely identifies the origin of this "new Republican way of thinking," it is possible that it stemmed from the National

---

[62] Marrs, Jim. *The Rise of the Fourth Reich: The Secret Societies That Threaten to Take Over America.* William Morrow Paperbacks; Reprint edition (June 23, 2009). ISBN-10: 0061245593. ISBN-13: 978-0061245596. Also see: Carlson, John Roy. *Under Cover: My Four Years in the Nazi Underworld of America.* Blakiston Company and Dutton and Company Publishers. December 1943.

Socialist philosophy brought into this country after World War II."

Introducing the experts in an autocracy Kerry R. Bolton, the fascist, and the anti-fascist Russ Bellant come to the same conclusions. Though other theatrics may attempt to show a Republican system intact, it was anything but. Julian E. Zelizer of *Time* places this into context on 7 July 2020. "The early stories included the claim that former President George W. Bush might not support Trump, though his spokesperson quickly announced that this was "completely made up." That entire conversation rests on a myth that the renegades have taken over the GOP. The truth is they did so decades ago. In the 1980s, "Party Gatekeepers"—the senior elected officials and party operatives who had the greatest influence within the party—made a Faustian deal with the burn-down-the-house mavericks that forever changed the character of the party. Until analysts reckon that there is no old-school Republican establishment anymore, we will never understand what the GOP has become to its core. Donald Trump is not an outlier. He is a perfect fit for the modern Republican Party… It all started forty years ago with Ronald Reagan's election as president in 1980, which was both exhilarating and frustrating for younger members of the party… The party gatekeepers of yesteryear opened the doors to all of this. In 2020, not only can the so-called "establishment" not contain the renegades, the renegades have become the establishment. If there are any establishment figures left who feel qualms about Trump's presidency, most will shove those concerns aside because Gingrich and Trump have helped maintain their power."

Since 1977, he was first invited to Republican Party insiders and President Reagan confidants by Dr. Armand Hammer in Palm Beach, Florida, who had well-known connections to the Soviet Union's KGB elite (Yuri Andropov). Donald J. Trump paraded his "new" wife from Czechoslovakia, a geographical pattern prescribed to blend into Republican preferences. Dr. Hammer and President Reagan had a significant role in arranging a meeting between Mr. Trump and General Secretary Mikhail Gorbachev during a White House dinner. Mr. Gorbachev invited Mr. Trump to Moscow KGB Headquarters. During Reagan, Donald J. Trump had complete access to the Soviet Union's KGB. For the Soviet people and particularly the Communist Party's high echelon, streams of access flowed through the government. Criminal careers were made on goods coming into the Soviet Union, where the government was consistently paranoid and hypervigilant about being invaded. Fear of invasion is inherited by its people, so obviously. Dr. Hammer was considered a Soviet thief at this stage and favored highly over one stranger from Palm Beach even with a criminalized background. Truth is, Donald J. Trump's biographical never matched success, and the belief Mr. Trump had that Hammer was filthy rich was a lie. He was just as bankrupt as Mr. Trump.

Dr. Hammer was identified as nearly a Soviet son, tied in by his history with Vladimir Ilyich Ulyanov Lenin, almost like his father. The Soviet-American commercial alliance was forming with concessionaire agreements and committees. Hammer took part in numerous of these arrangements in exchange for time with Lenin-Soviet-businessmen before Vladimir Ilyich Ulyanov Lenin's death. Was it not for the present taint of impropriety's shadows, the Russian-American relationship did have its time of cooperation. Nikolai Ssorin-Chaikov writes, "But as the historian of the US communist movement Theodore Draper puts it, it also epitomizes a paradox of mutual gifts of communism between Russia and America. Namely that while the "material basis of the Russian Revolution was in America; . . . the political fulfillment of the American economy was in Russia." Some of Lenin's own thinking about the American economy is reflected in his correspondence with Martens. But notes exchange about Hammer reveals a temporality of Soviet construction that is more complex than merely a combination of futures—the Russian political future and the American economic future." [63] The New York Times, December 12,1919, noted, 'There is, for example, an

---

[63] Ssorin-Chaikov, Nikolai. *Two Lenins: A Brief Anthropology of Time.* 2017 Hau Books, Chicago. ISBN: 978-0-9973675-3-9 LCCN: 2017934091.

exchange of telegrams in 1921 between Lenin and Ludwig Martens, a key Lenin lieutenant, and Bolshevik envoy, with Dr. Hammer watching over Mertens's shoulder.'

American oppression is best described as a flexible platform. It has coupled with theatrics and is more of an expression of frustration. At its core, it has a close similarity to a modern version of National Socialist politics, including the use of military and police force if required. There are also ways that National Socialism in the United States is different from the significant absence of "German prosperity." York University Professor Arthur Haberman stated in the *Toronto Star*, 28 July 2019, "The American Version of Fascism Is Alive and Prospering."

"The United States, as a whole, is not a fascist country. There are many places in states and localities where democracy thrives. The federal Republican Party, however, has become a fascist institution. The term "Fascism" gets thrown around too easily. In this case, it is not being used casually. Let's evaluate the Republican Party using the main characteristics of Fascism as it developed in the first half of the 20th century and as it exists now. Fascism is first characterized by a virulent nationalism, which is often either ethnic or racist. In the case of Trump, other leaders of the federal party, and many other Senate members and the House of Representatives, racist tropes are used all the time, most recently against several women of color in the Democratic Party. Republicans are nationalists, whether it is "America First," the insistence on the United States as the world's greatest country, or in a belief in American Exceptionalism, something that sounds as though it was coming out of middle Europe a century ago…. Fascists attempt to neutralize the courts and take away the independence of the judiciary. Republicans have politicized the Supreme Court, and the Republican-controlled Senate in the last few years has approved right-wing judges. Who do whatever is bidden by the party, many of them found not competent to serve by bar associations. There is a pretense to constitutional government, with manipulation in favor of the ruling party. The Senate, significantly, has changed or violated rules regularly. Mitch McConnell, the Republican leader in the Senate, is as fascistic as the president."

The fascist overhaul of the Republican Party Mr. Thompson sought, before his death on 3 March 2002, began as a notable donor to paleocons and extremist Conservative elements of the Republican Party. [64] During the National Socialists' attempt to influence the Reagan White House, Donald J. Trump made his presence known under the Democratic establishment's banner. He converted to Conservatism along with Rudy Giuliani, U.S. Attorney, during the President Reagan administration. Prominent fascist explains the targeting of Republican Conservatives and why they needed to be replaced. The fascists' insurgency began when Dr. Armand Hammer was heavily involved in the Reagan White House dedicated to stopping World War Three, which was also a goal of Harold Keith Thompson and other high echelons of the Nazis and Bolsheviks still alive.

"Why the Republican Party? At the time of the Reagan administration, there seems to have been an in-house contest for supremacy. Between what became known as neoconservatives and paleoconservatives. The "neo-cons," as we might call them, are neither "new" nor "conservative." They were Wilsonian-type liberal-Democrats and internationalists, or ex-Trotskyites who came over to the U.S. side during the Cold War in their hatred of Stalinism. The paleoconservatives, a term coined by Professor Paul Gottfried, were traditionalist Republicans of the Taft, America First variety. Including President Reagan's treasury secretary Paul Craig Roberts and Reagan White House

---

[64] Bolton, Kerry R. "H. Keith Thompson Jr." Profiles in History. *Inconvenient History.* Committee for Open Debate on the Holocaust. Vol. 6 (2014) No.2. See the Hoover Institution Archives for complete file.

communications adviser Patrick Buchanan." ---- Kerry R. Bolton, philosopher, academician, and prolific writer from New Zealand, is the author of "What's Behind the Anti-Right Witch-Hunt?"

American Harold Keith Thompson and his plan to reinstate National Socialism in Germany with Russia's assistance may still breed a new Conservatism. It is based on an event in history. When the Nazi Party ordered Vladimir Ilyich Ulyanov Lenin's financial support, the Bolshevik led to the Russian Revolution. The Nazi move illustrated that some extraordinary relationships among enemies are practical. Due to their compelling message, adherents in 2016 were willing to go back in time and become American Nazis. No public forum exists to address this.

This does not detract that Harold Keith Thompson kept his rank as Schutzstaffel, SS officer assigned, and operational. After the war, Mr. Thompson's retirement from the SS marked two critical events. That former CIA Director Allen Dulles politically engineered collaborative agreements with former recently "deactivated" Nazi SS officers. Mr. Dulles arranged for them immunity in exchange to work as covert CIA agents. In Germany, when Mr. Thompson called for an alliance with the Soviets, Germany had installed Dr. Hans Globke as their Secretary of State. Dr. Globke received notoriety when he disclosed that he was the same Globke, Nazi Interior Ministry's Office for Jewish Affairs, who authored the Protection of German Blood laws. The reasoning that would urge prosecutions for show then institute a release is the signature strategy led to the rise of the retired Schutzstaffel, SS, who viewed themselves as global police keeping their underground system intact.

Harold Keith Thompson was a pragmatist. He was from a pedigree of notable fascist Americans; there was only one significant character accusation during his career, having spanked members of the Marines for entertainment. Thompson never served one day in jail. The fascists have been working with Republicans for quite some time, as discussed by Kerry R. Bolton: I ask, "Why not the Republicans?"

"At the time, an "ethnic outreach" program by the Republican Party was recruited from among East European anti-communist émigrés who had fascist associations. The plan was headed by Laszlo Pasztor, founding chairman of the Republican Heritage Groups Council. He had been a member of the Arrow Cross movement of Hungarian National Socialists.

"The Heritage Council included Radi Slavoff, a Bulgarian supporter of German-American campaigner Dr. Austin J. App and Florian Galdau, a veteran of Romania's Iron Guard; Nicholas Nazarenko, a Cossack *Waffen S.S.* veteran; et al. This program campaigned vigorously against the Office of Special Investigations (OSI), established to hound elderly European émigrés with allegations of "war criminals," many having fought as partisans against Soviet incursions during World War II." [65]

Fascist ideology is disseminated in pieces in the United States in subtle matters. For example, Chris Hedges argues American Christians and particularly evangelicals are a fascist-inclined mob. [66] Evangelicals may refute this, but fascists are recognized throughout history as a group of individuals who abandon any former beliefs to attain state power. How else could anyone describe evangelical support for Donald J. Trump other than fascist-inclined if not committed to the cause? What we see is the coming together of fascist thinking widely expressed in evangelical movements for Trump. The Heritage Council was identified by the right-wing for decades as an organization dedicated to "displaced fascists."

It should be noted that after the Second World War, former Nazis were used by governments to spy on the Soviet Union in an attempt to slow the possibilities of another war. This was done by

---

[65]Ibid.

[66] Hedges, Chris. *American Fascists: The Christian Right and the War on America.* Free Press. 2006.

President Eisenhower, who fascists accused of hounding people with loose organization ties to Nazis.

A case study of the elite intellectual that drew on the subtleties of crowd ideology of fascism couldn't be a better example than Harold Keith Thompson (1922-2002). Still, many people would not accept him as an American, but he was. For this reason, Harold Keith Thompson serves as an American example of what Adolph Hitler's aim was in reaching out to Americans in their own country. His efforts directed operatives to create a state-sharing agreement that kept in place American flags and heroes' semblance. While the second objective was to keep the U.S. out of the war militarily, ensuring the Reich's potential to control the Heartland and Rimland. [67]

Mr. Thompson was a wealthy publisher along the lines of other famous fascists. History shows he did not speak much about himself and quickly rose to fascist prominence in his twenties. His father was a publisher in New York and was well-known among the rich and well-positioned in Washington, D.C. He was unwavering articulate, intelligent, and reflected a portion of the American political sentiment, aside from being a sharp opponent of President Dwight D. Eisenhower. When elites say they regard Adolph Hitler's American politics, Mr. Thompson often comes into the discussion. Mr. Thompson stated he sought a diplomatic relationship with Islamic politicians and made several inroads. Christian Science Monitor on 11 Oct. 2016 "Report: Germany's post-World War II government was full of Nazis." Fifty-percent of Germany's Justice Ministry in the 1950s and 1960s were former Nazis. Doing this work, "The Nazi-era lawyers went on to cover up old injustice rather than uncover it and thereby created new injustice." This added some discredit to Mr. Thompson's claim that former Nazis were being harassed and pursued relentlessly unjustly prosecuted.

Kerry R. Bolton remembers Harold Keith Thompson as a widely regarded fascist and dynamic grandson of researcher and

---

[67] Shevchenko, Vitaly. "Little green men" or "Russian invaders"? *BBC News*. 11 Mar. 2014.

innovator George K. Thompson. [68] Harold Keith Thompson, a New Jersey native, maintained friendships from the left and right spectrum. Such as with left-wing Mexican muralist David Alfiero Siqueiros. Thompson wrote an article on the case in Leftist publisher Lyle Stuart's magazine, *The Independent,* when Siqueiros was jailed in Mexico. Thompson also represented Left-wing artist Rockwell Kent and broke the blacklisting of Kent among publishers. By arranging for the production of Kent's *Greenland Journal* by Ivan Obolensky in New York. There was a different side of Harold K. Thompson, and it would reveal his philosophy and attitude toward the United States and Germany. His writing's central focus was to nudge and create doubt by the contrast between his optimistic view of National Socialism and a negative American outlook.

Thompson became a pivotal figure in Republican Party history and Conservatism. Not only because of his Republican and Conservative influence on significant historical events but for his stature and financial means. A friend of George Sylvester Viereck, a relative of the Kaiser and prolific Nazi writer, both were early American Bund and America First Committee/Party members. A close ally of Rear Admiral Richard Evelyn Byrd Jr., the Medal of Honor recipient, explored Antarctica in Operation High Jump. Rear Admiral Byrd thought that the center of the Earth was hollow based on a vision he had. Ironically this turn of events was discredited by a similar narrative Dr. Goebbels used to create mysticism and alternative aesthetic realities. Conspiracy theorists blew this out of proportion to the extent that theories of Germans living underground with dinosaurs and flying saucers obscured today's accomplishment of Rear Admiral Byrd and Harold K. Thompson.

Mr. Thompson was personally recognized and esteemed by Adolph Hitler and Heinrich Himmler. By Hitler's Oath, who made him a Special Agent of the Sicherheitsdienst (SD) Overseas Intelligence

---

[68] Bolton, Kerry R. "H. Keith Thompson Jr." Profiles in History. *Inconvenient History.* Committee for Open Debate on the Holocaust. Vol. 6 (2014) No.2. . See the Hoover Institution Archives for complete file.

Unit (a division of the SS) on 27 July 1941. Thompson was stationed in the United States and underwent foreign agent registration under the Socialist Reich Party. Mr. Thompson maintained his relationships with the Nazis and the Republican Party supporting Timothy McVeigh and the Oklahoma City bombing; 168 people were killed, including 19 children, and more than 500 were injured. This later compared to the Republican Party tolerance for Donald J. Trump's role in the 300,000+ deaths from COVID -19. This must-have placed Mr. Trump in high esteem with the Nazis because many victims were African Americans.

Historians first characterized Thompson as part of a Republican "fringe," often sweeping him aside. As this characterization became more synonymous with groups like the Liberty Lobby, Tea Party, and "freedom, faith, patriot" Libertarians and Sarah Palin Conservative, he was normalized. This psychological response will also be valid with Donald J. Trump, who will normalize radicals in his Republican Party though he was much worse than any Nazi in wanting to blow up the world. Followed by many socially acceptable labels compatible with the Conservative aspects of fascism. It was no longer possible to deny the "fertility," "apostasy," and contagion of those Nazism-Republican connections. Their beliefs went well beyond their so-called dual patriotism front and Americanism First followers. Republicans attempted to counteract the narrative as "socialist" by suggesting to Thompson to join the Liberty Party. He declined, surprised that they did not understand the Hitler Oath is exclusive. Mr. Thompson's involvement with Nazi war criminal Otto Skorzeny was not refuted in any historical account. Both worked on the ODESSA project to arrange the escape of the Nazi royalty and collaborator. Due to his elite status and Republican connections, Harold Keith Thompson has never been adjudicated as a propagandist like George Sylvester Viereck. Mr. Thompson played an important role in Nazi history because he was one of the only witnesses who knew the group's identity that engineered the link between the aging Nazi survivor in Eastern Europe and their resettlement to America.

What's behind the hounding of elderly European émigrés, according to Harold Keith Thompson? This involved the complex implementation of Holocaust reparations. A concern is that elderly Nazis needed some finances to survive, balanced by any Nazi loot surrender that arose during the President Clinton U.S. Holocaust Assets Commission Act of 1998. Also, Nazi Party divisions in the early part of Adolph Hitler's rise broke first alliances. Dr. Smelser, "…National Socialism pre-dates Hitler, and even after he entered politics in 1919, there were several National Socialists who still regarded themselves as the center of the movement by their seniority, of their political experience and success, and of their ideological development." (edited-RO) [69] History instructs us that after Adolph Hitler dominated the National Socialist Party, he transformed it by making it more criminalistic, evidenced by its evolving brutality.

Anti-fascist Russ Bellant, who agrees with Kerry R. Bolton's facts, "…tells us that an Eastern European émigré fascist network with direct ties to former Nazi collaborators has penetrated the Republican Party through its ethnic outreach program. He further argues that this network has played a significant role in shaping American foreign policy since World War II, to roll back the borders of the Soviet Union in an inevitable military confrontation." [70] In *The Beast Reawakens*, Martin Lee describes this Cold War period as a multifaceted neofascist restoration that gained disturbing energy within the post-Cold War era. A case in point, while President Bill Clinton's administration moved into areas concerning genocide in Serbia and financial recovery of Nazi treasure. One notable example of Slobodan Milošević's different philosophies entered the United States as Serge Trifkovic, a Serbian, Director of Lord Byron Foundation in 1995, and a famous writer. The United States, for many reasons, banked on the melting pot to cure many of the world's

---

[69] Smelser, Von Ronald M. "Hitler and the DNSAP: Between Democracy and Gleichschaltung." This is a revised Version of a paper presented at the annual Convention of the American Historical Association in Dallas/Texas, December 27—30, 1977. 1. Note: Gleichschaltung, the standardization of political, economic, and social institutions as carried out in authoritarian states.

[70] Bellant, Russ. *Old Nazis, the new right, and the Republican party: domestic fascist networks and U.S. cold war politics.* Copyright© by Russ Bellant 1988, 1989, 1999. ISBN 0-89608--41 9. Political Research Associates, 678 Massachusetts Avenue, Suite 205, Cambridge, MA 02139. South End Press.

ills. It turned out Serge Trifkovic was a Patrick Buchanan-type Conservative writing extensively about Islamophobia. The United States continued at its peril to invite unwelcome guests and share its freedoms and profits.

While Republican Party reactionaries and conservatives appear and function more like fascists, they place the world at risk. Either purposely or inadvertently, two actors in these theatrics are in the process of changing thinking patterns. Followed by changes in American identity will look more like foreign and emotional hate scenarios. Like the American fascist alters their strategy, so has Trump Organization incorporating these ideologies into their operations, providing them with the ability to share and synthesize criminal and ideological beliefs. ---the basis for financial cooperation with the mafia in sophisticated ways. There was still the mystery of why the respected Roy Cohn, Esq. that once was held in esteem by President Reagan for his history of locating fascists for Senator Joe McCarthy and Congressman Nixon changed drastically. Paul Manafort, Roger Stone, Donald J. Trump, who were well-connected insiders, reversed their stance, ultimately becoming alt-right pariahs.

Conservative Involvement in Europe

Rhetoric alone makes a fair speech campaign, but members have to be hardcore to start a new Conservative community movement. Yes, they can be trained as mob members, but one knows having the master who stokes his followers to breaking-bad have promising futures. This part of the alternative-right story leans backward to Paul Manafort's activities in Ukraine's right-wing politics. Movements do not exist in poverty, at least not ones involving intellectuals. In a fractured web of desperate financial gatherings, Mr. Manafort attempted to conceal millions of dollars he made while working on behalf of a pro-Putin political party in Ukraine. In 2005, Manafort was hired by Rinat Akhmetov, a Ukrainian steel magnate who wanted to burnish his international image. It is not just a random political outfit, but the one was working with Viktor Yanukovych and Aleksandr Dugin. To win the Ukraine right-wing ticket wishing to become integrated with the European Union infrastructure and possibly dismantle it. Once the plan fell through and collapsed, another route was selected.

That was Donald J. Trump and Conservatives appointing him as Campaign Chair, the perfect guise for continuing to leverage his value to Russia. Perhaps it was inevitable the emotional Trump-allure sent Mr. Manafort to prison. The theatrics of Russian political artistry should not detract from the likeness between the aspirations of neo-Nazis, the Fourth Reich, additionally, what the pilot Aleksandr Dugin conceived as The Fourth Political Theory. Just the fact that neo-Nazis are invited to be schooled in Moscow, Slovenia, Slovakia forests, and the United States on the merits of Russian affinity to racism speaks for itself. Conservatives were involved in Europe shipping Bibles and Christian literature to hosts propagandizing anti-abortion tools recently converted to an interest in money and Russian Oligarchy.

Russian criminal sources would not touch aluminum due to a discussion related to being killed. Knut Royce, for *The Center for Public Integrity* on 14 December 1999, wrote, "Kislin said Mikhail Chernoy tried to enlist him as "cover" or "legitimate front" in the plan to grab control of the aluminum industry, but that he declined. "I said aluminum is not for me," Kislin said. "I cannot do with aluminum because aluminum is a very dangerous business (in Russia)." Indeed, what followed has been dubbed "The Aluminum Wars" by the Russian press, as many businessmen, most of whom opposed the Chernoy takeover, were killed. Kislin said that the brothers obtained licenses "to buy the aluminum for $10 and sell it for $1,500" by bribing top Russian officials. "The corruption is unbelievable."

Senator Mitch McConnell recently was observed establishing an oligarch aluminum company in Kentucky associated with Russians. "He could be sending $200 million if you believe media reports. In what could very well be mobbed-up money to northeastern Kentucky to build a $1.7 billion aluminum plant on an old strip mine there.", according to *The Washington Post*, Max Bearak 30 October 2017. [71] Senator McConnell was working with what the West calls the white-collar mafia, the U.S. sanctioned Oleg Deripaska, connected to Paul Manafort. This avenue provides for direct communication between President Vladamir Putin and Congress in trade negotiations.

Seeming to agree with what is seen in the news, Aleksandr Dugin appears to take Harold Keith Thompson's identity, leaving the impression that his presentations have a quality of insincerity and conspiracy. [72]

"The 2014 Ukrainian crisis has highlighted the pro-Russia stances of some European countries, such as Hungary and Greece, and some European parties. Mostly on the far-right of the political spectrum. Predating the Kremlin's internet-inspired networks. The European connections of Alexander Dugin paved the way for the pan-European illiberal ideology that included fascism. Based on an updated reinterpretation of fascism. Although Dugin and the European far-right belong to the same ideological world and can be seen as two sides of the same coin, the alliance between Putin's regime and the European far-right is more a marriage of convenience than one of true love."-Anton Shekhovtsov, *Eurasianism, and the European Far Right: Reshaping the Europe–Russia Relationship.* 2014.

During the 1980s and 1990s, there were movements afoot that were recreating old paths formerly used by the Third Reich. Encouraged by the Presidential support out of the Reagan White House, the

---

[71] Pierce, P. Charles. "Surely It's a Coincidence That a Firm Tied to a Russian Oligarch Is Pouring Millions Into Kentucky." *Esquire.* 24 April 2019.

[72] Laruelle, Marlene. *Eurasianism and the European Far Right: Reshaping the Europe–Russia Relationship.* ISBN-13: 978-1498510707. Lexington Books (March 24, 2017).

white supremacist movement grew tenfold. In today's Turkey, Hungary, and Greece, American Front, where Steve Bannon, Aleksandr Dugin, and the white-collar mafia now are the most powerfully aligned fascist types in President Vladamir Putin's media network. Soviet Union's decline in the 1990s led to the resurgence of the "Third Positions" movement. During the Second World War, they were neo-fascists reorganizing and sophisticating their "centrist" viewpoint. They pursued a "National Bolshevik" ideology, which supported a revolutionary, ethno-nationalist model of Soviet-like governance in Western Europe. Contrasting their Third Positions to North Atlantic liberalism purportedly imposed by NATO. [73] This is in contrast to Bolshevism being illegal in Russia.

The extreme Conservative tactic here was to agree on the proposition ideologically akin to what is frequently heard of in *The Camp of the Saints* position and Gisèle Littman, who is Bat Ye'or. Gisèle Littman readily separates the ethnicity of political races by their eugenic capacity of "always being the oppressor" of American white supremacists alongside Jewish co-defenders. In this Apocalyptic battle on the side of Jews, Islam is ridiculed as a powerful force taking over the world. Perhaps to redress the actions of the Ottomans who entered Europe by extending the Islamophobia of this era? Using the twist in logic, on the one hand, she is a defender of American right-wing nationalism. Still, she doesn't appear to see that all nationalism has similar goals as domination. Gisèle Littman's angle endorsed the sublime fears in the idea of "Eurabia" --- that, in reality, is not easy to grasp unless you use another term to equate it, Lebensraum. See *Bibliography*.

Most of these viewpoints are marketed as "true tales" but are often used to fund trendy actions in the expanding fantasy within real "hate for-profit" industries. These Eurabia positions also correlate to pro-Zionist postures and are connected financially to what is known as the Islamophobia Industry. In 2011, The Center for American Progress

---

[73] Bevensee, Emmi and Alexander Reid Ross. "The Alt-Right and Global Information Warfare." Instructor, *Department of Geography, Portland State University*. Portland, Oregon, USA. Undated.

found the Donors Capital Fund gave a single block grant of $18 million to the Clarion Fund in 2008. In the same year, the group distributed 28 million copies of the Islamophobic film *Obsession.* Barack Obama was running for president, and conspiracy theories about him being a 'secret Muslim' abounded to make millions from revolutions, history informs, and consistent investments. This was the dawning of a new era where devotees could click hate messages, and their web hosts gained millions. The often-invisible Conservative became a cottage industry offering good incomes.

In cooperation with the former Soviet Union, Dr. Hammer stands out as a case in point. In his own way, Dr. Hammer played the Jackel. He managed to undermine American oil interests, never forgotten as a successful strategy. Note: There are no released records of why Donald J. Trump, Paul Manafort, Roger Stone migrated their similar ideologies toward oil-gas. [74]

"Hammer also happens to be Jewish (by background if not belief), yet Libyan strongman Col. Muammar el-Qaddafi has made him a major beneficiary of Libya's oil wealth. In the early 1970's, Hammer negotiated accommodation with Qaddafi that had the eventual effect of contributing to OPEC's growth and power, and that radically changed the oil business around the world. (Even though both Mobil and Exxon announced decisions to suspend production in Libya earlier this month, Occidental, the main channel of Libyan oil, declared its intention to continue production as usual.) Not incidentally, perhaps, it was also in Hammer's interest. His company was committed to shipping a million tons of concentrated phosphoric acid to the Soviet Union annually for the next 20 years. This would provide Soviet agriculture with the liquid fertilizers that it desperately needs to improve crop yields. The deal that Hammer reckoned

---

[74] Epstein, Edward J. "The Riddle of Armand Hammer." *The New York Times.* 29 Nov. 1981.

to be worth no less than $20 billion had been nearly wrecked by the American embargo."

Col. Muammar el-Qaddafi, under rabbinic law, was Jewish, a fact explored with Dr. Hammer. [75] There was also a claim that Russia promotes since the 1970s that always return to domination and wealth themes. President Nixon's ending of the free exchange of dollars for gold in 1974 was guaranteed by the US in 1944 at Bretton Woods. Writing on the Breton Woods agreement, Dmitry Kalinichenko wrote, "Grandmaster Putin's Golden Trap." President Putin was using his oil and gas to collect enough to buy the world's gold. [76] Mr. Kalinichenko, "The world will not survive if oil and gas from Russia are subtracted from the global balance of energy supply."

The Washington Post ran a piece that followed this theme, "100 years later, Bolshevism is back! And we should be worried." [77] Inarguably many of these Trump family associates were Soviet and Russian Jew émigré with old country connections to the Bolshevik-Communist era. Some had histories of collaborating with the Nazis. Before 2016, all right-wing extremists were welcomed into the Republican Party. Stephen Miller, a Trump White House Jewish advisor, had his behavioral spin.[78] Conceding by actions, he sounded like the specter of white nationalism in the White House.

Stephen Miller stated vehemently in what was his typical assertive posture. That since being dramatically exposed by writing 900 emails injecting white supremacy and its populism to Breitbart News, a Dr. Robert Mercer and Steve Bannon's media outlet. Mr. Miller accused his opponents of having anti-Semitic thinking. Miller has asserted

---

[75] The Economist. "Come and be an Israeli!" 10 Sept. 2011.

[76] Kalinichenko, Dmitry. "Grandmaster Putin's Golden Trap." *Information Clearinghouse.* 25 Dec. 2014.

[77] Applebaum, Anne. "100 years later, Bolshevism is back. And we should be worried." *The Washington Post.* 06 Nov. 2017.

[78] Behrmann, Savannah. "Advocacy group releases leaked emails from White House adviser Stephen Miller to Breitbart." *USA Today.* 12 Nov. 2019.

that government critics were attacking his Jewish faith and culture for his behavior as being racist against Jews. In contrast, it was evident by emails he condemned Jews himself through his anti-Semitic rants online and through policies. Miller, a Jew attacking Jews, then used the excuse they are anti-Semitic, absolved himself from being anti-Semitic. Serves as a prime example of a person of many social conflicts. But either move is undeniably not in his best cultural or religious interests. Is this future? [79] The new world order is questioned by *The Times of Israel.* [80]

"This all started much earlier. During and after the 1917 Russian Revolution, Lenin was putting together a Politburo and elite leadership with numerous Jews. About one-third in all, from a population of less than 3% of the Russian people. The names are familiar: Leon Trotsky, Grigorii Zinoviev, Lev Kamenev, Yakov Sverdlov, Maxim Litvinov, Karl Radek, and Grigorii Sokolnikov. Lenin, who had a Jewish grandfather who had become an Orthodox Russian – was fond of Jews. He declared, "Scratch an Old Bolshevik, and you will always find some Jewish blood.""

Still, *The Washington Post* claim seemed outrageous, but they have since been joined by others. Bolshevism is illegal in Russia. Many of them knew Vladimir Ilyich Ulyanov Lenin is dead, but they have inspired a new millennial following. This may be the reason why President Vladamir Putin keeps his connection to it concealed. Still, we know his father, Vladimir Spiridonovich Putin, worked for Vladamir Ilyich Ulyanov Lenin. Bertrand Russell defines the ideology, "Bolshevism combines the French Revolution's characteristics with those of Islam's

---

[79] Adelman, Jonathan. "Russians and Jews: The Odd Couple." *The Jerusalem Post.* 11 Oct. 2018.

[80] Surkes, Sue. "Oligarchs pumping money into Elkin Jerusalem mayoral campaign, filing shows." *The Times of Israel.* 24 Oct. 2018.

rise. The result is radically new, which can only be understood by a patient and passionate effort of imagination… There is, however, another aspect of Bolshevism from which I differ more fundamentally. Bolshevism is not merely a political doctrine; it is also a religion, with elaborate dogmas and inspired scriptures." [81]

What are the characteristics of political religion? There are simply an array of identifiable habits and loyalty systems found in the early Roman Church archetypes. Its main feature is the deployment of entryism and mainstreaming people, which the Republican Party under President Trump did exceptionally well to destroy themselves. This applies to the senior generation's efforts to maintain a corrupt, aging, rusting energy system Rachel Maddow describes in her book *Blowout* and Professor Kathleen Belew's study called *Bring the War Home*. First, readers should remember the previously mentioned *Threat Uncertainty Model* of Dr. Mehta. It describes the centrists' behavior, their hidden violence, and how useful the neo-Bolsheviks found Vladamir Lenin's approach destroying democratic mechanisms by making them helplessly weak from the inside of their institutional structure.

"As first stated, the theory of democratic centralism was based on the following reasoning as a political party's functional method. Social revolutionists needed not a mere parliamentary organization. But a party of action would function as a scientific body of direction, a vanguard of activists tied to the revolutionary masses, and a central control organon. The party should be an elite body of professional revolutionists dedicating their lives to the cause and carrying out their iron discipline decisions. No

---

[81] Russell, Bertrand. *The Practice and Theory of Bolshevism*. London, George Allen & Unwin. Ltd. Ruskin House, 40 Museum St. W.C. 1. Feb. 1921.

task too small; no sacrifice too great. Such a party could not be built from the bottom up but only from the top down." [82]

Some Mechanics of Bolshevism

The national security threat matrix against the United States is not understood outside the realm of democracies' positions. It's unnecessary to do the job as the Federal Bureau of Investigation could because the people's interrelationships are the most important. Bolshevism and the modern currents use are the same ones Dr. Armand Hammer exercised in creating Lenin's web of influencers and their pivotal employment role. The goal they want to achieve was aptly described by Professor Nikolai Ssorin-Chaikov's work on the Two Lenin's and the paradox of mutual gifts of communism between Russia and capitalist America.

Crimea was annexed in 2014 after a short war signaled by the fall of the Ukrainian president. In 2005, Manafort was hired by Rinat Akhmetov, a Ukrainian steel magnate who wanted to burnish his international image. The Orange Revolution unfolds in Ukraine. Mr. Manafort's involvement is not just a random political outfit, but working with aspiring-to-become President, namely Viktor Yanukovych. Previously Mr. Manafort worked with dictatorships, arms dealers and invested in a bank that crashed in Portugal, and in 2006 appears to be a consultant/operative for the Russian government. Caught in a swindling scheme, the variety of investments Mr. Manafort held after Mr. Yanukovych won the election then fled Ukraine (after the Euro-Maiden challenge) for Russia collapsed, but did not cut him off from Russia. Despite that, Mr. Manafort was in hock to prominent Russians who ultimately lost their investments. Eventually, Mr. Manafort clears about $17 million working as a foreign agent of a pro-Russian Ukrainian political party associated with right-wing backers.

---

[82] Weisbord, Albert. "Bolshevism, Fraudulent Practice Of Democratic Centralism." *"La Parola del Popolo"* November/December 1976.

This political process netted Russia millions after securing Crimea. It increased its net worth in dominating the small area, not for its cultural security but for developing it for a massive military base. President Trump sought a part of the action in a blackmail scheme against Ukraine that was made public. In 2017 President Trump appointed Michael Pompeo as Director of Central Intelligence Agency, then Mr. Trump repositioned him to the Secretary of State ostensibly to work with oil-rich Saudi Arabia. Ukraine Ambassador Marie Yovanovich attempted to resist influence, U.S. special envoy to Ukraine Kurt Volker did not hide the facts of what the Trump Presidency wanted to accomplish, which was identical in outcome to what Paul Manafort wanted for Russia. A Ukrainian state is sympathetic to the ultranationalist neo-Nazi right-wing Svoboda political party.

Although it first seems a motley mix of belief from neo-Protestant evangelicals anxious for the Apocalypse, neo-Nazis and preserving white people, Zionists, a Republican Party with streams of finances from Wall Street. They all had a significant problem in common. On the one hand, they were making money through the online hate industry. They were unified by their prejudices and hatred, some Jews, immigrants in general, those perceived as bad genes, and Arabs. This politics is a politics of individual superiority, preservation of privilege, resentment, and revenge. On the surface, this band of would-be ethnocentric lunatics are no longer confined but have an Office of the President to funnel their desires and wishes. Nevertheless, this set of beliefs was enough to invoke mass killings against Jews and kill Blacks on sight unavoidably is the terroristic outcome.

Conservative Gothic Against Women

Conservatives were enthralled with President Trump and became obsessed with their tentative masculinity in the Campaign that underscores their fears and sexual uncertainty. Being mostly dispassionate supporters, they were lashing out at liberals before they were faced at last by femininity, the needs of humanity, healthcare, and human nature. Finding their masculinity in danger, Conservatives conceived of frightening events in their campaigns. Such as imagined female spells, conjured female horrors, frenzies that visited them while Conservatives were asleep. Like a hidden hand caressing and chilling them up and down. This imagined darkness was a means of invoking slander and fear against challenges by women. I distinctly remember the turmoil Republican Conservatives went through at their first frightening glimpse of the Beetles and miniskirts, a Communist conspiracy. Since the 1960s, the Republican Conservative message about women turned toward narratives of violence and awe, e.g., the traumatic aspects of stress. This became frequent in the judicial system under the cloak of discussion about "preserving life" while being raped. The "raped" identity became standard in Republican politics and sometimes was used to associate it with environments, liberals, and politicians being raped.

Wilhelm Reich, MD, before his imprisonment in the United States, identified sexual repression as inseparable from the impulses of extreme conservatism he witnessed in Germany. It has long been a pattern of fascism that emerged under Nazism, was done by Soviet soldiers on Jews, and in Italy by Mussolini. Caroline J. (Kay) Picart and Cecil Greek, in their work "Introduction: Toward a Gothic Criminology," wrote, "Besides, sexual perversions are fundamental in Gothic literature because they are spawned by severe repression and, their imaginative exploration allows for the expansion of the parameters of sexual practice. Gothicism is drawn to all eruptions of unbridled sexuality, and the politics of gender involved in rape is as significant as the sexual aspect of the act. The contrast between the triumphant evil of the rapist and the helpless innocence of the victim accentuates the magnitude of the villain's power." This Gothic representation of power played out in Mr. Trump's Presidential candidate scandals, which were ignored despite the evidence. [83] This placed the image of rape and domestic violence as permissible and so allowable it could be done by the chief law enforcement officer of the United States.

---

[83] Biddle, Sam. "The Time Donald Trump's Ex-Wife Accused Him of Brutally Raping Her." 30 Jul. 2015. *Gawker.*

Gothic representation and grotesque mental images result from the unique medieval description used to horrify mental hospital confinement as a discipline method and keep the family's physical abuse secret. The masters of this gothic messaging were the Nazis. "Lock her up." is from this era, similar to the surrealism of "burn her." This is also true in Soviet psychiatry. Both the United States and Russia's legal systems have tried to intervene in emotional difficulty considered political dissent and classified under generic psychiatric classification like schizophrenia chronic undifferentiated type and "sluggish" schizophrenia in Soviet and Russian mental hospitals. [84]

In Republican politics and particularly since 2016, the use of confinement in psychiatric hospitals was repeatedly threatened under their rhetoric of the "madwoman" and an endless array of "lock her up" consensus by Mr. Trump allies. Suggesting there was something deliberately purposeful and fearful in his nature as the rapist coming for you. Declarations on Donald J. Trump that he is insane are along these lines. The psychiatric discovery of this or that diagnosis glosses over the real problem using gothic parallels. Society itself, its absolute positions, the rigidity of authoritarianism generates these "madness's," but they are hardly original.

Conservatives believed in legislative solutions for uncontrolled femininity. Women's harsh reality was that their children's infant mortality rates are about 3% higher during a typical Republican-presidential year than an average Democratic-president year. It is a numbing reality that fellow Americans are plotting the demise of unborn children they plan for and expect to die with too high infant mortality in Alabama. *Vogue Portugal* featured a "Madwoman Issue" in July/August, denoting a campaign for discussion that was renounced as the past. But is it? Soon this was underscored by the arrest of white slave trader Jeffrey Edward Epstein who ritualistically and suspiciously hung

---

[84] Reich, Walter. "The World View of Soviet Psychiatry." *The New York Times*. 30 Jan. 1983.

himself. It was a ritual following the criminal code to avoid talking to authorities, but it was uniquely conservative.

The worst of Conservative horrors during previous elections were revived when wives of Conservatives routinely dreamt. They have visions of being raped by different minorities seeking payment for the Conservative Confederates' oppressive deeds. Since keeping records of civil and criminal acts, Conservatives have used femininity to justify their terrorism, from 1923 Rosewood to 1955 Emmitt Till and recently in Charleston, South Carolina by Dylan Storm Roof. [85] This fear was made by tuning in to the political channels of their constituents. These imaginings amplified other questions. So, when strolling down roads, they might be grabbed into a back street. A few ladies felt this racial fear would lead to dark guys holding up beneath their beds in the fantasy of such an extraordinary event. Assaulting them when they came home at that point, impregnating them. In one recent case, this paranoia cost a man's life in Texas, and it is barely remembered. [86] By the end of this story, women and their consent will be a central theme as President Trump deploys this ritual, Gothicism. The feminist community would see Gothic attacks' unconscious impact on rape and horrendous pornographic displays that contaminate malleable American institutions.

"How could Nazism, which was represented by lamentable, shabby, puritan young men. By a species of Victorian Spinsters have become everywhere today… In all the pornographic literature of the world, the absolute reference to eroticism? All the shoddiest aspects of the erotic imagination are now put under the sign of Nazism?" ----Michel Foucault

---

[85] Gray, Emma. "The History of Using White Female Sexuality to Justify Racist Violence." *HuffPost.* 19 Jun. 2015.

[86] Morgan, Windsor. "Officer who walked into wrong apartment and killed man faces arrest: Authorities." *ABC News.* 07 Sept. 2017.

3. Social and Historical Context

"To them, you're just a freak, like me! They need you right now, but when they don't, they'll cast you out, like a leper! You see, their morals, their code; it's a bad joke. Dropped at the first sign of trouble. They're only as good as the world allows them to be. You'll see. I'll show you. When the chips are down, these, uh, civilized people? They'll eat each other. See, I'm not a monster. I'm just ahead of the curve. "----Joker (2019) Movie / Arthur Fleck aka Joaquin Phoenix

Organized crime families have their features and demographics. They leave their "signature" from their behavior. Their operative method is transmitted to family and members who are expected to imitate established traditions and values. Some crime families consider timing a golden rule, and some will not carry weapons, such as some financial mafia. True, we may never know what a person's thoughts are, but we know who they make friends with. This chapter will discuss a few of the stereotypical behaviors.

The worst of all crimes involve a little insanity while they are supported by sound judgment. In other words, people selectively choose a dark path and awake what is barbaric while appearing sophisticated and suave. This gives the sinister perpetrator a sense of control. They can choose to turn on their hatred and snakes in their head at will and direct it at "just the right victim." Usually, this involves the familiarity with the types of people to victimize repeatedly involving a pattern. Such as those people that are reminiscent of previous enemies and those who have harmed them. Sophisticated people trained by those not as maddened by these experiences can be found in the company and among friendships of crazier ones. They might have mutual feelings that irk them or the petty differences they resent in society.

When these types of criminals go public and operate on their whims, it is almost sure to clarify their emotional outlet and identify the types of victims they pursue. A person's higher authority may not just reflect the plot of murder that can be nurtured along but can become a national crime, where society is asked to participate. This is why hate crimes become dangerous because they can be infectious and easily inflamed. Americans have long believed in their goodness and morality. This chapter will show this is totally displaced and how cruel men brought about crimes under the banner of American patriotism.

There are corporate structures in Wall Street that are thinly veiled criminal organizations. Headquarters and the habitation of every sort of criminal from the mafia, intricate criminalist networks, thieves, and murderers. Those are just the ones the public knows. There are also thieves within the government. The ideal case study of how this type of economy thrives is no better an example than to select one corporation that epitomizes a microcosm of this problem. There are hundreds to choose from, each more enticing as a subject than another. Too enticing that it has captured the imagination of every aberrant and deviant business and political group. The publicity and boldness of the Trump Organization openly display their brazen model. It's just too much of an opportunity to ignore. Winner!

Trump's family is transparent about their dealing, but this is an intentional tactic to normalize the behavior. This book cannot feature all the examples of their efforts to undermine normality and encourage crime that present itself to the public. Instead, the family has stepped forward voluntarily by holding public office, thereby inviting scrutiny. This serves as more than a suitable case of how they incorporate criminal networks for profit. Overall, this chronicles the failure to pursue prosecution by a weak establishment too frightened to confront the underground. Since 1975 Donald J. Trump took over as family boss and had many escapades on the periphery of legitimate purpose until his involvement conjoined with foreign intelligence services drawing attention to an already established criminal network.

To briefly acknowledge underlying factors skirting the topic of how society's failure to maintain a stable regimen of truth has secreted from this family. In this chapter, readers should understand that the Trump Organization is some foreign business entity in New York and Washington, D.C. To the Trump family, it is their home. This is where several generations learned their family values, ate meals, went off to school, had their anniversaries and significant other relationships. The absence of social abnormality doesn't speak to any lack of psychological problems. For example, exposure to the dark world of organized crime figures during the formative years does much more to explain how moral code is transmitted in the family. This is particularly true when most endeavors you associate yourself with exhibit repetitive criminal associations like marrying into other criminals' families, perpetuating the family systems and secrets. The following information and social analysis will focus on family dynamics and their part in shaping American values.

For decades pre- and post-9-11, law enforcement in the United States refused to acknowledge any foreign organized crime operating here in reports of the highest order. Russian Organized Crime in the United States by James O. Finckenauer, Ph.D. from the *International Center National Institute of Justice,* is emblematic of this trend of denial. While law enforcement's higher echelon was priding itself on this belief, people on the street witnessed otherwise. In fact, there were thousands of "uninitiated members" of the global mafia's financial officers operating in cities across the Country.

The kinds of organized crime were often romanticized and misrepresented as a neighborhood problem. In reality, foreign organized crime was much more of a psychological issue. One in which foreign criminal culture was redefining American businesses, particularly the lucrative real estate sector, due to their dual role as mortgage banks. This chapter reveals a few of the main operatives working not only behind the scenes in their modest offices but documents their presence recreating and socializing with the nation's elites and celebrities. Consider the family history of "mining the miners" and "war profiteering," the profiteering criminal activities involved skimming funds from the government contracts program. This type of mentality asks, "is it really criminal to rob criminals?"

The naïve may, at first glance, not be able to see the interworking of different ideological groups that appear unrelated to one another. This is particularly true in the influential church community. That is until the spiritual insurgency model is understood. A spiritual insurgency can occur as Dr. Robert Bunker states, "Spiritual insurgency emerges from the personal and collective search for meaning in changing societies where traditional authority structures and social hierarchies had decayed or collapsed altogether."[87] In the United States, this type of insurgency is seen similar to Wall Street's commercial interests, the declining legitimacy of the neo-Protestant churches, generational changes in the Nazi generation, and fear of lost culture in white society. In the right hands elevating the hate in these groups can reap millions manipulating religious institutions.

Thief-in-law strength comes from its ability to reinvent and disguise itself according to a thief's code of honor. Thousands of different organizationally loose "subsidiaries" exist to support this effort, too numerous to track. This chapter provides a background on their features. Mainly how a principle of cooperation exists among these groups and their relationship to legitimate businesses. That is part of the mafia system of governance referred to as "the state within a state." Most people do not fully appreciate how the United States has been transformed from a "Federal Government" to a "Corporate State" within it. Segments of the corporate state are corrupted, with smaller outlying criminal groups on Wall Street similar to how the thieves-in-law operate.

France 24 media reported on 13 March 2019, "Russia's powerful 'Thieves in Law' face reckoning under Putin." That, "We must end this state within a state, and with it this romantic image that sometimes surrounds these 'godfathers' and presents them as heroes," said Otari Arshba, a lawmaker with the pro-Kremlin United Russia party and the prominent supporter of the bill amending Russia's criminal code. Arshba, a Soviet-era KGB officer who worked organized crime cases, said the key change in the law will be a provision making "the simple fact of being in charge of a criminal organization is enough" to

---

[87] Bunker, Robert et al. "Los Caballeros Templarios De Michoacán: Imagery, Symbolism, and Narratives." Los Caballeros Templarios de Michoacán: Imagery, Symbolism, and Narratives (2019). April 2019 *Small Wars Foundation*. Bethesda, Maryland.

convict crime bosses. [88] Mr. Arshba comprehends that crime is not the only business of the mafias. For the families to survive, they must also propagate their culture. Not only in their homeland Russia but imitate and replicate the formula overseas. Intergenerational families are significant replicators of criminal institutions, often undermining governmental authority or infiltrating.

A similar assessment of criminals' public perception was made to the "Waterfront Commission of New York Harbor (WCNYH) told Jane's on 18 April 2018. "The five families still run legal businesses, partner up with other criminal groups, run much of the show in town, certainly in the Ports of New York." Legal and criminal profit drives their enterprises. With FBI Assistant Director-In-Charge William F. Sweeney claiming at the time of the LCN (La Cosa Nostra) arrests, "The allure of gangland culture is often embraced and glamorized in movies and on television, where the threats posed to our economic and national security are seldom displayed." DIC Sweeny fell short of stating the mafias look to placing government under its control. [89]

In Russia, the country operates through a subgroup governing body of oligarchs and professional criminals as part of a corporate state model. Not only domestically but extends globally. This has attracted American corporations that seek the same influence of power and law evasion as they have in Russia within the United States. Complete with all the populist aesthetics, emphasis on male prowess, fraud, and Bohemian culture. These displays still persist today as a style of philosophy while they function as a social control mechanism. A continuation of Vladimir Ilyich Ulyanov Lenin's idea of developing capitalism in Russia today has Mr. Putin's position questionable.

---

[88] Lapenkova, Marina. "Russia's powerful 'Thieves in Law' face reckoning under Putin." *Agence-France Presse.* 12 March 2019.

[89] Sergi, Anna. "New York crime families survive and collaborate." Dr Anna Sergi is a lecturer in criminology at the Department of Sociology, University of Essex, United Kingdom, and Deputy Director of the Centre for Criminology.

"Mr. Putin's insistence that he be allowed to run Russia solely the way he needs and wants precludes meeting the population's demands for an end to abuse and privilege. His system does not merely permit those ills; it depends on them. It depends on cronyism, corruption, and abuse of privilege. Putin's system truly is a "gang of swindlers and thieves"—a widely used moniker, first given to the United Russia party by a prominent Russian opposition figure. That is not a side effect of the system Mr. Putin has created. As we have described, it is essential to the system's operation. This is how Putin controls the people who help him run the system. People at the center are swindlers and thieves because Putin's protection mechanism requires that they be swindlers and thieves. To keep them in check and remind them of the ruin they face if they try to cash out."[90]

Criminal and underworld American communities in the Soviet era relied on thief-in-law structures to control the growing number of criminals on the loose caused by the bureaucracy. Doing whatever is needed to survive, criminal worker bees and muscle among the thieves-in-law keep their criminal society intact during a crisis. [91] They have

---

[90] Hill, Fiona, and Clifford G. Gaddy. *Mr. Putin: Operative in the Kremlin.* Brookings Institution Press (November 27, 2012)

[91] Thieves-in-Law: The notion itself is a construct of two terms: the THIEF, in public perception clearly indicating the criminal sphere, and the LAW, that refers to notions, such justice, the state, legislation, legitimization, etc. Thus, the Thief-in-law is a notion, which regardless its inner structural controversy reflects a certain social reality, which is understandable for society and represents a part of a social structure. It needs explanation, which involves both understanding of historical roots and research of contemporary state of affairs. A *thief-in-law* (Wikipedia):(Russian: вор в законе, tr. *vor v zakone*) in the Soviet Union, the post-Soviet states, and respective diasporas abroad is a specifically granted formal and special status of "criminal dignitary" (kriminalny avtoritet), a professional criminal who enjoys an elite position among other notified mobsters within the organized crime

emerged with new energy and assembled from the time of Stalin's creation. Suppose they can continue to formulate a way to become a state-within-state in Russia. In that case, it spells trouble for Mr. Putin, significantly if they migrate into political positions that challenge his wealth. From the Eastern European perspective, how do they perceive the Trump family, investing time and money to create these close relationships.

Ivana Zelníčková married Donald J. Trump in 1977, and Melania Knauss Knavs married Trump in 2005, daughter of the Slovenia Communist Party Viktor Knavs. There is an allure to the Trump Organization environment in décor and familiarity and warmth of home. Both played an essential role in the image Mr. Trump had navigated about a mythical relationship with the Slavic people. Mr. Trump used his wives as a type of concierge between himself and Eastern European ethnicities. During these marriages, both women had a connection to the Communist Party. Neither revealed what their family was thinking concerning the invasions of their country by the Soviets. Not because they were not willing or incapable but treated like royalty was never asked. From the time of Donald J. Trump's attempt to disinherit the family from father Frederick, the family has been shut.

Arranged marriages are made between crime clans to bridge gaps in their operations and are considered an obligation for continuity. These marriages were a particular asset in working with Viktor Orbán, Conservative Prime Minister of Hungary, and the White House's adaptation of his Zero Tolerance policy. For example, this is an ideal situation for Russian agents to tap into personal and cultural loyalties in theory. [92] Donald J. Trump had never actually resided anywhere among

---

environment and employs informal authority over its lower-status members. The phrase "Thief-in-law" is a rudimentary, word-by-word translation of the Russian slang phrase "вор в законе", literally translated as "a thief in [a position of] the law", that can have two meanings in Russian: "a legalized thief" and "a "a legalized thief"". ---Gigi Tevzadze.

[92] Soldatov, Andrei and Irina Borogan. *The Compatriots: The Brutal and Chaotic History of Russia's Exiles, Émigrés, and Agents Abroad.* Public Affairs (October 8, 2019) ISBN-13: 978-1541730168.

any Slavic population outside the family. Where else would he be influenced to the extent he feels so harmonious with Slavic politics? Obviously, he reveals comparisons about oppressing and terrorizing Americans, stating they should honor him by subjugation. He defines the mystical and theatrical imaginings of the Russian type of fascism. In other words, clothing himself in the uniform of a high-ranking Russian official in a kind of theatrics. When he speaks freely about Russia and the world, he exhibits an interest by romanticizing the Soviet era's power and Moscow in particular. The tone and demeanor of his words and inflections are like a girl on a first date. Tired of Russophiles, he fluctuates to neo-Nazis as the other side of his coin. President Trump's imagination includes creating stories in the United States that play well in Russia, often boosting Mr. Putin's popularity.

The more Mr. Trump is publicly intimidated by Mr. Putin, he draws nearer. Mr. Trump was also influenced by the Slavic culture in New York, which was influential. President Trump has engaged in the imaginings as a Russian KGB have resulted in the behavior of unmarked police insignia, snatching defilers of authority from their home, controlling mail, things compatriots of the Russian Empire were horrified of.

One can tell the character of an entire nation from its clubs. Little Odessa, New York clubs had women in delicate garments in the bright native colors known in Czechoslovakia and Ukraine, some with folklore dresses. Their breath is entirely different than the crass men holding ashed cigars nearby. The women with green eyes over the age of eighteen were scented of peppermint and costly schnapps. The screeching elevated railroad passed through, with a faint aroma of raw steel that appeared to a drunk it had been annexed by Odessa, Ukraine. Smells in the air of hot potato salad fried briefly in bacon fat with chive. When it was part of the Russian Empire/Cold War just before their émigré departures here. This lifestyle and family environment, although it was shadowed with alley and backroom beatings, were familiar. In Soviet and Russian culture, familiarity was the essence of existence that

---

pulled the person to remain in this enclave. Though it is not the real thing, it is easy to see how an American finds this attractive.

This feeling of familiarity, in many respects, is being home—home in the imitative sense, a place with an unrealistic quality. The imitation of home in Little Odessa's bubble meant everything to an émigré, though, over time, the imagining became less as people acclimated. The expectation of speaking English in every transaction on the street. This fact makes Donald J. Trump's presence here out of sync. Instead of showing evidence of American acclimation, his actions showed someone quite comfortable living near Odessa. Almost intentionally desirous and pleased with what was a cruel and terrible era.

Not only was the Soviet-era a source of romanticism for Mr. Trump, but many American tourists allured by this darkness are shared by a specific request for Russian history monument tours. However, President Trump carries the appeal of Soviet dictatorship aesthetics to a different level exhibiting the former militaristic state tactics against civilians pulling on the worst theatrical levers. Still, there is a pathological aspect of this mindset. As can be expected, Donald J. Trump veers off in another direction, imagining himself as the enemy of the Soviet and Russian people playing Nazi. More surprising, the Russian President seems to enjoy this role too.

Odessa, Ukraine, and Czechoslovakia in Brooklyn, New York, wasn't just a night out drunk. A cultural picture of Berlin spoke more precisely about this lifestyle. While in Russia, Mr. Trump must have witnessed the likeness of Czechoslovakian culture. Mr. Trump married Ivana Zelníčková in 1977 when the country was under Soviet control, 1948 and 1968. Václav Havel released *The Power of the Powerless,* a testament to dissent in the Czechoslovakian Communist regime. The Soviet Union in 1977 was frozen in time when he married Ivana Zelníčková. According to the American media, Ms. Zelníčková did not exist before she met her husband since there is a total blackout on her past. The following should give readers some idea of the Soviet Union's feeling, if not its reality.

"Berlin, East Germany, 1978—My first impression of Checkpoint Charlie was that the East Germans hadn't evolved much since the Nazis were running the show. The uniforms and attitudes seemed the same; the only difference was these guys were commies. I was hoping to spend a few days in East Berlin, but these militaristic hard-asses clearly didn't want me there. They tore apart my luggage and tossed out a Blondie 12-inch record I'd brought as a gift for a friend. The commandant stared me down. *Das Commandant*, who by this point imagined me some sort of kindred spirit, stepped outside and confided in me. There was no human way; he informed me that I would be able to spend all that money in three days. He gestured toward a building a half-block away. That's a bar down there, he told me. And not just any bar; it was a kind of nexus between the East and West. It was a place where lovers drank before one or the other went back to the West through Checkpoint Charlie. Go there early in the day, he advised me, and attempt to drink up all your cash. If you can't, buy a round for the house. Seriously." [93]

Romanticism in Little Odessa, Brooklyn, New York. Once realizing the implication of looking back. Not what most people in the West see as their life. It was different in this respect for the Conservative, dealing with people behind that dark memory of the Iron Curtain that foreboding realization when the past met today in Berlin. These environs were where the Russ Bellant Eastern Europe émigré story began.

This is particularly frightening to the émigrés in the United States that were expected to watch President Trump's election since their former immigration and assimilation. It was pure torture for some. Totally shocking was Donald J. Trump's self-portrayal as one of their cheap, cheesy versions of a dictator on a flickering television of the

---

[93] Rice, Boyd. "Cold War Cocktails: Last call at Checkpoint Charlie." Blog. Dec. 06.

1930s. The theatrical version of their life in the old country during the evening news. Watching him at the podium is like being forced to attend a short movie as part of their citizenship. President Trump welcomes them to America.

Everyone who's an émigré wants to avoid this tear in time of President Trump's film. Staring at the vroom of motorcycle warriors who invaded Crimea, and the neo-Nazis welcome in Moscow and Charlottesville, Virginia. Plus, Eastern European émigrés that were Old Nazis watched Trump on television. Reimaging the familiar roles they and relatives played in the past as loyal Nazis viewed on television in 2020 in the White House. Mechanical men who take orders like machines without a sense of history using the scripts of Nazi's, "we were just following orders." Only Portland, Oregon, and Lafayette Square Park, D.C., were not in their old country. These scenes are familiar sights from the 1993 uprising staring Boris Yeltsin, whose brief intervention resulted in Vladamir Putin's rising. These events are being expertly choreographed. No one dares to say by whom.

The Portland, Oregon uprising, too, presented many political opportunities on both shores. Here are some possibilities. There is a strong message that is delivered to both coasts simultaneously to Russia via Portland. By midnight the scenes of the demonstrators being attacked and beaten by masked militia in the U.S. are the perfect visuals to relay a discouraging message to those seeking to leave Moscow to more fruitful careers in the West. It satisfied President Trump and Melania to have brought this snippet of history to real life while he could watch and drool over the violence and bloodshed. There was an added value for the President to watch as moms were riveted with projectile bullets, contaminated with gas, and beaten with clubs in what could only be described as sadistic. What a satisfying moment in time for Mr. Putin to relive the 1993 attempted coup in Moscow.

Distorted Norms of Privileged Individuals

In 2000 President Bill Clinton began an initiative on Wall Street known as the liberalized Commodity Futures Modernization

Act of 2000. White-collar criminals, and their murderous associates, were asserting themselves in Wall Street among the 300-500 million-dollar companies. Though Republican and Democratic parties publicly state they take prosecuting crime seriously, it only applies to street violations. They did everything in their power to absolve the wealthy families of crime stigmata at the approximate time of signing the crime bill against blacks and minorities to stop crack cocaine addiction and crime.

Michael Cohen, Esq, partially owned El Caribe Country Club, where Marat Balagula held court over other gangsters. Felix Sater, Paul Manafort, and others would be surveilled there by the FBI. Nothing would come from it. Russian operatives were tapping into specific groups to manipulate against America documented in *The Compatriots: Exiles, Émigrés, and Agents Abroad.* [94] Before 9-11, United States intelligence services may have thought Russia worked around its fringes. The following structure of interests shows that individuals working with the mafia made essential revenues, and the Security and Exchange Commission permitted them to become capital and stock investors.

The 5 New York Mafia families and experienced highly educated Soviet and Russian era thieves and formerly detained dissenters had younger members of interdependent networks, Lucchese, Bonano, and Colombo. U.S. Securities and Exchange in 2000 reported, "To further its manipulations, the enterprises infiltrated and gained control of certain brokerage firms. Including Monitor Investment Group, Meyers Pollock & Robbins, and First Liberty Investment Group." Violence was inherently part of the operation, "Violence turned the public's attention to possible organized crime involvement within the securities markets on October 26, 1999. Stock promoters Maier S. Lehmann and Albert Alain Chalem were found shot to death execution-style in a home in Colts Neck, New Jersey. At the time,

---

[94] Soldatov, Andrei and Irina Borogan. *The Compatriots: The Brutal and Chaotic History of Russia's Exiles, Émigrés, and Agents Abroad.* Public Affairs (October 8, 2019) ISBN-13: 978-1541730168.

Lehmann and Chalem ran an Internet web site, Stock investor. Com, which touted penny stocks. The SEC had previously sued Lehmann for his role in a penny stock manipulation." [95]

In "Paper Dragon Thieves," J.S. Nelson defined the Clinton legislation. Ms. Nelson stated, "Instead of hollow procedural shells, modern corporations should be understood as paper dragons in a parade. Costumes are animated by agents who are the dancers under the fabric that make it move. We focus on the dragon costume itself to the exclusion of recognizing the agents' presence and responsibility. Lack of agent accountability under the dragon costume encourages fraud patterns that caused the 2007–2008 financial crisis in which 45 percent of the world's wealth disappeared. Those patterns continue to be repeated." [96] Later, this wave of collapsed financial services may have caused migration increases and would be known as "the immigration crisis." It is an artificial crisis created by men at Davos to disenfranchise countries and suffocate nations by severely reducing their ability to pay their debts, correcting climate change, and spurring migration. Wealth, of course, does not disappear, but it can be stolen. No one will say by whom for fear of revolution.

A tremendous web of regulations was created by Congress to protect the privileged since 1940 passed in unnoticeable increments. These old laws are often referred to as "the system of privilege." Both parties admitted they could not control the influx of payoffs by corporate representatives. The United States has been on a type of suicide mission like a snake starting to eat itself by the tail. Undermining and decaying its former rigid no compromise judicial authority has

---

[95] Walker, Richard H. Testimony Concerning the Involvement of Organized Crime on Wall Street. U.S. Securities and Exchange Commission. 13 Sept. 2000. U.S. Congress.

[96] Nelson, J.S. "Paper Dragon Thieves." *The Georgetown Law Review.* [Vol. 105:87 2017} B.A. Yale University; J.D. Harvard Law School; Advisor, Center for Entrepreneurial Studies, Stanford Graduate. Note I have included (corporate)-R.O. Stanford Graduate School of Business; and Senior Fellow, The Carol and Lawrence Zicklin Center for Business Ethics Research, The Wharton School, University of Pennsylvania.

evolved, allowing "the right" and "smart" crooks to escape, but ensures the creation of crooks controlling lawmakers. Mafia has been pursuing relationships using Conservatives to remove all constraints.

"Second, form-hardening is strengthened by the intra-corporate conspiracy doctrine, which has quietly become widespread and powerful. The doctrine provides immunity from conspiracy prosecution to all types of associations and their agents. Based on the legal fiction that an enterprise and its agents are a single actor incapable of the meeting of two minds necessary to form a conspiracy. This formulation of the law allows the coordinated misbehavior of agents underneath that single actor's costume to escape without accountability. For example, the intra-corporate conspiracy doctrine now immunizes corporations from civil and criminal conspiracy under RICO in every federal circuit." [97]

The thief-in-law concept was relatively obscure in the United States. Then in a series of sightings, the white-collar mafia began to bleep on the radar post 9-11. What had developed post-9-11 were terrorist plots that combined efforts with organized crime as a funding source. [98] There are several international labels and trademarks of the criminal organizations that identify with *thief-in-law* at this American society level. Still, the next generation of mafia-related crime added a new complication for prosecutors. The conjunction of their white-collar organized crime thought to be isolated found only in the mafia's lower subcultures was wrong. It was proven a myth by the emergence of Nicodemo D. Scarfo Philadelphia Mafia, who pillaged a nearby Atlantic City mortgage company that involved banking products. Mr. Scarfo illustrated how easy it was to infiltrate the banking system and finance the white-collar economy's high echelons. Mr. Scarfo testified

---

[97]Ibid.

[98] Thachuk, Kimberley L and Rollie Lal, eds. *Terrorist criminal enterprises : financing terrorism through organized crime.* Praeger Security International. ISBN: 978-1-4408-6067-6. Copyright 2018.

in the above U.S. Securities and Exchange Congressional hearing investigation in 2000.

The unsurprising feature of this by Democrats was news by Peter J. Henning of *The New York Times* in the headline "Eric Holder's Mixed Legacy on White-Collar Crime." September 29, 2014, with a photo of President Obama and Eric Holder. Suffice to say, not one individual was prosecuted for a scheme that stole 45 percent of the world's wealth. Eric Holder, U.S. Attorney General busy with the 5 Italian mafia families, seemed to overlook crime at Trump Organization as it was happening. Holder totally missed it, and so did the U.S. Treasury. Seeing this under a micro view of New York crime dynamics, its general infrastructure is seen in the duopoly.

Knut Royce, *The Center for Public Integrity* on 14 December 1999, submitted this objective reporting, "Commodities trader Semyon (Sam) Kislin and his family also lavished thousands of dollars in contributions to Democratic Sen. Charles Schumer, to the Clinton-Gore re-election campaign, to former Republican Sen. Alfonse D'Amato and to several state and city politicians. Kislin sits on the New York City Economic Development Board. Kislin is not alone among émigrés from the former Soviet Union. They have successfully established themselves in the United States while law enforcement agencies, particularly the FBI, track their alleged associations with organized crime."

This problem had a history that included Rudy Giuliani, U.S. Attorney General for the Southern District New York, during President Reagan's law and order debut. During President Ronald Reagan's administration, Mr. Giuliani became Republican with Donald J. Trump during the Eastern European émigré recruitment program. Mr. Giuliani, known for establishing the Mafia Commission Trial, aka, in the *United States v. Anthony Salerno,* Mr. Giuliani operated from a prosecutorial myth that getting the top organization's leaders would thwart the rest of the mafia. The Attorney General failed to focus their prosecutorial expertise on removing the entire echelon. A move that would be typical practice in the 1930s in that case, the whole superstructure would have collapsed. Instead, this self-assessed valiant effort against crime bosses was given up.

Meanwhile, the Russian mob filled the void created by Italian vacancies. Marat Balagula, remember, was the first publicized record of Russian thieves-in-law incorporating itself with the Italian families and Trump Organization. This eventually led to the bleached blonde actor remaking himself as Aryan, with his daughter bleached blonde Ivanka, and two borderline intellectual sons to base a percentile of their income on these criminals.

The Ukrainian-born Jew Semion Mogilevich, aka "The Boss of Bosses" in the Russian mafia, had headquarters offices in New York. He attended clubs with Donald J. Trump, who suggested he only knew Semion Mogilevich, who admired Mr. Trump so much that his enthrallment led to an autographed photo between them. There were indications Mr. Mogilevich had ties to Marat Balagula and David Bo-gatin. Still, he was not a thief-in-law rather a Russian mobster and thought one of the smartest businessmen in his sphere. Some records indicate Mr. Mogilevich is interested in financial products, investment, casino industries, and perhaps stocks along the futures speculator's lines. In some ways, Semion Mogilevich, an alleged expert in internet crime, is similar to the New York archetype villain Murray Wilson. He was coined "America's Last Jewish Gangster" by the *Village Voice*. [99]

Since Donald J. Trump's Presidency, an effort has been made to blot out knowledge about the Russian mafias in what appeared to suppress expertise. He has sought to retaliate against the FBI to fire those that were also well-known authorities on Russian crime, includ-ing those experts on Semion Mogilevich. Bruce Ohr, a Justice De-partment lawyer, and Lisa Page, who were part of a broader strategy, some observers report, to fully comprehend how Semion Mogilevich interacted with Russian government officials. Mr. Mogilevich, who is publicly known to hold deep Russian interests, while business-friendly to the Iranian arms dealers they liaison with. Mr. Mogilevich was

----

[99] Bastone, William. "The Last Jewish Gangster." *The Village Voice* online. 26 Jun 2019.

considered a class of his own as a white-collar boss with an Italian connection, including the Sicilian Mafia, Italy, competing with him by educating its young white-collar criminals in finance.

Using the appeal of populism to seize government was not a new feature. Their tactics were well-devised and strategized experimenting on smaller foreign governments for decades. One only has to peruse their intrusion in Chile and Brazil. Particularly considering the UN International Convention for The Suppression of Financing of Terrorism and President Trump's attempts in degrading, reducing the effectiveness of completely disassociating the United States from this legitimate UN convention. The International Criminal Courts might help identify funding sources of domestic terrorism like the Ku Klux Klan, neo-Nazis, and Islamic groups. Specifically, when terrorists operate overseas with American passports. The current Presidential administration's resistance to investigations of any kind that might cause an inquiry into Conservative bastions and think tanks has been a kind of Conservative preoccupation. These actions are not about his media image but keep silent on what information investigations might glean about international Conservatives.

Authorities have yet to explain the use of conscious parallelism in the Trump Organization. [100] The evidence shows the Organization was not only a criminalist organism, a place to train the mafia, but connected to the thief-in-law finances. By definition, the family itself served organizations and networks of individuals while facilitating criminal endeavors. There are hints as to why in Democratic and Republican mayoral administrations did not prosecute the Trump family. The 5 families controlled a staging area for high-level criminal

---

[100] "Conspiracy: Evidentiary Value of Conscious Parallelism." Doyle explains," The difficulty arises determining what sufficient truth of the existence of a conspiracy is and then actually obtaining the necessary quantum of proof. It is not essential to prove a conspiracy by direct evidence of an express agreement, written or oral. Circumstantial evidence has always been enough. Evidence of a formal contract is unnecessary and was the law; otherwise, such conspiracies would flourish...." See Twomblyet al. v. Bell Atlantic et al., 425 F.3d 99 (2d. Cir. 2005) briefed, argued and submitted to the Supreme Court in November 2006.

activities because the FBI made arrests there. Known to spies as a criminal hub like businesses in Old City Hong Kong. There is evidence that each illegal activity that resulted in arrests involved a corresponding set of transactions to purchase or lease suites from public records. In any other country by any other intelligence service, this behavior would be classified as a safe house for terrorist and criminal networks. Unfortunately, operating on a 9-11 myth that criminals use within networks and terrorists within ideological platforms, the FBI's deficit prioritized prosecution for hard evidence cases. Instead of gaining expertise on criminals exerting their soft power of peddling ideologies against the United States that could develop into a terrorist network like white supremacist individuals, they opted for physical evidence cases. Fortunately, FBI Director Hoover did not follow this path but considered both the ideological and criminality of American Nazis.

In this process, the Trump Organization was overlooked as an intercorporate conspiracy case. Despite all the known criminal owners' applications had to be screened, credit checked, and various other references obtained according to New York State law. Can the Organization be held responsible for hosting these illegal activities? When an Organization's investigation is done, it stood to gain from the criminal activity, like a monetary benefit, then there is justification for filing conspiracy charges. Due to the repetition of these activities by several people buying prestigious suites, it can be assumed they had to be working in concert with the owners. Circumstantial evidence should have been presented with a pattern, but no charges were performed, and no papers were filed.

Gillman wrote, "The Twin Insurgencies: Plutocrats and Criminals Challenge the Westphalian State." [101] This is a new approach in a white-collar criminal enterprise. That the superrich could not at the same time become a super terrorist like a lawyer's son, evidenced by Ilich Ramírez Sánchez, known as Carlos the Jackal. It is telling how durable and resilient the system of privilege has been established deeply

---

[101] Gilman, Nils. "The Twin Insurgencies: Plutocrats and Criminals Challenge the Westphalian State." PRISM. *National Defense University*. 25 Oct. 2016.

in the law. In fact, it was so predictable for foreign agents to take advantage of it.

"...On the other hand, there exists a plutocratic insurgency. In which globalized elites seek to disengage from traditional national obligations and responsibilities. From libertarian activists to tax haven lawyers, to currency speculators, to mineral extraction magnates, the new global super-rich and their hired help are waging a broad-based campaign. That aims either to limit the reach and capacity of government tax collectors and regulators or to manipulate these functions as a tool in their own cutthroat business competition."

The former swift justice system for foreign actors on American soil has deteriorated, and the courts, investigators, have ignored the warnings of the 9-11 alerts. Virtually there is not enough improvement in how the United States Justice system restrains its white-collar criminals, as J.S. Nelson stated. [102]

"While the cost of white-collar crime continues to rise, the number of white-collar cases being brought is at a twenty-year low. White-collar prosecutions have declined more than 36 percent since 1995—prosecutions of individuals for the white-collar crime ...are infrequent. Professor Brandon Garrett documents that, between 2001 and 2012, the U.S. Department of Justice (DOJ) failed to charge individuals at all for crimes in 65 percent of the 255 cases it prosecuted. Public figures such as U.S. Senator Elizabeth Warren have said it is "time to stop recidivism in financial crimes and to end the "slap on the wrist" culture. That

---

[102] Nelson, J.S. "Paper Dragon Thieves." *The Georgetown Law Review*. [Vol. 105:87 2017} B.A. Yale University; J.D. Harvard Law School; Advisor, Center for Entrepreneurial Studies, Stanford Graduate School of Business; and Senior Fellow, The Carol and Lawrence Zicklin Center for Business Ethics Research, The Wharton School, University of Pennsylvania.

exists at the Justice Department and the [Securities and Exchange Commission (SEC)]."

Whether the chosen political venues are left or right to the centrist, there is little doubt of the United States' enforcement weakness. The criminal code since 1940 has been adapted and persistently amended by Congressional white-collar criminal sympathizers. [103] To the degree that capitalism allowed white-collar criminal lobbyists, this self-interest created the political foundation of funding populists. President Ronald Reagan was of this revolving door school of thought. This criminality, instead of prosecutions, removed penalties from the very rich. Inevitably on election day in practically every community, the economic disparity is played out clearly as white-collar crime is ignored. A homeless person who stole a loaf of bread almost always received a beating and a few years. Barclays is the case study to emphasize this approach to justice and its failures.

"Indeed, one reason why Barclays may choose to go to trial rather than settle for damages from the financial crisis. Is that its behavior is repeated so precisely in the foreign currency exchange manipulations? ...As the December 22, 2016 complaint details, Barclays' financial crisis behavior allegedly reveals that the bank was on notice of fraud. Did nothing to report it and even aggressively "pump-prim[ed]" the system... Barclays not only acquired and securitized billions of dollars of loans. It knew it had material defects, but it also extended billions of dollars in financing to lenders it knew was originating loans. Without regard to the ability of the borrowers to repay them (including, in many cases, fraudulent loans) ... Investments that the bank peddled as trustworthy it knew were instead "craptacular," the "scariest collateral," and possessing the "distinct aroma of default." It was Menefee who admitted that the loans were

---

[103] Sutherland, Edwin H. "White-Collar Criminality." *American Sociological Review*. Volume 5 February, 1940 Number 1.

"about as bad as it can be," that the risk "scares the sh*t out of me," and that the credits of Wells Fargo pools were so bad that "we have to eat their sh*t loans." [104]

During the Campaign of Donald J. Trump, he made a trip to Wall Street for funding support. Organized crime had infiltrated Wall Street being investigated by the Securities Exchange Commission. [105]

"Wall Street protests showed a "fine line between smart and illegal" in financial crimes. But the difference between "smart"-yet-damaging trading strategies and illegal behavior would start to collapse with additional information and prosecution of (corporate-RO) agents. While the public is in the dark about what traders at the five banks pleading guilty in the LIBOR scandal did. Other traders may be pumping their colleagues at these banks for details. Of how to set up their versions of such "smart" trades, whether the entities for which those traders work eventually become willing participants or not. As a hedge-fund employee who improperly pressured a rating agency to approve investments wrote to his peers. "We all do all this for one thing, and I hope promotions are a given. Let's hope big bonuses are to follow." As a trader justified his request to another trader to fix exchange rates, "Don't worry, mate—there's [sic] bigger crooks in the market than us guys!" As a third trader summed up, "if you ain't [sic] cheating, you ain't [sic] trying." "Smart" is making money. "Illegal" is getting caught and absorbing personal repercussions."

---

[104] Ibid.

[105] Nelson, J.S. "Paper Dragon Thieves." *The Georgetown Law Review.* [Vol. 105:87 2017} B.A. Yale University; J.D. Harvard Law School; Advisor, Center for Entrepreneurial Studies, Stanford Graduate School of Business; and Senior Fellow, The Carol and Lawrence Zicklin Center for Business Ethics Research, The Wharton School, University of Pennsylvania. See also, Sally Quillian Yates, Deputy Att'y Gen., U.S. Dep't of Justice, Memorandum to Assistant Att'y Gen., Antitrust Div. et al. (Sept. 9, 2015), Also, Hiding in Plain Sight: The Spiraling Cost of White-Collar Crime, Comprehensive Fin. Investigative Solution (Aug. 19, 2015).

The mistake of the presidential supporters was known by almost all educated law enforcement officers. I have used some sociological analysis in the descriptions of the thief-in-law. I hoped to communicate the impact of what Dr. Gigi Tevzadze wrote on the Soviet and Russian crime era. Namely, the importation of crime and specifically organized crime under the category of "outlaws" to divert attention away from corporate insurgencies. This move should be viewed as inventive and created/participated in by the state. It has moved from street crime alone from the "thief-in-law" to the professional and political sphere in the "legalized thieves inside the law," gaining in sophistication and educational level where corporations and white-collar citizens participate openly as "syndicates of influence." President Trump has been quite fluent in using the strategy, including terrorist channels, in and outside racial purity constituents.

"Organized criminals find that to mobilize sufficient power to resist the state, they must move their organizations beyond pure criminalist. With its limited appeal to most citizens and add elements of political protest. In this way, they legitimize their activities in many people's eyes, not otherwise inclined to support them. But those who are frustrated by the existing politico-economic system. From Robin Hood through "Pretty Boy" Floyd to Carlos Lehder and Pablo Escobar. Criminals have shrouded themselves in vaguely populist, anti-establishment political rhetoric to generate sympathy or outright support. Their immediate followers find personal meaning through wealth, and their sympathizers find fulfillment through seeing the regime made to look impotent and helpless." [106]

For the state, this creative talent may appear within the range of political appointments to the general administration of governance.

---

[106] Bunker, Robert et al. "Los Caballeros Templarios De Michoacán: Imagery, Symbolism, and Narratives." April 2019 *Small Wars Foundation*. Bethesda, Maryland.

These individually corrupt corporations can be understood as the polity that contracts with government controlling functions needed to deliver services. The contracts are notoriously lucrative. In what could be called "the privatized self-model," as long as thieves adhere to thieves' code, offer a monetary reward to their boss, and maintain order within the criminal network, people may seek to imitate various illegal franchises. [107] The most objectionable aspects of this financially motivated criminal endeavor are that Wall Street and Davos conferences pick the winners and losers. One affinity to a fantasy of Nazi beliefs is enough to spread it throughout the world. Either through passivity or evangelically, the most significant blockage to drawing on lessons of the Holocaust turns out to be Holocaust Centers.

Where high-level elites suppress discussions on world genocides that they say diminishes past Jewish annihilation. Still, the truth is their suppression of such meetings actually encourages such genocide in the future. Case in point Mein Kampf distribution is much more significant in the Middle East than anywhere else. Therefore, holds more potential to become acclimated into the culture. To no surprise, even among Sicilian mafias, a type of marriage has been consummated between neo-Nazis and the mafia.

Mafia's Useful Cousins

Mr. Martin Kerr was in charge of the New Order headquarters of the neo-Nazis. It was located in the American Heartland of New

---

[107] Franz Kafka. "In it, a protagonist known only as "K." arrives in a village and struggles to access the mysterious authorities who govern it from a castle. Kafka died before he could finish the work, but suggested it would end with K. dying in the village. The castle notifying him on his death bed that his "legal claim to live in the village was not valid, yet, taking certain auxiliary circumstances into account, he was permitted to live and work there." Dark and at times surreal, *The Castle* is often understood to be about alienation, unresponsive bureaucracy, the frustration of trying to conduct business with non-transparent, seemingly arbitrary controlling systems, and the futile pursuit of an unobtainable goal." ---Wikipedia

Berlin, Milwaukee. [108] Harsh reality check for Conservatives. Some remnant of this is an integral part of your new voting bloc. The infrastructure of this faction of society is undergoing significant change, and a coalition has formed surrounding a modern extremist Conservatism. We know what the future will be like with the Ku Klux Klan, neo-Nazis, and other criminal and religious elements taking over the government's control. The intent of these theatrical politicians is not to hang the Swastika but think in empathy to it. Same financial "fixes" and race-baiting but suave and uniquely Western. The Trump family is not unique but part of the lower echelon of a network of financiers and logisticians. Let me introduce you to some of these publicly infamous figures.

Though it was not immediately made public, the Alt-Right in the White House instituted censorship in conservatives' name. It was equivalent to raising a flag of extremism from the most significant institution housing historical memory. Borrowing a practice of President Putin's regime, the newspapers had these headlines of recent censorship, "National Archives exhibit blurred images critical of President Trump." To pledge their loyalty and apparently the first national censorship. [109] This characterized how deeply extremist Conservative influence went. They could impact institutions once thought impervious to propaganda. National Archives is a center of national memory and knowledge. This illustration of dominion over small pictures seemed foolish initially—he who controls the masses is the master.

Semion Mogilevich, a Ukrainian-born Jew who immigrated to Israel (known as the Brainy Don), and Marat Balagula (The Russian Tony Soprano), were almost interchangeable. Both gangsters were versions of Murray Wilson, described as the last Jewish gangster and link between the Mafia and the Russian Mob. William Bastone says,

---

[108] Murphy, Bruce. "City a Leader in White Nationalism: New Berlin is headquarters for Neo-Nazi party founded by George Lincoln Rockwell." *Urban Milwaukee.* 01 Nov. 2018.

[109] Heim, Joe. "National Archives exhibit blurs images critical of President Trump." *The Washington Post.* 18 Jan. 2020.

"Wilson quietly sits at the crossroads between Howard Beach and Brighton Beach, perhaps the only man to be identified by law enforcement officials as a high-level associate of both the Russian *Organizatsiya* and the Italian *La Cosa Nostra*." [110] In reality, Murray Wilson was from the old school of the mafia, surviving the bosses. No one would actually locate him, and the FBI offices thought he was dead. That speaks to his obscurity, almost like the soldier that knew too much, then one day vanished.

The network of the mafia's supporters who did administrative and financial investment work was apportioned according to specialty. Murray Wilson and his family were thanked for their financial giving as donors by the Hasidic Chabad-Lubavitch, whose prestigious-members and close associates include President Vladamir Putin, Jarod Kushner, and Ivanka Trump. Mr. Wilson's association with the Russian mob did not preclude his investments in restaurants and legitimate businesses that return profits into millions. He was able to keep the FBI field investigators informed but at arm's length. Following the Meyer Lanksy way of building financial empires, Murray Wilson was considered an *uninitiated associate*. This title boils down to function as a stockbroker/ financial advisor for mafia organizations operating in the grayish neutral zone.

Over the years, his social-climbing in the mafia led to open links to other investors where he hid "investor money" in legitimate businesses. These world travels led to contacts with different criminal types of his own caliber, like the shadowy Shabtai Kalmanovitch, a financial advisor to the Sierra Leone government about diamonds. It turned out that Shabtai Kalmanovitch was a cold-blooded KGB spy and Israeli immigrant shot in Moscow in 2009.

Mafia going through this kind of financial advisor makes investment on their behalf to take over a company. This impact would have to be managed. Thus, the need for Murray Wilson to represent the mafia while helping the company find investors. On the one hand,

---

[110] Bastone, William. "The Last Jewish Gangster." *The Village Voice* online. 26 Jun 2019.

it fulfills society's requirement in doing the function of recirculating dirty money. Then by bringing it back into the system and legitimizing it, making use of it to pay salaries, eventually ending up in legitimate banks. In the second benefit, not many companies can find investors. The transactions hid companies' identity needing investors for a wide range of projects, including big-ticket items like real estate. One could even say Mr. Wilson was a financier.

Marat Balagula, visible in the Jewish community, may have been the first to reach his goal due to his Thai drug connections while supporting women's group Hadassah, who used the establishment for meetings and fundraising dinners. True Marat Balagula once met Murray Wilson. William Bastone explains the old to new, "Though certainly never the financial genius he has been made out to be, Lansky — like the thousands of uninitiated associates who followed him — helped maintain the Mafia's financial backbone. Today, this network of associates — which far outnumbers "made" men — continues to help generate, hide, and invest organized crime's illicit profits. A Mafia affiliate like Wilson — a highly prized moneymaker for the Genovese gang — is required to kick back funds to the family he is "with."

Daniel Pagano, an influential Westchester-based Genovese member, and Alex Zilber of Odessa, Ukraine, a Wilson associate, was investigated by journalist Robert I. Friedman about a Marat Balagula gas scheme. It got Alex Zilber's brother killed. Marat Balagula and David Bogatin, a Jewish émigré, taught the FBI a thing or two. Defining their signature crime activity as a multi-million-dollar oil and gas scheme in 1987. In cooperation with gas stations, they controlled and reached the halls of corporate offices in the United States.   Despite the fact, it was mentioned in the television series *The Sopranos*. Such a profitable scam spanning continents had to be imitated by others once connected to the Soviets before the Union reorganized.

The deterioration of the Soviet Union in 1993 caused the abandonment of organized crime gangs throughout the world, where they had a government interest in the drug trade. Marat Balagula's gas scheme was done by associates of "José Antonio Yépez Ortiz (aka "El Marro"), who was arrested by elements of the Mexican Army (Sedena) in Guanajuato on Sunday, 2 August 2020. "El Marro," which means the sledgehammer or mallet, is the Cártel Santa Rosa de Lima (CSRL). The CSRL are widely known for their role as 'huachicoleros' or participants in the illicit fuel trade. The CSRL has been mobilized for the past year as government forces sought its leader's arrest. It fought against its rival the Cártel Jalisco Nueva Generación (CJNG) to control Guanajuato's illicit economy." ---John P. Sullivan, *Small Wars Journal*, Mexican Cartel Strategic Note No. 30.

"The grandeur of the thieving falsity is larceny, the fall of cities." — Justin K. McFarlane Beau

One year after President Putin took office, Alec Luhn's 2013 reporting showed the Russian mob's criminal intent inside the Trump Organization. The corruption that ensued went throughout this high-class echelon from wealthy enclaves for "a night out." [111] What was the Russian thief-in-law doing so comfortably with the American financial sector's upper stratus at Trump Organization? No one would publicly name the thief-in-law player, not even prosecutors.

"The April indictment in New York of 34 conspirators involved in gambling and bookmaking reads like the 1998 poker flick Rounders screenplay. With high-stakes games, Russian mafia dons, and thugs breaking bones to collect from losers too deep. The leading players include a notorious Russian *thief-in-law* (the equivalent of an Italian mafia don). A billionaire art mogul, a J.P. Morgan banker, a Hollywood poker hostess, and the Russian-born ringleader --poker pro-Vadim Trincher, who lived in the Trump Organization in a $5 million apartment housed directly beneath that of "The Donald" himself. "From his apartment, he oversaw what must have been the world's largest

---

[111] Luhn, Alec. "International Russian Organized Crime Ring Does Old-School Gambling in a New Way." *The Organized Crime and Corruption Reporting Project* (OCCRP); is a global network of investigative journalists. 13 May 2013.

sportsbook," Assistant U.S. Attorney Harris Fischman said during a hearing. A judge ordered Trincher, facing nearly a century behind bars if convicted, held for trial without bail. The whopping 84-page federal indictment spells out how the conspirators fit into two related rings that operated since 2006 out of Kyiv, Los Angeles, Moscow, and New York. The men were charged with heavy-duty counts of racketeering, extortion, money laundering, and operating an illegal gambling business. The organizations laundered at least $100 million, the indictment said. Most of the charges are related to the transfer of money in the course of their operations."

The cartels in New York since 1990 were building high rises when internationally known wealthy invested their money in them to avoid tax. 112 The interest generated from Mr. Luhn's reporting was the method and manner of the old school's crime and was not technological. The venue was not located in Marat Balagula's El Caribe Country Club's secure offices, and it was unguarded. The charges of operating an illegal gambling business reveal the true nature behind the financial mafia's crime. 113 Hosted by the Trump Organization, the setting had all the earmarks of being a recurring event as casual as other daily corporate functions. None of the books and accounts of the Trump Organization revealed any of this, causing suspicion the critiques were part of a publicity mechanism to cover up the real purpose of a roque's palace.

Frederick Trump's associate appeared in photos from tatted Gulag prisoners that explained each tattoo's meaning. In particular, Boris Nayfeld was rumored in the heroin trade with the Five Mafia families splitting the imported drug with Latino street gangs similar to

---

[112] Holmes, Steven A. "A Drug Dealer Finds Many Eager to Launder His Drug Money." *The New York Times*. 24 Jan. 1990.

[113] Santino, Umberto. "The financial mafia. The illegal accumulation of wealth and the financial-industrial complex." Centro Siciliano di Documentazione "Giuseppe Impastato." Undated.

David Bogatin. [114] In great detail, "the Mafia life" of cross-relation-ships surrounding the sphere of Little Odessa extending into the far and profound political intrigues of Paul Manafort's Ukraine and So-viet-era and Russian crime families. Marat Balagula's association with Michael Cohen and Felix Sater, Paul Manafort, emanated from a cas-ual business that the familiar participants' uninventive practices re-peated one another's crimes. Each one of the dually criminal and political parties had inside ties to Republican Party interests. Namely, they started their initiation in the Reagan White House.

Few people in the mafia world have had such intrigue and lived as long as Marat Balagula. This was not by chance. Marat Bala-gula knew people in high places and was extremely intelligent, reveal-ing in this biographical that his impact on shaping politics went deeply into Moscow's leadership. Doing so explained his value to politicians and foreign analysts. The account itself had to be released through au-thorization. John William Tuohy, an undercover journalism source, explains Marat Balagula's relationship to Moscow and a thief-in-law's ascension. This is sensitive because the biographical note offers a view into another part of the cooperation with Eastern European émigré criminal networks that entered the United States and their travel route through cover that could be afforded by Central Intelligence Agents. Communists at high levels courteous, notably that one has to be po-lite, not rude, and abide by underground culture to survive. [115]

"The Soviet government granted (Marat Balagula's hero father) a management position in the lock factory in Odessa after the war. Marat himself served on a hitch in the Soviet Army, who mistakenly placed him in charge of a food cooperative,

---

[114] Pearson, Jake. "Notorious Russian Mobster Says He Just Wants to Go Home." *NBC* Universal Media, LLC. 27 Jan. 2018.

[115] Tuohy, John William. "John Tuohy Russian Mafia Gangster Blog." My Writer's Site. Bloglapedia Family of Blogs. John William Tuohy lives in Washington DC. Accessed 05 Oct. 2019. "Unverified" source.

essentially introducing him to the lucrative Russian black market. He was so powerful that, according to Balagula, that future party chief Mikhail Gorbachev was on his kickback payroll. Once out of the military, he attended night school receiving his diploma as a teacher in mathematics. Then returned for a second degree in mathematics and economics. After that, he returned to the exploding Russian black market. He married in 1971 and in 1977, moved to the United States as an oppressed Jew. He laid low at first, working for minimum wage as a textile cutter, and then moved to Brighton Beach and went to work for local mob boss Evsei Agron as hired muscle. Far more intelligent and educated than Agron, Balagula had been the Godfather's chief advisor and financial guru for several years. In the aftermath of Agron's murder, he blamed Agron's inability to get along in the Brighton Beach neighborhood. Balagula took over as the gangster in residence in Brooklyn. However, local and federal authorities placed the blame for Agron's death squarely in the Balagula camp. One of his first projects as the boss was to build a massive scam to collect gasoline tax from selling gasoline, which turned him into a multimillionaire. When Balagula's men started to get shaken down for cash by members of the Colombo and Lucchese crime families, Balagula met with Lucchese boss Chris Furnari. Entering into a working agreement with the Lucchese, Balagula and his gang had a junior partner status with the Mafia. Using a maze of dummy companies, Balagula organized a massive gasoline-bootlegging scheme that evaded billions of dollars in sales taxes. Adding on about 2 cents on every gallon that went to the Italian Mafia for protection. Generating them an income of over $100 million per year for the Mob. By 1985, the Balagula operation included over 100 gas stations run by Russian Jews, oil tankers, seven oil terminals, several dozen gasoline trucks, and oil-refineries in Eastern Europe. Balagula then went international and formed networks with other gangsters from Russia, Eastern Europe, and Asia. Balagula and his friends all but ran the African nation of diamond-rich Sierra Leone. Genovese gangsters, who had toured the Russian Mafia country courteously, had underwritten President Momoh's 1985 presidential campaign. Including several Genovese soldiers stood with Momoh on the podium as he was sworn into office. The hood took diamonds out of Sierra Leone and traded them for heroin in Thailand."

Marat Balagula, Ukrainian, the pivotal man, three days before his sentencing in November 1986, fled the country. 116 Ralph Blumenthal reported, "A criminal underworld of Soviet émigrés, some of them skilled in white-collar crime and hardened by Soviet prison and labor camps is reaching beyond its base in Brooklyn. It uses extortion and violence in its own neighborhoods and engages in multimillion-dollar racketeering schemes on an international scale." 117

David Bogatin, grandson of a Talmudic scholar, owner-of-record in Platinum Energy, also a Soviet army veteran that served in North Vietnam for the Soviets in an anti-aircraft unit and associated with the Marat Balagula family, by this time a publicly known Little Odessa mafia figure, and boss, an associate of both the Lucchese and Trump families. Invariably had no problem closely associating with a Soviet soldier who may have shot down American jets in North Vietnam. When it was learned from reliable sources in the Soviet Union that the United States was monitoring their organized crime families in New Jersey, all eyes were placed on Wall Street and the banks. [118] That's how serious the national security issues were. Arrested in Poland, David Bogatin said, "for my success" and a scheme to open at least 200 banks. [119]

---

[116] Ibid.

[117] Blumenthal, Ralph, and Celestine Bohlen. "Soviet Emigre Mob Outgrows Brooklyn, and Fear Spreads." *The New York Times*. 04 Jun. 1989.

[118] State of New Jersey, "Executive Summary, The Tri-State Joint Soviet-Émigré Organized Crime Project, The Nature of Russian-Émigré Crime."

[119] Horrock, Nicholas and Lynette Myers. "Extradition Target Says His Real Crime Is Success." *Chicago Tribune*. 03 Apr. 1992.

The work of Drs. Kimberley L. Thachuk and Rollie Lal's made a significant contribution to the interrelationships between terrorism and crime. [120] On the one hand, they explain how a criminal enterprise's financial networks can follow the dispersal to terrorists in the chain. Sometimes unintentionally, resulting from routine business dealings that, in my words, is similar to the Conservative theory of trickle-down economies.

In a surprise move, the new thief-in-law boss became crowned. The new *Legalized Thief in the Law*, Shakro Molodoi, is expected to take his post in Uzbekistan; the organization is alleged to have heroin and several criminal enterprise portfolios. Treasury Department's Office of Foreign Assets Control states, "…Thieves-in-Law has "grown into a vast criminal organization which has spread throughout the former Soviet Union, Europe, and the United States." [121] Criminal investigators can only imagine how much money will come into the United States economy, making the financial sector soft and without the legitimate equity or collateral to base mortgages and loans. This can be investigated using link prediction. [122] They seek people like Murray Wilson to serve as the backbone of their criminalist endeavors. Umberto Santino spells out an additional feature of political and financial hierarchies that could help develop an identification process with criminal syndicates and the political power in many parts of the world. Such basic standard features conclude that various criminal organizations are becoming increasingly 'mafia-like,' vertically integrated with

---

[120] Thachuk, Kimberley L and Rollie Lal, eds. *Terrorist criminal enterprises : financing terrorism through organized crime.* Praeger Security International. ISBN: 978-1-4408-6067-6. Copyright 2018.

[121] Synovitz, Ron and Sirojiddin Tolibov. "'Thieves-In-Law' Syndicate Crowns New Crime Boss From Uzbekistan." 18 Apr. 2019. Radio Free Europe.

[122] Berlusconi G, Calderoni F, Parolini N, Verani M, Piccardi C (2016) Link Prediction in Criminal Networks: A Tool for Criminal Intelligence Analysis. *LoS ONE* 11 (4): e0154244.

national and political systems. [123] The opposite is also possible; national and political systems use the mafia to operate.

Legalized Thieves Inside the Law

More complex crimes such as international banking and commodities scams, money laundering, and dealing in strategic metals may be beyond the scope of the thief-in-law foot soldier. In this case, what is needed are some people part of the law. This type of criminal category is those in public offices or essential positions to a government permitted to break the law, have immunity from local police, are corporatists, or align with them. Recall what Umberto Santino stated, "increasingly 'mafia-like,' that is, vertically integrated with national and political systems." See Appendix C for an excerpt.

Dr. Hammer unknowingly represented what international criminal networks would become. Forward leaning profits from the downfall and ruin of nations. Alive today, Hammer would be indispensable to the Republican Party and Conservatives who want to deal with Russia, as they did with China. Though the current President is not as sophisticated as Dr. Hammer and Vladamir Ilyich Ulyanov Lenin. Vladamir Lenin's philosophy, vis a vis the Hammer relationship, was compatible with President Reagan and Trump. The belief and tactics of Lenin's right-wing are used to exploit revolutionaries then, after use, discard them. This reveals the present intent of President Putin and Trump while being popular in Republican Conservatism. From the looks of things, President Trump is happy with the idea of discarding his most loyal subjects so long as it fulfills his finances. Should he leave office, the right-wing vision of developing Russia by American corporations that were so self-destructively not in American interests may still be in the works for the sake of portraying presidential unity "for the people."

---

[123] Santino, Umberto. "The financial mafia. The illegal accumulation of wealth and the financial-industrial complex." Centro Siciliano di Documentazione "Giuseppe Impastato." Undated.

Ms. Bevensee stated, "…The American Conservative—indicates a widespread willingness to engage in a far-reaching effort uniting ideological positions in favor of a "new detente" with the Kremlin, vis-a-vis a coalition spanning far-right and radical left." [124] Like the cartels in Central, America populism offers a substantial and useful diversion. Potentially due to their lack of understanding and susceptibility to emotionalism, they can be marketed for billions.

The modern legalized thief from Russia and Eastern Europe may be distinguished from thief outlaws by completed college or university before or after being a prisoner. Many are accustomed to working within the system. They can be the most astute suspects of intelligent criminals who may constitute an unusual problem over the long term. [125] They are educated in upper-tier education and scientific institutes. Some experts believe that the legalized thief still dominates the traditional criminal world in Russia through Solntsevskaya Bratva. But, a legalized thief, the gangster bureaucrat, or diplomat criminal, with their intertwined links to the government, will dominate the social, economic, and political structures of the former Soviet Union. [126] As those pursuits grow in size and sophistication, it is expected that these

---

[124] Bevensee, Emmi and Alexander Reid Ross. "The Alt-Right and Global Information Warfare." Instructor, *Department of Geography, Portland State University*. Portland, Oregon, USA. Undated.

[125] A thief-in-law (Wikipedia):(Russian: вор в законе, tr. *vor v zakone*) in the Soviet Union, the post-Soviet states, and respective diasporas abroad is a specifically granted formal and special status of "criminal dignitary" (kriminalny avtoritet), a professional criminal who enjoys an elite position among other notified mobsters within the organized crime environment and employs informal authority over its lower-status members. The phrase "Thief-in-law" is a rudimentary, word-by-word translation of the Russian slang phrase "вор в законе", literally translated as "a thief in [a position of] the law", that can have two meanings in Russian: "a legalized thief". ---Gigi Tevzadze.

[126] Etter Sr., Gregg W. Ed. D, and Ms. Stacia Pottorff. "The Russian Mayfia: Examining the Thieves World from Thieves-In Law to Thieves in Authority" Journal of Gang Research. Volume 23 Number 4, Summer, 2016.

criminals will look to expand their interests toward the United States. [127] Due to recent developments, they would likely consider a career in government and welcomed by extremist Conservatives. This may also indicate that terror groups will continue to eye criminal enterprises, corrupt corporations as funding sources for their sustenance. [128] The U.S. Dept. of the Defense system of large civilian contractors are not immune from what Refinitiv found.

Refinitiv is a "global provider of financial market data and infrastructure." Its recent survey found that 1) 72% of financial industry professionals know that financial crime is taking hold in their own global operations.2) 41% of survey respondents have never screened their third-party vendors, suppliers, or partners 3) 49% of all detected financial crime is reported internally and, for the most part, said externally. [129] Therefore, corporations and businesses almost entirely rely on symbolic enforcement and legislation. That thus far has been unwilling to prosecute corporate financial schemes pointed out previously by J.S. Nelson and others. Currently, Refinitiv does not publish the adjudication of financial crimes nor the worth of physical loss in terms of stolen intellectual property, software, and inventory. Like the real estate market, financial crimes blight efforts to deliver legal corporate and business services. A top priority of corporations surveyed admitted they experience trouble detecting financial crimes as they occur. [130]

A weak government is defined as an arrangement between the financially astute and resource-rich. Who take their influence to new levels, dictating to the government on what legislation to approve on their behalf. The International Monetary Fund stated to Refinitiv, "Weak governance goes hand in hand with corruption. Only by

---

[127] State of New Jersey, "Executive Summary, The Tri-State Joint Soviet-Émigré Organized Crime Project, The Nature of Russian-Émigré Crime.".

[128] Thachuk, Kimberley L and Rollie Lal, eds. *Terrorist criminal enterprises : financing terrorism through organized crime.* Praeger Security International. ISBN: 978-1-4408-6067-6. Copyright 2018.

[129] Cotter, Phil. Managing Director, Risk, "Revealing the true cost of financial crime" Refinitiv. 2018. Publication No. RE903599/12-19.

[130] Ibid.

working together with renewed determination at a global, national and individual level, in both public and private sectors, can we create an environment in which there is nowhere for criminals abusing the financial system to hide." A criminal enterprise's more significant problem is their felonious pursuits and the blight they impose on communities.

From Germany to Slovenia, the mafias, plutocrats, and wealthy bandits, have teamed up with the new Nazis sharing one another's platform and disinformation highway. It would be expected that the visibility of anti-American sentiment within the country will grow as it gets more corrupt. Discouragement toward its credibility to reliably protect its citizens has given way to a new attitude—the extremist questions the moral, ethical, and legal basis of society's structure. Extremists have expanded into the financial markets, becoming more like opposition parties on their exterior, hiding their real mafia interior. American criminal organizations wish to band together and merge to bring down the government. A commercial corporation would be an ideal place to bring them together.

Plot by the Conservative Establishment

What differentiates Mr. Trump is that he is chief law enforcement official for the United States and Commander-in-Chief of military forces. Expletive! This subchapter illustrates the development of several physical and psychological features in his organization. Mr. Trump became intimately familiar with Eastern Europe's living conditions and politics, the politics associated with it now taken over by the alt-right Republican Party, and his interest in financial survival. His empire's future solely depended on profiteering from criminals in the same work as Murray Wilson and a thousand other links that supports the mafia.

Even under the Trump ownership of Frederick that stole from World War Two and other veterans in New York, a minimal price was paid plus the embarrassment. An immunity and silence were extended to his unintentional second-choice heir Donald J. Trump by leaders in the Republican and Democratic Party politicians. Using similar schemes to pursue a thieving and confident man's practice, he began the route to cozy up to Soviet interests, then graduated to Russian operatives in the business world. Thus far, the Trump family was physically untouched. Still, they incite and engender many white supremacist's civil unrest and mass murders, and a 20% increase in white terrorism.

This is the type of power only a political party has. Mike Schmidt of *The New York Times*, on 3 Nov. 2020, Mr. Schmidt reported, "The Justice Department secretly took steps in 2017 to narrow the investigation into Russian election interference and any links to the Trump campaign. According to former law enforcement officials, keeping investigators from completing an examination of President Trump's decades-long personal and business ties to Russia." [131] Evidence shows that numerous times a complacent Republican establishment more interested in their seizure of power ignored and protected the Trump Organization's legacy of ill-gotten gain.

The Jackson-Vanik Amendment of 1974 under President Barack Obama was changed into The Magnitsky Act, which meant to criminals that they could not freely migrate to the United States unfettered. Additionally, the U.S. Department of the Treasury's Office of Foreign Assets Control (OFAC), on 22 December 2017, designated the Eurasian criminal entity, the thieves-in-law, and 10 individuals, two entities linked to the thieves, under Executive Order (E.O.) 13581. Targeting significant transnational criminal organizations (TCOs) and their supporters.

No need to inquire why they had it in for President Obama's Executive Order (E.O.) 13581 initially ended an era where Russian organized crime invested its money without being subjected to laws in the United States vis-à-vis Trump Organization. As the record shows, President Trump continued in relationships with groups and individuals connected to terrorism in Crimea and acting as Russian agents while in office. As president of the United States, he continued to seek and conduct transactions with Spetsnaz Russian special forces. There has not

---

[131] Schmidt, Mike. "Justice Dept. Never Fully Examined Trump's Ties to Russia, Ex-Officials Say. *The New York Times*. 3 Nov. 2020

been a change of attitude by the extreme Conservatives to push back on the corporatist crime networks in the United States. Instead, they place this burden on the citizenry, but Conservatives could not fool the world about the actual identity of terrorist networks and how they were built.

"Commercial insurgency, by contrast, melds crime and politics. It is an easier or more effective way for people marginalized in the existing economic system to acquire wealth and the power and sexual attractiveness it brought. Commercial insurgency is related to old fashioned banditry. The criminals portray themselves as heroically fighting against an unjust system rather than simply thieves—think Robin Hood or Pancho Villa. Like many purely criminal gangs, criminal insurgencies provide their members both a sense of community and a source of income, rationalizing what they did by allusion to higher purposes like addressing injustice or protecting their communities. Examples include the late-stage Armed Forces of the Resistance (FARC) in Colombia and Sendero Luminoso, both of which moved into narcotics production and trafficking; the smuggling and kidnapping funded al-Qaeda in the Islamic Maghreb; and the Abu Sayyaf kidnapping gang the Philippines." [132]

Taking it from the top of his career, Donald J. Trump portrayed fraud as socially acceptable. Not just backroom conspiracies, but supporting the kind of global racists that kill. Confirming what most of society knew that racists, given the lead, will gladly admit their racism openly. A criminal feature Conservatives were willing to accept. Mr. Trump's family narrative is a failed empire waning, from his University scheme to inauguration, those steaks, the wine, then there was the

---

[132] Bunker, Robert et al. "Los Caballeros Templarios De Michoacán: Imagery, Symbolism, and Narratives." April 2019 *Small Wars Foundation*. Bethesda, Maryland.

Panamanian debacle, not to mention the pandemic crisis and insider interests in oil. Instead of the Trump portfolio as a mastermind, he seems only an extraordinary alt-right criminal thinker. Now in terrorism, that is something he can do to scare the people while using terror for profit. It must be admitted that there are supporters who still believe in overthrowing the government for profit. The following number of cases were not followed by any Trump family prosecution.

Dr. Aleksandr Burman was convicted of Medicare, and Medicaid fraud, a Ukrainian from Kiev who scammed the U.S. government out of $26 million in health care bought into Trump properties. Aleksandr Burman, "For several years, Burman worked as an undercover informant for the FBI; on two medical fraud trials in the Manhattan federal court in 2004 and 2009. In 2007 and July 2013, similar charges brought him ten years. Lawyers asked for leniency, referring to the fact that while living in Kiev, Burman could suffer from a radioactive release in Chernobyl. (No doubt a derivative expected of Dr. Armand Hammer.) He was impacted by the anti-Semitism he was subjected to in the Soviet Union, that he was seriously ill and a drug addict. Burman said he spent 20 years on opioids. The prosecutor's office rejected these arguments, noting that many Jews suffered from anti-Semitism. Still, few of them chose the criminal path." [133]

Donald J. Trump and his family continued lengthy relationships with those he facilitated in purchasing his properties. The energy sectors. "Igor Romashov, chairman of the board of Transoil, a Russian oil transport company subject to U.S. sanctions, paid $620,000 upfront for a unit at a building adorned with the future U.S. president's name in Sunny Isles Beach in 2010. Buyers connected to Russia or former Soviet republics made 86 all-cash sales. According to an analysis shared with McClatchy, totaling nearly $109 million — at 10 Trump-branded properties in South Florida and New York City. Many of them made

---

[133] Forum Daily. "Former Kiev resident earned millions of dollars on insurance fraud in the USA." *Voice of Russian Speaking America.* 17 Nov. 2017..

purchases using shell companies designed to obscure their identities." [134] A tactic used by drug lords, by obscuring names and locations. Convictions and investigations were conducted during the Conservative Presidencies of George W. Bush and Obama, making them knowledgeable about Mr. Trump's criminal and political activity. [135] Igor Romashov, an oligarch, was Deputy Prime Minister of Russia in Vladimir Putin's cabinet.

Konstantin Simonov explains the relationship between Igor Romashov and President Putin. "The fact that the connections between Timchenko and Yakunin are retained is proved by appointment in July 2006, of Igor Romashov. Who earlier used to be Director-General of Transoil and Link Oil SPb companies, connected with Timchenko, to the Federal Agency of Railway Transportation. Most likely, the appearance of this alliance and its consolidation was supported by President Vladimir Putin." [136]

The global news office, *Reuters Investigates*, Nathan Layne, detailed, "A Reuters survey found that in any event, 63 people with Russian travel papers or addresses have purchased $98.4 million worth of property. In seven Trump-branded luxury towers in southern Florida… People from the second and third tiers of Russian power have invested in the Trump buildings as well. One recently posted a photo of himself with a Russian motorcycle gang leader sanctioned by the United States for its alleged role in Moscow's seizure of Crimea… One wealthy Russian buyer was Alexander Yuzvik. According to Florida property records, in 2010, he and his wife bought unit 3901 of Trump Palace in Sunny

---

[134] Kumar, Anita. "Buyers tied to Russia; former Soviet republics paid $109 million cash for Trump properties." *McClatchy Reports, D.C.* 19 Jun. 2019.

[135] Nazaryan, Alexander. "Trump is Leading the Most Corrupt Administration in U.S. History, One of First-Class Kleptocrats." *Newsweek*. 02 Nov. 2017.

[136] Simonov, Konstantin. "Russia 2006 Report on transformation." President The Center for Current Politics in Russia, (Moscow). III EUROPE–RUSSIA ECONOMIC FORUM Vienna, April 23–24, 2007. Publisher *Fundacja Instytut Studiów Wschodnich Foundation Institute for Eastern Studies ul.* Solec 85 00–382 Warszawa. ISBN 83–60172–01–3.

Isles for $1.3 million. The three-bedroom apartment has 2,100 square feet and panoramic views, according to an online real estate listing. From 2013 to 2016, Yuzvik was a senior executive at Spetstroi. This state-owned company has carried out construction projects at military facilities. The Spetstroi website says the firm was involved in construction projects at the Moscow training academy of the FSB, Russia's primary civilian intelligence service, and the KGB successor. Spetstroi also did construction work in the administrative building of the GRU's general staff, Russia's military intelligence service." [137] What happens once you don't have political protection? When President Trump says he knows a few great individuals in Ukraine, Mr. Balagula will, without a doubt, be remembered.

Mr. Marat Yakovlevich Balagula died on December 19, 2019, at age 76. Organized white-collar crime is still prevalent in New York, supported by Trump Organization history. Comparatively speaking, ten days before Marat Balagula's death, the Gambino family appeared in federal court. Authorities alleged organized crime had participated in the construction of the XI buildings. It housed a hotel, and 234 condos for up to $25 million, rising to take their place in the city skyline. [138] Following the Trump template, in contrast to Trump's getaway, they were charged for mob looting and tax-breaks. Not so for Donald J. Trump. Without Marat Balagula, President Trump announced he would make Palm Beach his new headquarters.

Three years before Marat Balagula died, President Donald J. Trump established the same financial arrangement in New York at Palm Beach with political protection. The Trump Organization brought his Slavic associates to Trump properties in Florida. Where the Republican Conservatives built an infrastructure for his activities, any crime

---

[137] Layne, Nathan and Ned Parker, Svetlana Reiter, Stephen Grey and Ryan McNeill. "Russian elite invested nearly $100 million in Trump buildings." *Reuters News Agency*. 17 Mar. 2017.

[138] Smith, Greg B. "Mob Looted Tax-Break Towers Rising Along The High Line: Feds." *The City*. 09 Dec. 2019.

organization is envious of. The assets included a friendly political and police enforcement environment. Pam Jo Bondi, 37th Florida Attorney General from 2011-2019, who refused to testify in the Trump University case and Congressman Ron DeSantis, now Governor, who served in Congress from 2013 to 2019 who had a career with complete affinity to the Republican Party and extreme Conservatives during his subsequent political status. [139]   Add this influential hub to the President's fortunes and their collaboration with the Russians. The security to protect a former president ensures that the criminality will be protected using the latest technology.

Mr. David Bogatin had bought millions worth of suites in the Trump Organization, proceeds from the gasoline-bootlegging project. [140] Mr. David Bogatin was released and busted again. These criminal associations were among a long list of Trump Organization transactions with organized crime. [141] How is it not ironic, the entire Republican Caucus in the House of Representatives and the Senate did not mention Trump Organization in the Russian Investigation. Where Mr. Trump knew he made profits off of the Russian annexation of Crimea. Leonid Zeldovich had an extensive business in the Russian-annexed area of Crimea. Buying four Trump units outright at the cost of more than $4.35 million, three of them in New York City between 2007 and 2010 when George W. Bush and Barack Obama were President. There would be other infractions involving Ukraine and Trump Organization swept aside by the bi-partisans.

The Night Wolves' biker gangs supported retired Spetsnaz special forces that recruited youth from Slovenia's forests used as "little green men" baby faced soldiers in Crimea. Igor Zorin, a mid-level Russian bureaucrat with $75,000, winds up near Mar-a-Lago buying 8

---

[139] Wilkie, Christina. "Trump Held Fundraiser for Pam Bondi at His Palm Beach Mansion After She Passed On Lawsuit." *Huffington Post.* 09 Jun 2016.

[140] Fearnow, Benjamin. "Viral 'Crime Infested' Trump Organization Thread Details Convicted Criminals, Russian Mobster Tenants Over The Years." *Newsweek.* 01 Aug. 2019.

[141] Johnston, David Cay. "Just What Were Donald Trump's Ties to the Mob?" *POLITICO.* 22 May 2016.

million in Florida real estate. He partnered with Svyatoslav Mangushev, a retired Russian intelligence officer and Floridian practicing real estate investment nearby. Both were involved in creating a new Floridian biker gang named *Spetsnaz MC* comprised of Russian expatriates. Svyatoslav Mangushev bought into a Trump property through a relative for 1.5 million. [142] His operation was affiliated with the Night Wolves, a paramilitary force in Ukraine. In the United States, they are affiliated with Zorin in Florida.

Charles P. Pierce, "U.S. officials said the Night Wolves had abducted a Ukrainian border guard, stormed a Ukrainian naval base and smuggled a senior Ukrainian official out of the country. Also, "the Night Wolves have been closely connected to the Russian special services [and] have helped to recruit separatist fighters," a Treasury news release said." [143] The gang members are in line to eventually apply for citizenship. How did a terrorist group get U.S. State Dept. approval in an environment of illegal currency exchanges?

Hunter Wallace of Occidental Dissent of Eufaula, Alabama, explains Donald J. Trump's attraction on March 03, 2017, in *Tom Woods: The Alt-Right.* "President Trump humiliated the mainstream Right. What's more, we're nowhere near as isolated as the paleocons. We have smartphones and social media and can easily fight back against mainstream narratives. If that wasn't the case, President Trump would have been taken out a long time ago. We don't need a television station to propagate our discourse at the expense of the "mainstream."

Airing a primary internet and online media blitz did not negate a higher reality. In the real world, Donald J. Trump was not totally intrigued by criminalist profits to propel his dogma. Mr. Wallace explains the new theatrics of Hitler's Russian-culture. Under this formula,

---

[142] Dobrovolskaya, Lily and Nicholas Nehamas. "Russian official linked to South Florida biker club spent millions on Trump condos." 28 Jun. 2017. Miami Herald.

[143] Pierce, P. Charles. "The Russia Scandal Was Desperately Missing a Biker Gang Subplot. Well, Here It Is." *Esquire.* 26 Jun. 2017.

it does not matter whether Donald J. Trump is impeached, he gets kicked from office, or ends up living in a bush under a bridge.

"The more identities a man has, the more they express the person they conceal." -— John le Carré, Tinker, Tailor, Soldier, Spy

Hunter Wallace stated he leaves Occidental Dissent to become a Republican. Greg Johnson explains to Wallace, "Thank you for being so diligent about reposting the material to Reddit. That kind of quiet but sustained activity ultimately has a real effect on the *Zeitgeist*. Ever wonder how ideas discussed a few years back only at VDARE, AMREN, and even more radical sites have steadily infiltrated the mainstream? This is how."

Distorted Identity and Cultural Norms

In 2020 there are few stories about the jealousy between the elites, but decades ago, the elites seemed rare and few. Feuds existed and were reported in minute details in glossy headlines and photos in Hollywood. In passing decades, the paparazzi's significant intrusions dwindled in number as the wealthy individuals surpassed all expectations. Playboy and National Enquirer (the newspaper that reported women gave birth to a fish) reflected the disdain, pettiness, and smallness of individuals involved in stories about elites. In the Bowery, among dilapidated community buildings, a few people still carry on the elite-generated funds of the 1920s-1960s. Due to psychological problems and eccentricity, people continue to be vulnerable and captive to the dark events caught between emotional disorder and modernity that shed from erotic expose.

Take the unpredictable jealous depth of Mr. Trump and his competition with the Clinton's. Suspicion by Donald J. Trump and the "that should be me" and "no future for you here" was a vital component of his well-being. Trump's family could not maintain the lifestyle and reputation required in Manhasset, New York, where many corporate and international power brokers lived. The steady incline in this city is roughly double of American households. So, Trump did the next best thing and began to insert relatives there. Starting with John Walter, a nephew and family historian, to aspiring Manhasset-Born Sean Spicer and Anthony Scaramucci, a recent new resident. Yet, psychologically, Trump's dynastic attraction to Brighton Beach (Little Odessa), Brooklyn, New York, where they were exiled by the Manhasset super-elite. The gatekeepers to the easy money were Anthony Casso (Gaspipe) and Marat Balagula (The Russian Tony Soprano), who lived in Little Odessa. Anthony Casso (Gaspipe) was sentenced to 455 years.

Though not as elegant as the Manhasset Country Club, the El Caribe cafe was still comfortable in Little Odessa. No one would have known that in Greenwich, Connecticut, they would turn around the crime family's storyland image and try to ban Donald J. Trump and his family through an action on the 2020 City Council, degrading their stature by asking them to leave. Trumps are being booted out like a person living under the bushes publicly humiliated in the process. This blow was one of several as Trump's world of imagined prestige became outside of the real-world.

The underworld-connected remember Brighton Beach as Little Odessa. Others recall the open-door policy of the place that is open to everyone regardless of status. Warm welcomeness underscores the relationships here. Little Odessa has the largest population of Russian immigrants in the Western Hemisphere. There is also the same specter of criminal and present or former intelligence service officers as in the Soviet and Russian Empire. There is a dark side to choosing a Ukrainian city as the "sister city" of Brighton Beach. No one would expect this once sleepy section of the metropolis would be the hub of former Soviet and Russian intellectuals who specialize in American government fraud.

Inhabitants from the Little Odessa enclave included former prisoners in the Russian justice system, international drug cartels, and mafia thieves-in-law. Shrewdly, President Donald J. Trump barred all information about visitors to the White House. Vast untraceable money, diamonds, and all manner of the flesh trade have empires here.

Even the drug lords of the Iron Triangle of Eastern Thailand, where Laos and Cambodia meet and all the way to the mountains and jungles of Colombia, have representatives in New York. Every one of them requires housing and specific accommodations and discuss, as Melania Knauss Knavs-Trump said, 'Locker room boy stuff.' Italy ten years ago, the Cosa Nostra, the Camorra in Naples, and the 'Ndrangheta in Calabria — earned 75 billion+ in euros a year from the protection racket and loan sharking. They have come to New York to work and payout to friends.

The election of one of Mr. Trump's best friends, President Bill Clinton, a centrist, and "the first black president" and "I don't know you any longer." What to do about this crisis? What of the sanctity of Democratic Party racism that welcomed Trump? His friend had sided with the enemy for votes. Still, it was apparent Clinton, a civilized man, would toss him overboard the first chance he got? Because of his experience as an on-screen character and position as a government official. Mr. Trump urgently attempted to rethink the Clinton story during the presidential campaign. He decided to make the Clintons black and criminal in a play of words. The Trump family tried to transform Ms. Clinton into a prostitute. Though it may seem childish at first in the years to come, Donald J. Trump would get back at Bill Clinton in numerous ways by punishing the country while fulfilling his emotional needs.

Like Bill Clinton, this was part retaliatory and vendetta while always remembered for sliding a stake in the hearts of left-over Nazis and Mr. Trump favoring them. President Bill Clinton signed the U.S. Holocaust Assets Commission Act of 1998 to recover the world's looted Nazi gold. Some total the estimate as a $1.25 billion settlement. The significance of this event had a domino effect on global white supremacist and extreme Conservative institutions. Those trying to profit or con their way into modern Nazi financial networks felt this impact on National Socialism's future. President Clinton's actions pulled out the financial rug underneath their hopes to expand their movement. [144] This was also a blow to Right-wing Conservatism directly connected to apartheid, the New York illegitimate diamond and gold trade.

Next is also hard for him to take. The shock of the financial downfall of apartheid in South Africa and President Frederik Willem de Klerk DMS seemed to change the picture even more. During Bill Clinton's Presidency, the economic course in 1994 of America's racist community and their finances were once again disrupted. This was one year after the breakdown of the Soviet Union economy. A tremendous amount of wealth between the United States and South Africa was bottled up in pension funds, stocks, state investment, and minerals. This arrangement of profits from the slave economy was like those who invested in World War Two industries built from the concentration camps. The interface between apartheid profits turned upside down anyone invested in the global white supremacist regime. It specifically impacted the Orthodox Jewish communities in Brooklyn and Lakewood, New Jersey, working in the diamond district. The latter group has a long history of supporting extreme Conservatives and apartheid.

Twenty-one years after Germany fell, JAB Holdings and Benckiser admitted to Holocaust participation. Their name brands are Panera Bread, Stumptown Coffee, Bally, and Coty. For the participant in the limelight like Donald J. Trump in an advantaged society or among that class, desperate for attention, Conservative individuals routinely looked to traverse from the way they were viewed with privilege and began transcending to radical public figures. Gaining notoriety fulfilled some particular need, but it gives insight that some of the most notable terrorists in the tabloids were from this upper societal stratum as Greenwich, Connecticut, making trouble for lower classes. Often justifying government law enforcers to round up minorities to save the Republic.

---

[144] Blee, Kathleen M. and Kimberly A. Creasap. "Conservative and Right-Wing Movements." Department of Sociology, University of Pittsburgh, Pittsburgh, Pennsylvania 15260.

People reasoned less than a dozen captains of industry held the United States captive. Corporate statism in fascist countries is supported by those in democratic societies. The wealthy town of Greenwich, Connecticut, historically an enclave of international bankers, Wall Streeters, old money, is an excellent example of this occurrence. [145] The prominent members of the village were foremost in their support for special financial consideration by first-tier politicians. Can we also see that it's accurate Mr. Trump chased after them? In Greenwich Republican tradition and history, Prescott Bush's life was closely followed, who publicly rejected fellow Republican Conservative extremist Senator Joseph McCarthy.

By November 1942, American authorities seized the Bush affiliated Silesian-American Corporation to supply coal to the Nazi government. [146] This was not the only infraction working for the W.A. Harriman & Co banking George Herbert Walker and his son-in-law Prescott Bush engaged with relationships with Fritz Thyssen, an enthusiastic German financier of the impending takeover by the Nazis. When the United States declared war Harriman bankers were seized for financial and business collaboration to prevent them from being taken by the court on behalf of the Nazis. This was done as the Third Reich attempted to acquire these loyal and devoted companies as German property on American soil. The outcome would be a problem of visibility. American corporations and industry supported Nazis as their soldiers died, so some traversed South America and German concentration camps.

Conservative extremists had dangled financial privileges to small Republican groups in Greenwich. The Trump family was eager to incorporate them into their support base, saying, "This might be the right place for me, given this history? Perhaps unwitting at first,

---

[145] Osnos, Evan. "How Greenwich Republicans Learned to Love Trump." *The New Yorker.* 03 May 2020.

[146] Marrs, Jim. *The Rise of the Fourth Reich: The Secret Societies That Threaten to Take Over America.* William Morrow Paperbacks; Reprint edition (June 23, 2009). ISBN-10: 0061245593. ISBN-13: 978-0061245596.

the Greenwich elite established continuous funding streams. They were now positioned in a sort of chess game. To sustain their privileged status, Greenwich also had to financially support Conservative extremists. Readers may have heard extremists protesting their right to catch the coronavirus; in attendance were organizations associated with the Klan, neo-Nazis, and several other revolutionary causes. Most of the lockdown protests originate from well-funded small Conservative enclaves. [147] Greenwich's communities were pulled in now by the Trump family's presence with the notorious Klan and neo-Nazis in a comparable place as Prescott Bush.

"For the powerful, crimes are those that others commit."
— Noam Chomsky, Imperial Ambitions: Conversations on the Post-9/11 World.

Take the case of some of the upper classes' *pristine* examples—upright meticulous citizen Patty Hearst, pardoned by President Bill Clinton after being "captive by blacks" and notorious bank robber of the Symbionese Liberation Army (SLA). From scantily dressed and attractive cheerleader Angela Atwood to General Gelina, who was killed in an attack with the Symbionese Liberation Army (SLA). Jane Fonda, aka Hanoi Jane, used theatrics sitting on an anti-aircraft gun when David Bogatin shot down American jets. More often than not, the incentive to choose to live in a subculture does not subtract from an ambition to achieve and aspire to criminal status. One may want to be the best thief in capitalist culture or dine at the best club like Al Capone. Marc Rich, King of Oil, a hedge fund manager, pardoned at the last moment. Despite their position, the white-collar terrorist is often protected by the police or their own security forces in some places. Then why does the vast majority of Americans consider Donald J. Trump an "anomaly" instead of this natural flowing stream of terror?

---

[147] Vogel, P. Kenneth, Jim Rutenberg and Lisa Lerer. "The Quiet Hand of Conservative Groups in the Anti-Lockdown Protests." *The New York Times*. 21 Ar. 2020.

Americans have come to anticipate discussions of death saturating film and entertainment. Though most of the deceased does not occur to the wealthy of any race. Where do people become assimilated into white extremism? Among the youth that has become a storage medium, "Much of the Alt-Right's international outlook stems from international correspondence groups forged through affinities among fascists during the 1980s and '90s." [148] In the Russian conversation about the Victory Day history, Kseniya Kirillova of Euromaidan interviewed a foreign agent of the Central Committee of the Communist Party (CCCP) who alluded to the conspiratorial nature of Russian intelligence services. During the Presidency of François Maurice Mitterrand and President Reagan's administration, the French underwent a right-wing extremist attack by the Nazi's. Sanctioned by the CCCP. [149] This interview highlights what different ideologies may be used to extend the interests of Russia. Before President Vladamir Putin added to the validity, Russian history has tangible examples of discrediting and nullifying its heroic role in the Second World War. [150]

"On the other hand, sometimes it seems that modern Russia is even more successful than the USSR. Because, not having a real ideology, it nevertheless offers various "ideologies for export" abroad for both rightist and leftist groups. The Soviet Union could only attract the extreme left…Let's just say this: Russia has become a sort of fascist country, and therefore it is friends with all the fascists worldwide. But

---

[148] Lebourg, N. "Arriba Eurasia?," in Eurasianism and the European Far Right: Reshaping the Europe-Russia Relationship, M. Laruelle, Ed. Boulder, CO: Lexington Books, 2015, pp. 125–142. In Bevensee, Emmi and Alexander Reid Ross. "The Alt-Right and Global Information Warfare." Instructor, *Department of Geography, Portland State University*. Portland, Oregon, USA. aross@pdx.edu. Undated.

[149] Kirillova, Kseniya. "I was told we should work with fascists: former KGB officer Zhirnov." *Euromaiden*. 03 Dec. 2018.

[150] Grossman, Vasily. Robert Chadler Ed. *The Road: Journalism and Essays*. NYRB Classics; 1st edition (September 28, 2010) ISBN-10: 1590173619. Also: Khiterer, Victoria and Abigail S Gruber. *Holocaust Resistance in Europe and America: New Aspects and Dilemmas*. Cambridge Scholars Publishing. 2017.

I do not think that its activities abroad are so successful. Of course, if people are dissatisfied with what is happening in their own country, they may seek some kind of support elsewhere. And Russia, in this sense, may be of interest to them. And in France, too, some people are interested in Russia and believe in Putin. But, let's say, after the recent spy scandal in Austria, Austrian Foreign Minister Karin Kneissl, who danced with Putin at her wedding, now refuses to go to Moscow."

Edward Hunter, in 1958, described how psychological warfare was the predicate for the Soviet Union to change American thinking. They believed a change created a fantasy that the Soviet Union/Russia was not America's enemy but its best business partner. This view comes with the price of increasing the Soviet's industrial capability. [151] Strangely, the same psychological motivation of commercial interest that the Soviets of the 1950s remain the same.

"This is a strategy. The Kremlin is merely giving the United States a choice in surrendering by the voluntary change of attitude, to avoid more destructive ways of surrender. Unfortunately, in the United States, large elements, mainly among our non-Communist population. Have been softened up into believing that it will take care of itself if we can stall in this situation. The Reds have succeeded in inducing business communities to look to Soviet trade to restoring prosperity."

Ideologically, in the pursuit of Aleksandr Dugin, according to Emily Bevensee, "In Dugin's influential 1997 text, *Foundations of Geopolitics*, the National Bolshevik explicitly developed the strategy for intriguing. Within the social and political dynamics of the North Atlantic to bring about the disintegration of liberalism. Utilizing the

---

[151] Hunter, Edward. *Testimony.* Committee on Un-American Activities, House of Representatives, Eighty-Fifth Congress, Second Session, 13 Mar. 1958, Printed for the use of the Committee on Un-American Activities United States Government Printing Office, Washington.

geopolitical notions of the Eurasian "Heartland" and Atlantic "Rimland" initially conceived by British geographer Halford Mackinder. Dugin layered fascist myths of the Aryan "Sonnenmensch" over an idea of a united Eurasia to promote a global Russian empire from Dublin to Vladivostok and southerly to the Indian Ocean." [152] To meet this Dugin objective, Mr. Trump recruited the Jews that surround him. Many of Aleksandr Dugin's propositions are repaved over the Cold War's views by Harold Keith Thompson and those described as pre-internet fascists in correspondence groups.

Criminal types used crime to establish their matrix of influence and robbed assets, banks, and national treasures. This criminal hegemony is now practiced in almost all countries touched by the 1993 Soviet decline. The error in American thinking that the Slavic does not share is that Russia clearly identified a psychological need of Donald J. Trump they could fulfill. It might be accurate to say that there were needs of depths of darkness the United States could not meet, so they had to go outside and find a historical reference that would satisfy. Not only psychologically but sensual---to lie down in bed with fantasy then awake with Adolph Hitler in his bed. During Donald J. Trump's strange trip in 1987 Moscow visit, he slept comfortably in Vladimir Ilyich Ulyanov Lenin's bed that was now a shrine. This honor was previously given exclusively to Dr. Armand Hammer but did not come with Hitler. [153] In this evolution of closeness to Russian operatives, conservatives' desire to find another China to exploit became so strong that the greed gave them cause to select Russia for exploitation.

FBI documents stated that Dr. Armand Hammer took direct orders from the Central Committee to the Communist Party (CCCP), unsettled President Reagan's White House staff. Restricted to

---

[152] Bevensee, Emmi and Alexander Reid Ross. "The Alt-Right and Global Information Warfare." Instructor, *Department of Geography, Portland State University*. Portland, Oregon, USA. Undated.

[153] Harding, Luke. "The hidden history of Trump's first trip to Moscow." *Politico*. 22 Nov. 2017.

financial matters and seemed to sustain the CCCP contacts through-out the world. [154] He accomplished this by having Soviet and Russian bankers and financial operatives put too much money in Dr. Hammer's hands for too little work. Then he made out checks and deposits for KGB spies in the United States from Palm Beach to New World College. That he later admitted but was never prosecuted, Dr. Hammer claiming the Soviet agents had no other means and would starve in the United States while attempting to access the Urals' jewel mines.

A particular casual and unsettling character surrounding Dr. Armand Hammer were puzzling to the FBI, unaccustomed to the coldness and satire. [155] No allegiance to American values, not any specific Communist aggressions, just an interest in helping a low Soviet economy and substantial poverty from a European Embargo. Nikolai Ssorin-Chaikov, "When the train halted for a few hours at a whistle-stop east of Ekaterinburg, Hammer and other passengers went for a walk toward a nearby village and passed a small hut where an old man was making a coffin for himself. "I am all alone, you understand, and I have food for three more weeks only, and then I must die. But before that, I will have made my coffin and will lie in it to await death so that I shall not be buried like a dog in the bare ground." [156]

Due to the interference campaign between the United States and Russia, aggressiveness has increased tenfold as President Trump's threatening behaviors. Mr. Trump projects hostile gestures to almost anyone. To a great extent, this projection of threats in a moment of nuclear and pandemic danger comes from a lengthy social history. His surroundings have been a source of pathological schemes against the government for decades, which has involved Russian partners in crime. One could even say this behavior was genetic. Still, one of the nuances

---

[154] Federal Bureau of Investigation. Subject: Armand Hammer/Occidental Petroleum. File No. 61-280. 14 June 1921.

[155] Epstein, Edward J. "The Riddle of Armand Hammer." *The New York Times.* 29 Nov. 1981. See FOIA Request CIA.

[156] Ssorin-Chaikov, Nikolai. *Two Lenins: A Brief Anthropology of Time.* 2017 Hau Books, Chicago. ISBN: 978-0-9973675-3-9 LCCN: 2017934091.

in Mr. Trump's personality was his ability to gain a persons' confidence in the sense that while undermining the country and placing them in personal danger, they believed he still had their interests at heart. This was evident in his mass killings during COVID 19, where individuals in his presence never thought they were in jeopardy. Although they actually were in a great deal of danger, they thought nothing could happen to them like they were somehow an exception to everyone else. It was a strange way of thinking, witnessing people who Mr. Trump could put on fire and telling them they weren't as they died before everyone and still deny it was happening. Soviet-Russian went through that in the old days, happening more irregularly now.

"I felt as if I had no control over what I said as if loathsome, ugly words were waiting inside me like snakes and toads looking for a chance to sneak out before I could stop them." — Gloria Whelan, Summer of the War

The thieves-in-law of Marat Balagula fame originated in Stalinist prison camps among the criminal and political prisoners. Among this population are some accomplished intellectuals and dissenters. Its members are initiated or gifted a "crown" after demonstrating an "ideal" criminal biography and take an oath to uphold a code that includes living exclusively off their illegal profits and supporting other thieves-in-law. From that era, as gratitude from elders, the new Russia brings younger recruits from the "left-behinds" in society. This new gang member is a near-true NextGen example of white supremacist and neo-Nazism because these organizations are available and inclusionary. The Stalinist era is romanticized by the younger mafia; the following account is a picture of the initial thief-in-law period---the NKVD mentioned is the secret police.

"When I was hired by the NKVD, I was terribly proud, he said. 'First time they paid me. I bought myself a nice suit... '...What was the work like...What can you compare it to? It's something like war. But for me, the war was like a holiday. You shoot a German; he screams in German. These people screamed in Russian . . . They're practically your own people . . . It was easier to shoot Lithuanians and Poles, But the ones screaming in Russian, "Cretins! Idiots! Hurry up and finish!" (expletive) . . .!! We were always covered in blood. We'd have to wipe our hands on our hair. Sometimes they gave us leather aprons. That's what the work was like—the job. You're young . . . Perestroika! Perestroika! . . . [my ellipsis] I slept with a gun under my pillow . . . always prepared to put a bullet through my forehead. Everyone lived like that in those days! Soldiers and marshals alike. In that, we were equals. When war broke out, I immediately asked to be sent to the front. It's not that frightening to die in battle. . . [my ellipsis] I liberated Poland and Czechoslovakia. . . [my ellipsis] after the Victory I was arrested. . . They gave me seven years. And I did all seven. To this day, I still wake up as I did at the camps at six on the dot. What was I in for? They never told me. What was I in for! (expletive)...!!!" [157]

White-collar organized crime is a competitive business, and to some extent, a gift to the underground. News reports say that real estate was produced from recycled drug money. These transactions contributed significantly to the economy. Taken off the streets, not going directly to terrorists is a lie Americans liked to tell themselves.[158] Soviet officials had a high impact on New York enclaves when they released their Gulag émigrés. The notion of "criminal culture" is reminiscent of French and Creole prostitution in New Orleans. They ran liquor by moonshiners to manufacturing in New York City. Mr. Trump was based in New York but knew of almost every significant narcotic deal in Asia that would undoubtedly come in handy through connection with David Bogatin. After the devastating change extremists had gone through inflicted by the Bill Clinton family, another black President

---

[157] Donovan, Stewart. *Not Built for Peacetime*. A review of *Secondhand Time* by Svetlana Alexievich London: Fitzcarraldo Editions, 2016, pp. 694.

[158] Hudson, Michael, et.al. "How New York Real Estate Became a Dumping Ground for the World's Dirty Money." *The Nation*. 03 Jul. 2014.

gave another executive order.   Legal action surely to follow. President Barack Obama was elected twice!

The U.S. Department of the Treasury's Office of Foreign Assets Control (OFAC) on 25 July 2011, designated the Eurasian criminal entity, the thieves-in-law, and 10 individuals and two entities linked to the thieves, under Executive Order (E.O.) 13581. Noticeably they omitted Trump Organization. Targeting significant transnational criminal organizations (TCOs) and their supporters. The thieves-in-law is being targeted for their involvement in dangerous illegal activities. Today's action generally prohibits U.S. persons from conducting financial or other transactions with these individuals and entities, freezing any assets they may have under U.S. jurisdiction. It was signed by President Barack Obama. Automatic war on him by Sen. Mitch McConnell, who was receiving plans for a Russian aluminum plant.

Michael Rothfeld of *The Wall Street Journal* wrote before, "In 1981, a young and ambitious Donald Trump sat down with federal agents. And discussed his calculation in entering the mob-infested world of Atlantic City casinos. "If people were like me, there would be no mob, because I don't play that game," Mr. Trump said. He called himself "the cleanest guy there is." Like David Duke, he changed completely. By the 1990s, Mr. Felix Sater, a close Donald J. Trump associate, became connected to Moscow's investors. He was involved in a Mafia-linked scheme to pump up underperformed stocks, dump them on unsuspecting investors, stash the profits abroad. This scheme also worked in reverse in India. The system relied on gangsters from three mob families for protection, said a Justice Department news release. It quoted the 2016 New York police commissioner at the time as saying the operation could have been called "Goodfellas Meet the Boiler Room." [159]

---

[159] Rothfeld, Michael and Alexandra Berzon. "Donald Trump and the Mob." *The Wall Street Journal.* 01 Sept. 2016.

"The demise of the Soviet Union and its transformation to a market economy ignited a great deal of currency exchange activity with the United States and western Europe by Russia and other former Soviet republics. During the last few years, a massive influx of money originating as rubles has been exchanged for United States dollars via financial institutions and leading companies in this country and Europe and then transported back. Fearful that the funds are being used to support criminal organizations, terrorist groups, and drug cartels. Law enforcement officials are trying to determine how much of this activity is legitimate. More than thirty people involved in the Russian banking system have been murdered during the past year. Russian authorities believe these events are the result of organized crime efforts to control the banking industry." [160]

This environment of loose money is aggravated by Mob Wars. Dr. Etter: *The Great Mob War of 1992-1994 and The Continued Violence of the Russian Mafia.* [161]Thief-in-law's first case was in New York in 1995 during the Presidency of Bill Clinton. This was an attempt by various Russian Organized Crime Groups and the organized affiliated groups of some of the former Soviet Republics of Eastern Europe to dominate the former Soviet Union's criminal community. By now, Dr. Armand Hammer and Frederick Trump had died. "The 'Great Mob War' was fought mostly in Moscow, but its echo was heard in Vladivostok, New York, Chicago, and California. Dr. Etter: "One famous analogy of what was happening in Russia at this time was that of a car wreck—a vehicle stuffed with dollar bills crashes, the money is scattered on the ground, and the bystanders push one another away, trying to grab the most significant bundle. Both the older mob bosses

---

[160] State of New Jersey, "Executive Summary, The Tri-State Joint Soviet-Émigré Organized Crime Project, The Nature of Russian-Émigré Crime."

[161] Etter Sr., Gregg W. Ed. D, and Ms. Stacia Pottorff. "The Russian Mayfia: Examining the Thieves World from Thieves-In Law to Thieves in Authority" *Journal of Gang Research.* Volume 23 Number 4, Summer, 2016.

(the thieves-professing-the-code) and the younger 'gangster business-men' engaged in a savage struggle with one another to stake their claim." Dr. Etter traces this scenario, one faction included the Solntsevo Brotherhood and their allies, operated from New York as the Slavic Brotherhood.

Lone operations generated their own popularity in Latin America with little if any funding since the Soviet collapse. They had to continue their gangster businesses and thief-in-law expertise from Soviet intelligence services. Dr. Stephen Mets explain the Western perception of the problem, "It treats insurgency as military, political, and economical, but it overlooks or underestimates the importance of psychology. It is a psychologically and culturally sterile approach rooted in Western Enlightenment notions of political legitimacy and power. That is why it sometimes fails." [162]

The psychological approach to understanding President Trump's corporate dictatorship is reminiscent of Ms. Omorrosa Manigault stating numerous times, a White House project of his personal dark side of revenge politics. Conservatives have simply adopted the Trump family to place the United States government at their disposal to exercise their hate against specific individuals and groups in exchange to fulfill their goals. Mr. Trump insists on participation in a crime. Revenge and betrayal had happened on different micro-levels. The primary one began during President Reagan, who took revenge on the government for what he perceived as an overreach that harnessed businesses from meeting their potential. From that idea, militarism, fear of nuclear war, homelessness, and uncontrolled capitalism was unleashed. It was "normal" that from the ruins came other actors, populists, deinstitutionalization, and government contractors. In this atmosphere, it was entirely acceptable even for his supporters and those designated as threats and sources of fear for Mr. Trump to

---

[162] Bunker, Robert et al. "Los Caballeros Templarios De Michoacán: Imagery, Symbolism, and Narratives." *Small Wars Foundation*. Bethesda, Maryland. April 2019

operate within a sphere of paranoia. One in which he could protect himself from imagined "hidden hands" and the concern and paralysis of a possible conspiracy against him. Ultimately leading him to become President Trump, where he would find safety and protection from the U.S. government.

By 2016, the President with the world economic engine at his disposal, including the mechanisms to finally fulfill what Omorrosa Manigault asserted about Mr. Trumps' ego. "Every critic, every detractor, will have to bow down to President Trump," she said. "It's everyone who's ever doubted Donald, whoever disagreed, whoever challenged him. It is the ultimate revenge to become the most powerful man in the universe." ----Interview for a PBS "Frontline" special on the 2011 White House Correspondents' Dinner. Ms. Manigault recites a scene from the Count of Monte Cristo to reward those who are kind to him and his father, then punish all those responsible for seeking his imprisonment.

Ms. Manigault is also reflecting on what predicament the Republican Party finds itself in. It has latched onto gambling with "death" and decline. William Cummings, *USA Today*, on 20 Oct. 2016, "A flash of anger comes over Trump's face, and he appears to grit his teeth as he angrily rips a page from his notepad. He then appears to collect himself as Hillary Clinton crosses the stage to shake hands with debate moderator Chris Wallace." Psychologically, the political program carefully created a spectacle and depth of spite, anger, and hatred, creating a dissent wave, one that threatened to eventually overcome Mr. Trump. To illustrate this fear's depths and the problem of being discovered, Fyodor Dostoyevsky writes about spite. Spite against authority, parents, women, matriarchy, despite being spiteful.

In his *Notes from the Underground* (Underworld) in 1864, Fyodor Dostoyevsky narrates the sick, isolated, resentful, and conservative thought using the mask of spite. "When petitioners used to come for information to the table at which I sat, I used to grind my teeth at them and felt intense enjoyment when I succeeded in making anybody unhappy. I almost did reach. For the most part, they were all timid people--of course, they were petitioners. But of the uppish ones, there was one officer, in particular, I could not endure. He simply would not be humble and disgustingly clanked his sword. I carried on a feud with him for eighteen months over that sword... That happened in my youth, though. But do you know, gentlemen, what was the chief point about my spite? ...I was inwardly conscious with shame that I was not only not a spiteful but not even an embittered man, that I was simply scaring sparrows at random and amusing myself by it. I might foam at the mouth, but bring me a doll to play with, give me a cup of tea with sugar in it, and maybe I should be appeased. I might even be genuinely touched, though probably I should grind my teeth at myself afterward and lie awake at night with shame for months after. That was my way. I was lying when I said just now that I was a spiteful official. I was lying from spite."

Republican Conservative extremists exhibited nationalism and fascism in The Beast's recent emergence in their graphic campaign in Charlottesville, Virginia. What of the uproar? Commemoration of the Confederacy is as much a ritual as a commemoration of the dead. It fulfills psychological needs to identify with what is a *Day of the Dead* in Mexico. Alt-Right beliefs encase the imaginary to make death rise again, become together with them, and act for them, with a historical reference to Eastern Europe and admiration/idolatry. [163] Death to the dying is a relatively new phenomenon in modern America relegated to the Dust Bowl, World Depression, and food lines. This era's psychopathic thinking child feels an irresistible pull to revisit the scenes that his father witnessed firsthand in adulthood, perusing the cemetery and battlefield as symbols of evil reverence and places of consolation below.

"It is well known the dead soldier became in all European countries an icon that carried the meaning of the war back home, an

---

[163] Neocleous, Nicholas. "Long live death! Fascism, resurrection, immortality." *Journal of Political Ideologies* (February 2005), 10(1), 31–49.

emblem in the political culture of ancestor worship that constitutes a crucial dimension of nationalist politics. But where for most political movements, the question of the dead and the practice of commemoration centered on the theme of 'homecoming' or the 'return' of the dead to their homeland, of 'putting the dead to rest' in their own soil, the emerging fascist movements more forcefully raised as a political and historical issue the meaning of these deaths. In the two major countries in which fascism was to eventually triumph the cult of the fallen took on a special significance, becoming central to the 'nationalization of the masses' and thus the consolidation of fascism as a political ideology. Therefore, initially, in the name of the war dead that fascism sought to defend the nation and build a movement for achieving national greatness again. Part of this special significance was to turn the dead into heroes. Even before the Nazi seizure of power, those on the far-Right proclaimed the political and historical importance of those who died at Langemarck. Josef Magnus Wehner gave a speech of dedication at one memorial in 1932: 'The dying sang! The Stormers sang. The young students sang as they were being annihilated: "Deutschland, Deutschland u"ber alles," u"ber alles in der Welt" ... The dead heroes became an omen for the German people.' Fascism turned such ideas into a philosophy of life, with the coming new age founded on the heroism of the dead. The myth of Langemarck, for example, quickly became a primary component in the repertoire of National Socialist propaganda, with annual ceremonies and eminent figures such as Martin Heidegger addressing rallies on the historical event (in November 1933)."

David Duke

It's not difficult to grasp why neo-Bolshevists would be attracted to the Good Hitler theory. Considering that Nazism provided Bolshevists their early financing even though they may not immediately have realized it. Later it was an unavoidable fact the Reich had created them as an enemy for their purpose. Then the Soviets turned this around and dominated them. The Russian leadership seemed to have this uncanny ability in their DNA. That is, appearing they are duped, then capturing and destroying their enemies. This behavior is actually Biblical in Proverbs 26:27. This behavioral feature made such a compelling character and actor-politician.

Frederick Trump was onto something in the 1920s, associating himself with the Klan active in Queens, New York, a reactionary electorate. The Ku Klux Klan's case sheds light on its adaptability through the decades and its durability as a Trump family ally and a terrorist organization. Myths of the Ku Klux Klan as an undereducated band, underpaid, and disconnection from society all worked to benefit the Klan. Under the hood, one of their perpetual abilities is to hide in the Republican and Democratic parties. Frederick Trump was curious about the Ku Klux Klan, and later, Donald J. Trump established firmer organization ties. What attracted the Trump family to the white supremacist organization? During the 1920s, the Ku Klux Klan was connected to substantial economic resources and acted as homegrown terrorists.

The Klan's own affinity to neo-Nazism went back to their limited comprehension of Adolph Hitler, a populist who called their practices "the beginning of a high German racialized state!" The notable similarity between the Ku Klux Klan and the National Socialist party gained approval when Adolph Hitler adopted their verbiage. Today is no different as the Klan finds itself promotes and exerts itself in foreign affairs through the modern Republican Party for Mr. Putin. A glimpse of the Klan's Americanism was a white society ruled by its intellectuals and elites with a centralized planning committee. An intricate part of the belief system was eugenics and race/gene purity.

"We in the lead found ourselves with a following inspired in many ways beyond our understanding, with beliefs and purposes which they only vaguely understood and could not express, but for the fulfillment of which they depended on us. We found ourselves, too, at the head of an army with an unguessable influence to produce results for which the responsibility would rest on us -- the leaders -- but which we had not foreseen and for which we were not prepared. As the solemn responsibility to give right leadership to these millions, and to make the right use of this influence, was brought home to us, we were compelled to analyze, put into exact words, and give purpose to these half-conscious impulses." -- Hiram Wesley Evans, "The Klan's Fight for Americanism," *The North American Review* (March-April-May 1926).

The New York Times decided to advertise a historical series of articles on the Ku Klux Klan entitled *The New York World's exposé of the Ku Klux Klan* on 6 September 1921, posting new items in an everyday series. This ultimately shattered misconceptions about the Ku Klux Klan being a poor, incapable organization of the lower unemployed and working classes. What seemed to be the impetus for the articles was a 1,000 member Ku Klux Klan rally in Jamaica, Queens, New York. Frederick Trump was arrested during the rally. The Frederick Trump family was forever stigmatized; instead of public repentance, they blamed the government. [164] The Klan's old image was dissipating as a financial model, giving way to more profitable territories. Namely, to avoid legal complications and conspiracy charges of gang-related activities, it instituted interdependent relationships among the political class.

The Ku Klux Klan is deeply embedded in society. Roland G. Fryer, Jr, and Steven D. Levitt wrote the following examination of the Klan individuals. Many believed that the Klan was a social club despite their violence and lynching. They assert the Klan has long been different from common perceptions. It was the gold mine for Frederick Trump during economic instability and uncertainty, performing like a hedge fund by investing in its underworld future while reaping the

---

[164] Bump, Phillip. "In 1927, Donald Trump's father was arrested after a Klan riot in Queens." *The Washington Post.* 29 Feb. 2016. See Wikipedia under *New York World Expose of the Ku Klux Klan.*

rewards in selling them goods and places they needed. [165] Frederick Trump could use the KKK to fill some of his housing and not be concerned about minorities.

"The results we obtain using our new dataset on members of the Klan are, in some cases, quite surprising. Individuals who joined the Klan were better educated and more likely to hold professional jobs than the typical American, reinforcing earlier findings of some historians on the subject." [166]

The research pointed out Klan officials' dual personality, businessmen by day, and lynches in the evening. Today the public portrayal of white supremacist organizations like the Klan ranges from liberals and intellectuals who each have their reasons to support the Klan. Disguised insurgent groups operated like a penny stock investment in the Klan through small donations and merchandise. A kind of Trump era marketing effort that significantly compares to the National Rifle Association (NRA). A self-portrayed social club turns around to get matching funds from big donors and get maximum return on marketing violence. People would laugh at small items the Klan marketed. The Klan, though, the threat they pose is their ability to mobilize voters who support their racist candidates running primarily on Republican and Democratic platforms. The content of their publications and aim is close to those of American neo-Nazism that is found worldwide in similar Conservative enclaves, including Europe.

"The Klan's true genius lay in its uncanny ability to raise revenue. We estimate, at the peak of the Klan, initiation fees, dues, and profits from robes in the state of Indiana alone generated nearly $4 million (in 2006 dollars) annually for the national

---

[165] Fryer, Roland G. and Levitt, Steven D. "Hatred and Profits: Under the Hood of the Ku Klux Klan.", *The Quarterly Journal of Economics*, Volume 127, Issue 4, Nov. 2012, Pages 1883–1925.

[166] Ibid.

Klan leader, $2.4 million for the head of the Indiana Klan, and over $300,000 each for the national head salesman and the salesman responsible for Indiana. Per capita income in the United States at this time was roughly $8,000 in 2006 dollars."[167]

Marketing fanaticism and racism helped the Klan gain a foothold each subsequent decade and linked to the Ku Klux Klan Internationals' go*als. The *hooded Klan, for almost 8 decades,* were able to conduct their business model in secret. Telling lies to white voters about how racist they weren't kept their individual style out of view. The new tactic of the hanging Klan was the patriotic American Klansmen. Still, this hood was taken away too by an unlikely source when Donald J. Trump attempted to out Bernie Sanders. Then exposed operatives and his supporters as Mr. Trump's "too loyal white nationalists" criticized by the media as too racist or too similar. Sanders was also a transition candidate for "something better" than Mr. Trump that was not brought to fruition by underminers.[168]

Where does the Ku Klux Klan find itself in 2020? It attempts to modernize and expand into Eastern Europe's hate industry. Worthy of attention by extreme and moderate Conservatives who want to preserve "the legacy of white people." Under the umbrella of this supposed noble endeavor, it has made itself attractive to "The Camp of the Saints," a fictional fantasy turned white racist movement, including Renaud Camus' "The Great Replacement movement," a fictional white identity book, for Islamophobic groups, and white terrorists. [169] Because of the uncontrollable nature of what is essentially a dynamic

---

[167] Ibid.

[168] Cheney-Rice, Zak. "Bernie Sanders and the Lies We Tell White Voters." *Intelligencer*. New York: 11 Nov. 2018.

[169] "Camp of the Saints Worldview" combines moral conflict and physical combat to illuminate the ideological and religious roots, and deadly consequences Jean Raspail's French novel Camp of the Saints and the Eurabia Project writings of Egyptian Jewish exile writer Bat Ye'or. They are, respectively, the "intellectual forefather" and the "matriarch" of the counter jihad or "rising Muslim tide" movement.

movement steeped in overreactions to regular changes in society, its position in the communities it purports to assist can become entwined with those who can be motivated by one of the oldest frauds. Gather an audience whose discontent has reached unfathomable levels and disgust, then suggest a way out. Keep them so busy they won't realize you're the type of person who helped create their problems. It was an old version of Trump's brand, make a problem, yell about it, then offer a solution to a problem that doesn't exist.

This is where fictional theatrics meets reality. Could this kind of politics realistically climax in acts of terrorism? Instead of being a beacon for its purported goal to preserve white people, it actually places its members in a more violent susceptible status. President Trump's counselor Kellyanne Conway from Atco, New Jersey, expresses it accurately, "There are facts, and there are alternative facts." It's certainly true when it comes to Donald J. Trump's attempt to create an alternative biography beyond his glossy print. This is certainly true when the Ku Klux Klan gets into business with Trump. President Trump's message has been a violent one, "You know what solves it?" Trump said of America's alleged troubles during a 2014 interview. "When the economy crashes, when the country goes to total hell and everything is a disaster. Then you'll have a [chuckles], you know, you'll have riots to go back to where we used to be when we were great…" [170] Mr. Trump incorporated violence into his Make American Great Again platform alongside his role as a corporate statist and his anti-Semitism program. It didn't matter that if the economy crashed, it would be on top of his supporters, but from his attitude, one could readily see he enjoyed that possibility. This eventually led the Klan to Moscow. Like many elites suggesting violence, he never intended, it might impact him, just his supporters.

Pastor Thomas Robb, Ku Klux Klan leader, and Christian Identity pastor, was also the national director of The Knights Party,

---

[170] Boland, Stephanie. "This 2014 Donald Trump interview hints at a new kind of special relationship." *New Statesman America*. 17 Nov. 2016.

also known as the Knights of the Ku Klux Klan, taking control of the organization after David Duke. Not revealing himself as in Jean Raspail's *The Camp of the Saints.* With enough effort, it was possible to triple the Ku Klux Klan's membership and money, making it attractive again to millennials who vote for Trump. The Russian polity reestablished global alliances with elder Nazis and neo-Nazi organization factions. Ms. Bertrand, in 2016, "A model for civilization": Putin's Russia has emerged as " a beacon for nationalists' and the American alt-right." [171] Mr. Putin's strategy is theatrical, using nationalists, "where they are," supplying and guiding them. How did David Duke become famous in Moscow? Why did he ditch the Americanism stance for an offer of foreign nationalism?

Like Donald J. Trump, this last visit to Moscow significantly changed his identity. David Duke, his influential ethnic speeches, hefty politics of hate and division. And his enthusiasm to promote white people was reversed. All of a sudden, a man emerged not at all as the David Duke everyone knew. He no longer spoke openly over the radio of the poor mismanagement and discrimination. Instead, David Duke became more of a functionary, a peddler of Vladamir Putin's ideology, much more conservative. He assimilated Mr. Putin's enthusiasm for (occultist, Heartland, and Rimland) views of world dominion. Behind Mr. Putin awaited a more sedate and intellectual David Duke, a graduate of a Ukraine university more of a Dugin type of philosopher and not a proponent for a white Americanism as DDS Hiram Wesley Evans, but a compliant operative. [172]

"During his hiatus from U.S. politics, Duke wrote, and he traveled several times to Russia to promote his book, *The Ultimate Supremacism: My Awakening on the Jewish Question.* While

---

[171] Bertrand, Natasha." A model for civilization': Putin's Russia has emerged as 'a beacon for nationalists' and the American alt-right." *Business Insider.* 10 Dec. 2016.

[172] Thompson, A. C. (2001, January 6). "Ex-Klansman David Duke Sets Sights on Russian Anti-Semites." *Los Angeles Times.*

there, he became enamored with the strongman ethnic-nationalist ethos of the newly elected Russian President Vladimir Putin. Duke's anti-Semitic book, a top seller, is featured in the bookstore in the Russian Duma (Congress). Eyeing a potential new ally in highly motivated, post-Soviet Russia, Duke left Louisiana and moved to Moscow in 1999, where he rented a flat and lived for five years. While living there, Duke became acquainted with Aleksandr Dugin, a former sociology professor at Moscow State University. Branded "Putin's Rasputin" by former Trump White House chief strategist Steve Bannon. Dugin rose to prominence as a policy advisor to Russian President Vladimir Putin's top political and military leaders after the Soviet collapse. The privileged son of an intelligence officer, Dugin, is an avowed fascist who subscribes to the ideology of neo-Eurasianism. A school of thought believes Russia and the former Soviet Republics are neither part of Europe or Asia. And that "Greater Russia" must reclaim these lost territories and redefine itself as the Russian Orthodox ethnic-continent. Dugin's book, *Foundations of Geopolitics*, is allegedly required reading for new members of the Russian General Staff Academy."

Alexander Dugin's Eurasianism, like Dr. Andranik Migranyan's Good Hitler philosophy mentioned in this book's first Volume, it turns out, is not an original theory but from rejected knowledge repackaged for his President an idea of Harold Keith Thompson Jr., a former Schutzstaffel (S.S.) member in the United States.

4. IMPORTING AND EXPORTING ESPIONAGE

"When the enemy enthusiastically embraces you, and the fellow countrymen bitterly reject you, it is hard not to wonder if you are, in fact, a traitor."----Ursula K. Le Guinn, The Left Hand of Darkness

This chapter defines different parts of influence campaigns in America. Each of the subchapter topics is interrelated to one another in a web designed to facilitate unrest. The U.S. Dept. of Defense has been penetrated by the right-wing extremist and foreign financial interests. No extremist group can be financially adept without support from the internet. This is also true of the Republican National Committee once it was melded to the Trump Organization that finds its financial stability in data mining and hate-bait. The silence from the Republican Party led to jeopardizing the Department of Defense. This relationship opened the door to civic and cultural intrusions.

The Russian bureaucracy is asking numerous questions about the U.S. Dept. of Defense. Some of these are serious inquiry such as whether the Dept. of Defense has complete control over its computer system and a false signal can cause nuclear conflict. Part of these questions surrounds the issue of why Israel's nuclear weapons are not monitored. Republican and Democratic Party officials decline to answer Russian inquiries. In the following pages, readers will understand Russian concerns raised by Yuri Vladimirovich Andropov, as Second Secretary of the Communist Party of the Soviet Union to President Reagan.

Revisions to the Trump Organization's revenue stream had, through various criminals formerly invested in his property, were drying up due to partial enforcement of Executive Order (E.O.) 13581. However, President Trump and Kellyanne Conway's theatrics were receiving benefits. To transcend the federal monitors and surveillance, devising a project to circumvent them using old tricks from the Ku

Klux Klan playbook. Developing a means by which he could apply a levy on supporters after they were emotionally manipulated to a "click-bait," where a stream of revenues would go to an American hedge fund investor. The arrangement instigated the hate-for-profits scam. Perhaps in the most diabolical scheme yet, the Trump family never intended to build a political movement based on the alternative-right. Instead, Trump's duplicated the Trump University and foundation fraud. Mr. Trump used the numbers he gathered during his speeches in different ways to con his supporters to send him cash that he turned around, converting it on the internet as "hate clickbait." At one point, slipping and called them "disgusting." The con involved routing all the haters and conspiratorialists to specific websites and apps to collect small fees amounting to millions. Their clicking never ended in his supporter's emotional excitement, making Trump's, Steve Bannon, Dr. Richard Mercer, and Kelly Ann Conway, to name critical elements, millionaires.

Thomas Mann wrote about Germany, stating, "the mystery and precept of our age is not liberation and development of the ego. What our age needs, what it demands, what it will create for itself, is—terror." ----The National Interest Jacob Heilbrunn 14 August 2019.

Justice Robert H. Jackson said the framework of this type of legacy is "…sinister influences that will lurk in the world long after their bodies have returned to dust. We will show them to be living symbols of racial hatreds, of terrorism and violence, and of the arrogance and cruelty of power." The folk surrealism cannot be compared without considering the impact of emotions he awakes. As Leon Trotsky and Ku Klux Klan leaders discussed, racial rallies and mass gatherings are a circus but is specifically focused. [173] Not to say the content is not stern, it is, but the material is devised to excite and detract from reality. This type of ploy establishes the speaker's hierarchical position

---

[173] O'Malley, JP. "Trotsky's day out: How a visit to NYC influenced the Bolshevik revolution." *The Times of Israel.* 19 Sept. 2016.

while separating apart the followers. It confirms who is in charge. It is a surrender of the will under specious terms.

Who were the men aroused by Mr. Trump that helped to define America as a failed state? The Evil Twins, Steve Bannon, a Jew by birth, once a liberal, produced over 18 films and primarily cult flicks. Their distortions of content tampered with national events like the Civil War. Being an unusually educated and cunning man and experienced in propaganda films, Bannon and Dr. Robert Mercer, a hedge fund cohort, took their scripts from Nazi film. [174] Mr. Bannon appears as the evil double of Michael Moore. Steven Mnuchin, son of Robert Mnuchin, was a partner at Goldman Sachs and a traditional Jew. Steven Mnuchin made significant income as an award-winning executive producer of over 35 highly rated films. At first, it seems contradictory for them to support the Confederates and neo-Nazis, but they do for the reasons stated above. Neo-Protestants have long been in conflict over the evangelical movement's direction, often comparing it to the Southern Strategy. The other side of this psychological dynamic is the sympathetic Jew to white supremacy; some speculate with an identity to neo-Bolshevism. Being a Jew does not excuse their anti-Semitism.

Historian George Mosse lamented over liberalism, "We failed to see," Mosse once wrote, "that the fascist aesthetic itself reflected the needs and hopes of contemporary society." [175]

Masculinity, European psychologists later recognized right under military analysts' noses that man was not just brutal in his fascist state but saw himself as impossibly vain, graceful, and beautiful. Not in ways liberalism imagined in his gracefulness of living, but in his choreography of destruction and ultimate death. This description fit

---

[174] Spotts, Frederic. *Hitler and the Power of Aesthetics*. Harry N. Abrams; 1 edition (January 6, 2003). ISBN-13: 978-1585673452.

[175] Mosse, George L. The Fascist Revolution: Toward a General Theory of Fascism (New York: H. Fertig, 1999).; Saul Friedländer, Reflections of Nazism: An Essay on Kitsch and Death (Bloomington: Indiana University Press, 1993).

Kühn and his company, a chemist by trade, quickly becoming a valuable Nazi asset and visual artist. Like American populists today, Mr. Kühn could not control his criminal propensity. He was convicted and deported as a fraud and conman who robbed his own agencies. According to the Hitler Oath of the SS, George Sylvester Viereck was imprisoned to keep Harold Keith Thompson totally liberated to pursue a project. The kidnapping of this theatrical concept took place way back to President Mitterand in France when the Central Committee to the Communist Party (CCCP) ordered its KGB agents to work with the fascists. [176] This applies today because the Trump Tower inclinations run purposely parallel to these views.

Matt Pearce, a writer in Los Angeles, reported on Conservative Steve Bannon's behavioral shift toward fascism as it happened. Mr. Pearce wrote, "Today, Bannon represents a new ideological force inside the Republican Party. An anti-establishment activist and businessman propelled from the fringes of the GOP to its very center. Seen by his critics as the proverbial barbarian who has breached the gates." Speaking about Julia Jones Bannon, Pearce addressed who began imagining, "At one point, the pair developed a proposal for a TV show. To feature philosophers from a wide range of traditions, including non-European mystics and shamans."

Steve Bannon went into paganism, citing how great the fantasies were of Leni Riefenstahl's *Triumph of the Will*. The Nazi propagandist, "Bannon, has cultivated an archvillain image, recently declaring apocalyptic beliefs, "Darkness is good," and praising Dick Cheney, Darth Vader, and Satan as emblems of power. (One "Saturday Night Live" actor played Bannon by wearing a Grim Reaper costume.) Bannon's remarks succeeded in further enraging his liberal critics, who see him as the master enabler of a demagogue." [177] This established the racial-hate message of blood and soil, and the "voice of

---

[176] Kirillova, Kseniya. "I was told we should work with fascists: former KGB officer Zhirnov." *Euromaidan*. 03 Dec. 2018.

[177] Pearce, Matt. "Stephen Bannon found inspiration in ancient thinkers, Ronald Reagan and Nazi propaganda." *Los Angeles Times*. 09 Dec. 2016.

the Bannon devil" was a routine message. Using Germany's approach in the 1920s, they updated and revised it creating old feelings on new formats always directed at youth, possibly due to their propensity of violence and undiscipline. Bannon and Mercer's propaganda efforts were based on Nazi and Bolshevist doctrine, but probably not the one he wants that Hitler described as poisonous.

"Hitler publicly swore that in time the German youth would not even remember "the infection of our poisonous party system... They will not even understand the language of the alienage... [and that youth] has been consigned to us and has become our body and soul. They live in this proud Germany of the swastika and will never again let it be ripped from their hearts." – Adolf Hitler to the Hitler Youth, September 8th, 1934, quoted from the film Triumph of the Will, *Triumph Des Willens* (Reichsparteitag-Film, 1935.)

Pearce continues as Bannon shows himself to be generally aware of the Eastern European émigré recruitment, "The next documentary co-directed by Bannon and Watkins. "In the Face of Evil," released in 2004, uses similar dramatic imagery and praises Reagan as "a radical, with extreme views" on government. Among filmmakers, Bannon describes his journey as a Jew. "The film also offers a clue as to why Bannon seemed so at home in liberal Hollywood, where he would create new conservative documentaries. A narrator praises the Hollywood of the 1930s as "the most powerful crucible on Earth." A "brutally efficient industrial process" was run by Jewish refugees with "ruthlessness and uncompromising patriotism" that reinforced the values of Western civilization with stories of "order versus chaos, good versus evil." [178]

Leni Riefenstahl's *Triumph of the Will* affected her subconscious, which underwent distress similar to a fascist orgasm. "I had an almost apocalyptic vision that I was never able to forget. It seemed as if

---

[178] Ibid.

the Earth's surface were spreading out in front of me. Like a hemisphere that suddenly splits apart in the middle, spewing out an enormous jet of water, so powerful that it touched the sky and shook the earth." Ms. Riefenstahl played different roles where she imagined herself as a goddess. Vulnerable to the point of irresistibility, sexual in nature, she then abruptly tells someone her ability. Ms. Riefenstahl realizes it is possible to see human nature in her productions and Adolph Hitler's sublime. She imagines giving birth to him, nurturing him through youth, and enhancing his 1,000-year reign.

Riley Folsom critiques, "It is the fact that Hitler intimidates Riefenstahl that draws her to him. Riefenstahl decides to join Hitler and his entourage, becoming a lone female in an all-male pack of wolves. She travels in an exclusive circle, positioning herself always in a safe distance to the alpha male, the Führer. She decides to prove the ones who distrust her. She will make a film worthy of his greatness, as good as any demagogue could desire." [179] Steve Bannon chose her as his idol in filmmaking as an example of his subjugation to Trump. Bannon suggested when he furnished his office in the White House, he would bring an essential tool for Donald J. Trump, the pocket version of *My New Order*. Steve Bannon was booted from the White House and replaced by a neater, tidier, and quieter married white supremacist Stephen Miller a Jewish counterpart.

Steve Bannon and Dr. Robert Mercer have strong connections to the hate industry and will not disclose their investments. On 7 Jan. 2014, and 10 Mar. 2015, the Southern Poverty Law Center reported on William W. Williams's efforts, a special forces officer with two Vietnam tours, with a Russian wife 24 years younger. Mr. Williams has become "head Nazi in Charge" of the National Alliance, the oldest neo-Nazi organization in America with an organization established for global impact complete with publishing. National Alliance played a

---

[179] Folsom, Riley. "In the Land of Gods and Monsters." In Hoy, Pat C. 2013. *Mercer Street 2013-2014: a collection of essays from the expository writing program.* New York: Expository Writing Program, New York University College of Arts and Sciences.

crucial role in the Democratic Party, assisting Governor George Wallace, a "born again Christian" and segregationist. Mr. Williams' approach is also a revamped National Socialism designed to enlist more moderate youth attracted to Nazism. From the Presidential election of 2016, the counter-culture Nazi trend has increased. It was partially fueled by the absent voter turnout by the Democratic Party and apathy or the disbelief that racists were deep within the Republican Party. After purifying the membership, Mr. Williams eliminated riff-raff and the Jewish-Christians he is tired of meeting at supremacist events.

Casey Michel reported, "Despite reports that Putin's intimates routinely referred to former President Barack Obama as the n-word or "monkey." [180] This is how Mr. Putin intimidates Trump, who quickly succumbs to him. American white supremacists had connected with Russians long before his presidency. American Conservatives did not acknowledge they played a pivotal role in agitating racism decades ago as part of a longitudinal program. Conservative extremists (like George Sylvester Viereck and Harold Keith Thompson) had much more in sync with American conservatism than the party cared to admit. Only when they must, Conservatives will come out against these Russian-culture attempts to reincarnate Nazism. Still, it's rare, according to Mr. Williams, Jewish-Christians also support a wide range of white supremacist ideals.

Surrealism is vital to keep the fascist myth alive. Hans Fritzsche said this, "The artist, the writer, each creative artist is free. He wants to bind them from below; after years of direct influence streaming in from different directions, he wants art to again be rooted in the soil of the homeland, in the soil of the people. This binding is no chain but rather a liberation and fruitfulness. For each German, ethnicity must be the absolute reality. From this ground and no other, creatively artistic and cultural forces must rise. The deeper art's roots

---

[180] Michel, Casey. "Russian attempts to woo American white supremacists have backfired." *Think Progress*. 20 April 2017.

are in the soil of the nation, the greater will be its international significance." [181]

Though National Socialists changed the culture, they did so not to save it. Self-destructiveness was built into their formula; it was made into their psyche as Hitler said a "poison" youth could drink and absorb. Dr. Goebbels, a surrealist, was in the habit of reinforcing the spoken word of a glorious German legacy to films of perseverance, persistence, and the Heroes Death.

"Gentlemen, in a hundred years, they will be showing another fine color film describing the terrible days we are living through. Don't you want to play a part in this film, to be brought back to life in a hundred years? Everybody now has the chance to choose the part that he will play in the film for a hundred years hence. I can assure you that it will be a great film, exciting and beautiful, and worth holding steady for. Hold out now, so that in a hundred years; hence, the audience does not hoot and whistle when you appear on the screen." -Joseph Goebbels Reich Minister of Public Enlightenment and Propaganda ("Volksaufklärung und Propaganda"), Speech to the Propaganda Ministry in Berlin, 17 April 1945, thirteen days before his suicide.

The inner workings of the Nazi emphasis on commemorating what is dead near the end of the Reich and which Germany will soon die from are illustrated by Sophie Wunderlich. [182]

---

[181] Hans Fritzsche (1900–1953) was head of the radio division of the German propaganda ministry. A relatively minor propaganda ministry official who had not held a policy-making position, Fritzsche was included in the dock at Nuremberg in the absence of the deceased Joseph Goebbels and to mollify Soviet authorities, who held him in their custody.

[182] Wunderlich, Sophie. "We See into the Distant Future, Because We Know What It Will Be" Destiny, Utopia, and Apocalypse in National Socialism." *Williams College.* Williamstown, Massachusetts. 16 Apr. 2018. Thomas Kohut,

"These Apocalyptic fantasies reflected their devotion to self-mythologization. If they could not be the founders of the new world order, the world would end with them in the most horrifyingly beautiful way imaginable. Rather than fizzle out in humiliating defeat as in the First World War, the Nazi leaders imagined themselves as great heroes destined to fall in battle, their final acts ones of valor and sacrifice, enacting a romantic Heldentod (hero's death). This imagination was centered on death's mythical ideas, uniting their yearnings for sacrifice and resurrection into an emotional, romantic, and terrifying image of the regime's collapse. Friedländer characterizes the resulting aesthetic as a "kitsch of death," which found beauty in the high emotions and horrifying images that dominated Nazi thought in the Third Reich's final days. Nazi leaders abandoned reality for these Romantic scenarios. In these imaginings, they could remain world-historical figures. Rather than the architects of a better world, they would become the choreographers of its dramatic final act. As Goebbels declared at Nazi martyr Horst Wessel's funeral in 1930, "Perhaps we Germans don't know much about living, but as for death—that we do fabulously!"

Dr. Joseph Goebbels's last appeal for unity and going down with the ship also emphasizes the problem with Nazism. Adolph Hitler's view of Nazism drew on people that had many different perspectives on nationalism. It was not destined to be as eternal a fixture his commanders portrayed. Therefore, what came about were many other Nazi dystopias according to individual imagination. Though different historians try to emphasize, it was not chaotic and was orderly. The image of preciseness was portrayed influentially by achievement in industrial power. Still, precision rarely went beyond industry and military forces. Few mechanisms of Nazi governance were natural. Dr. Goebbels mused, "Perhaps we Germans don't know much about living, but as for death—that we do fabulously!" Rituals of

---

Advisor A thesis submitted in partial fulfillment of the requirements for the Degree of Bachelor of Arts with Honors in History.

commemoration and remembering the dead's meaning projected a dire image of suicide, lack of hope, and fatalism.

"Hitler's dictatorship differed in one fundamental point from all its predecessors in history. His was the first dictatorship in the present period of technical development, a dictatorship that made full use of all technical means to dominate its own country. Through technical means like the radio and the loud-speaker, eighty million people were deprived of independent thought. It was thereby possible to subject them to the will of one man."[183]

Neo-Bolshevik Bagmen

When he first appeared as Donald J. Trump on an escalator, one could almost imagine the song "Springtime for Germany," a piece in the film *The Producers* by Mel Brooks. The early phase of President Trump's administration initially seemed ludicrous. An objective assessment leads everyone to a similar conclusion Mr. Trump is cunning and intelligent. Marketing and hotel management does not make a President. Apparently, though, his remarks on "good people on both sides" were somewhat reminiscent of President Reagan's statement at the Bitburg SS Cemetery.

The Confederate Klan and neo-Nazi messaging were being dumped into the video sphere. All Mr. Trump's rants and racist remarks were put on social media programs. One initially thought this was to win the 2016 election. Instead, it was a complete fraud designed and orchestrated to drive an audience to "clicks" where vast

---

[183] Speer, Albert. "His final statement to the Nuremberg court." 31 Aug. 1946. Trials of The Major War Criminals. Before the International Military Tribunal. 14 November 1944- 01 October 1946. Published Nuremberg, Germany 1947. See Khoshkish, A. *The Socio-Political Complex: An Interdisciplinary Approach to Political Life* (Pergamon international library of science, technology, engineering, and social studies). Pergamon; 1st edition 22 Oct. 2013.

amounts of revenues were collected then distributed among Mr. Trump and staff. His supporters generated so many videos and so much income that aligned with Mr. Trump's positions. When discovered by a whistleblower, they quickly dispersed millions in revenues. This was in addition to corporate size and small donations. It was almost impossible to get an accurate sketch as to what happened. The following is that explanation.

This may have been how the first term would have ended, with the United Nations' audience laughing at Mr. Trump's statement as "best President ever." This public image gave way to staff firings and inexperienced staff's insertion representing white supremacism, a self-admitted fascist, the usual assemblage of opportunists, and cronies with Wall Street ties. All the efforts were to create revenue streams as one might expect from a criminal operation. The unexplainable contradiction to the racist and bigoted opinions was that key members making policy had Judeo-Christian and religious backgrounds. Conforming their spiritual experience to the politics at hand, perhaps a cursory acknowledgment of the Trump family's intent to co-opt the alt-right and rob the neo-Nazis in a type of pyramid scheme over the internet. There is some dispute whether Mr. Vladamir Putin, the Russian President, has taken an interest in this.

The Republican National Committee and Federalist Society had hand-selected the staff, actors, an entire mechanism, and Chiefs of Staff that administrated the government and politicians in a well-choreographed beginning. Even David Duke expressed privately he could sit back to watch the Trumps operate to increase the Klan's members. In fact, it was too well-planned for it not to be noticed that many regular government employees were suddenly unsuitable, requiring their careers to be destroyed. This would become a type of psychodrama. What campaign content was developed was repeated on Facebook. These efforts and their connections are narrated here. It appeared from the start that the White House's operation and the nation's security were secondary to an old-fashioned robbery.

Trump family finances since their campaign were derived from brandishing old routines of hate and glory. Their white supremacy and nationalism stood on the past framework of "the master race" belief. Still, the Trump system sounded superficial, obfuscating essential resources from services intended for the public to Trumpian seniors like millionaire Wilbur Ross. It was difficult to swallow that the grand replacement theory of terminating federal employees served the public well. It did, however, serve as a distraction. Mr. Putin was observed speaking to President Trump during his White House lunch. This ignited various rumors, one of which I am sure is historically accurate. Turns out President Vladamir Putin also exploited the alt-right.

Since Premier Nikita Khrushchev, the stories have grown greater under President Putin. Tales that psychiatric treatment was becoming tied to mysticism and spiritism, visions of a renewed Russian Empire as heavenly born. In this dream, the integration of military totalitarianism and psychiatry had never wholly been abandoned from the Soviet Union; still, the Premier warned of cults of personality and their devastating effect. He implied the use of these cults is an apostasy. [184]

Theatrics and oral presentation continue to play an essential role in public exhibitions by shaping thought patterns and influence campaigns using film. [185] Before any Third Rome coronation, the platform had to be imagined, then imitated and created. Russian psychiatry, one of the most volatile professions in the Soviet Union, was overtaken by the Marxist philosophy of fluctuating and confusing medical standards in the 1980s. [186] Since then, the psychiatric work has struggled to gain independence from its connection to the state's

---

[184] "Khrushchev's Secret Speech, 'On the Cult of Personality and Its Consequences,' Delivered at the Twentieth Party Congress of the Communist Party of the Soviet Union," February 25, 1956, History and Public Policy Program Digital Archive, From the Congressional Record: Proceedings and Debates of the 84th Congress, 2nd Session (May 22, 1956-June 11, 1956), C11, Part 7 (June 4, 1956), pp. 9389-9403. Wilson Center Archive.

[185] Polyakova, Alina. "How Russia Meddled in its Own Elections." *The Atlantic*. 18 Mar. 2018.

[186] Reich, Walter. "The World View of Soviet Psychiatry." *The New York Times*. 30 Jan. 1983.

affairs. For political dissenters in the Soviet mental institution, there were no impactful mental health advocates. No civil commitment process with lawyers as all these mechanisms was subject to enforcement of keeping the apparatus intact. [187]

Political prisoners in Russia are incredibly knowledgeable about the psychiatric approach to silence dissent. The sluggish schizophrenia diagnosis was much like America's schizophrenic diagnosis of "chronic undifferentiated type." Psychiatry can function as a religion within the state, a mixture of atheism and Christianity fluctuating while striving for a place in modern medicine. Elena Volkova, "…Trump's dream-the oppressive authoritarian regime with a quasi-religious foundation, a hybrid of Communism and Christianity that is ready to sacralize the leader and demonize his enemies, approve of any aggressions abroad or repressions within the country." [188]

President Reagan began dismantling the Dept. of Defense, replacing military personnel with civilian contractors, called civilianization. In financial investments, the Dept. of Defense involved itself in a contract /outsource scandal. Wall Street's President Trump investors, Steve Bannon, and the Mercers bought the Strategic Communication Laboratories (SCL) offshoot of Cambridge Analytica (CA) that President Reagan's work made possible. [189] CA was started by Steve Bannon and Dr. Robert Mercer and was purchased with some of the Dept. of Defense software intact. It operated out of the U.S. because it would be illegal in Europe with its stricter privacy laws.

---

[187] Bloche, Gary. "Law, Theory, and Politics: The Dilemma of Soviet Psychiatry." *The Yale Journal of International Law.* Volume 11, Number 2, Spring 1986. Author: Columbia Presbyterian Medical Center, New York; J.D. Candidate, Yale University, 1986.

[188] Volkova, Elena. "Communist Christianity as Russian Political Religion: Does Putin's Dystopia look like Trump's Dream?" *Journal of the European Society of Women in Theological Research* 27 (2019) 279-298.

[189] Whylie, Christopher. *Mindf*ck: Cambridge Analytica and the Plot to Break America.* Random House (October 8, 2019). ISBN-13: 978-1984854636.

The firm cut its teeth on campaigns for Brexit and the failed Sen. Ted Cruz's Presidential pursuit. The United States once again conceded the use of subversive activities from within. Aleksandr Kogan, aka Dr. Spectre, was a data scientist at Cambridge University who developed an app called "This is your digital life." Possibly the most anti-privacy program in existence that hoped to reach the technologically undereducated. Like many other seemingly reasonable apps, it was easily corrupted and used as a fraudulent method to control people.

CA used this app with an informed consent process to reach several hundred thousand Facebook users who agreed to complete a survey for academic use. According to Facebook, this scholarly research was approved. However, CA used this app to turn it into an insurmountable privacy problem by collecting personal information on the people who agreed to take the survey. Through this survey, CA had information on 87 million users with over 5000 data points each. CA then modeled those personalities until they found enough "persuadable" in the swing states that could affect the Presidential election." – *Smith Hanley Associates.* 29 Aug. 2019.

The Cambridge Analytica purchase's first act showed that the corporate forces and Wall Street supporting the Republican Nationalists who selected Ted Cruz's Presidential pursuit pivoted toward Donald J. Trump. Emmi Bevensee, "Amidst the resurgence of fascism and authoritarianism in popular culture, there is a concurrent global information war afoot. State super-powers are warring through manipulating the information sources and social media discourses of different political groups in foreign nations. Our initial data suggests that the Alt-Right leans heavily on Kremlin-controlled media sources as a critical backbone of their ideology, thus playing a role in their attendant violence."

Secondly, Facebook Mark Zuckerberg, Jewish by background, is the son of a psychiatrist. Facebook was only too eager to provide an avenue for Russian profit. The unity of beliefs behind Facebook's attitude is an ideological one, "*Victory is not won, but given freely to those destined to take it.*" —Volkssturm. Money was accessible through the convenience of social media's available audience. In Mr. Zuckerberg's actions, it appears his familiarity with behaviorism served an entire theory, practice, and platform of psychiatry to shape public opinion while creating revenues for himself.

Thirdly, Cambridge Analytica made almost a billion dollars on "hate bait." It was apparent that the app, "This is your digital life," was used to locate psychological matches of people. Cambridge Analytica took the data and identified what misinformation had the most impact based on personal backgrounds. This was how Russian hackers knew how to mobilize actions matching them to individual characteristics. Namely, the more nervous a person is, the easier they are to manipulate. Russian hackers only had to use the online marketing tools available on Facebook to businesses. Then convert them for their use. This was not only foreign meddling but supported by the rank-and-file Conservatives in Trump Campaign.

Facebooks' campaign followed the psychological system of Ernst Hanfstaengl, nicknamed "Putzi." A Harvard graduate who helped Reich leaders in speechmaking and song creating Nazi Stormtrooper marching songs. He said to war crime investigators, "There is only so much room in a brain. So much wall space, as it were. If you furnish it with your slogans, the opposition has no place to put up any pictures later on because the apartment of the brain is already crowded with your furniture." [190] Illustrating the use of hysteria in the Adolph Hitler speech, Ernst Hanfstaengl understood mania as a fundamental basis for mass manipulation. It serves the current social media blitz in Russia's psychological warfare and influence campaigns traversing Facebook's platform. An added feature was employed to reach people on social media who were not susceptible to the app, "This is your digital life."

Psychologists used Neural Linguistic Programming (NLP) to influence social media users in what appears to be a confidential agreement to market NLP and CA tools. NLP was initially developed by

---

[190] Langer, Walter C. Psychological Analysis of Adolph Hitler. CIA File. Central Intelligence Agency. Declassified August 1999.

Richard Bandler and John Grinder in the 1970s, from a combined psychoanalytic, occult, and New Age world in the 1980s. In other words, it was primarily conceived as a technology that had religious devotees, based on positive and magical thinking toward a "better" enlightened world using friendly "touchy-feely" language.

The New Age theory was universally known as the essential strategies of terrorist organizations like ISIS that used psychographic tools in recruitment and propaganda to develop cult followings. NLP is a perfect tool to impact the imagination to have people create a feeling of invulnerability, an invaluable resource for extremists. But the question that exists is whether NLP was also used on President Trump to direct his actions. NLP psychologists and psychiatrists that worked with CA were never subpoenaed by Congress. One could argue the Conservative advisors in the Trump campaign had every right to use NLP and other real estate marketing companies. [191] Still, this did allow Cambridge Analytica to go on its own and market its programming to misuse American elections and obtain citizen emails for political purposes and profiteering. This also made it possible to make the unimaginable contract to train Russian military personnel.

Dr. Robert Mercer and their daughter Rebecca who made their wealth on Wall Street from hedge funds, like Facebook's Mark Zuckerberg, expanded into the misinformation industry. Once the head of the CNBC's reported Anglosphere Society, Dr. Robert Mercer's father led their attention to market privileged white people, under the moniker "celebration of the Anglo-American experience." [192] In 2012, Steve Bannon, then using the title of a cultural Jew and born again Christian, Wisconsin GOP operative Mark Block, Jewish, and Alexander Nix, a British citizen CEO of SCL -an affiliate of Cambridge Analytica

---

[191] Bolstad, Richard, Ph.D. "The Day The Tide Went Out: Using Neuro-Linguistics on a Global Scale." Transformations International Consulting & Training Ltd. Browns Bay, North Shore, Auckland, New Zealand.

[192] Schwartz, Brian. "GOP megadonor Mercer family donated to nonprofit conservative group that focuses on historic values of 'English-speaking people." 13 Mar. 2019. CNBC, Inc.

and Dr. Robert Mercer, the generous funder of Jewish philanthropy, and Rebekah Mercer had already laid plans to initiate a civilian equivalent to psychological intelligence warfare operations commonly known by the military as Psy-Ops. They employed online propaganda tools, including psychographic modeling techniques, on behalf of the Trump campaign.

Widening the spectacle's circle, the fourth party to election interference emerged as one Nigel John Oakes (born July 1962), a British businessman. The founder and CEO of the Behavioral Dynamics Institute and SCL Group (formerly Strategic Communication Laboratories), the parent company of Cambridge Analytica. Nigel Oakes used to market his company as an election service for the Dept. of Defense. Branching out as a government contractor, he created a behavioral institute comprised "to help orchestrate a sophisticated campaign of mass deception." [193]

Dan Sabbagh reported, "SCL, Cambridge Analytica's parent company, had access to secret UK government information. According to documents released by MPs, the UK Ministry of Defense was singled out for praise by the UK Ministry of Defense for training provided to a psychological operations warfare group. An endorsement from an official at the 15 UK Psychological Operations Group dated January 2012 concluded that they would "have no hesitation in inviting SCL to tender for further contracts of this nature." [194] No public reports showed that the FBI had done any investigations on whether the United Kingdom data went directly to the Russians or Steve Bannon and Dr. Mercer for sale to Middle East investors. [195] Colin Dwyer of National Public Radio 0n 21 Jul. 2020 wrote, "The Parliament's Intelligence and Security Committee said it can't determine whether the Kremlin tried to influence the 2016 Brexit referendum because the

---

[193] Whylie, Christopher. *Mindf*ck: Cambridge Analytica and the Plot to Break America*. Random House (October 8, 2019). ISBN-13: 978-1984854636.

[194] Sabbagh, Dan. "Cambridge Analytica parent company had access to secret MoD information." *The Guardian*. 29 Mar. 2018.

[195] Ibid.

British government hasn't even tried to find out." Inadvertently the UK Ministry of Defense and their American counterparts shared in their work for Mr. Putin.

It can now be speculated with some certainty they had decided to use theatrics in their messaging for Trump Campaign. What kind of messaging? The sort of imagery most familiar to this group's history in film making. Impactful non-intellectual, unreasonable, and emotionally reactive dark films and images bordered on pornography, suggesting sex and intense surrealism. Like the snuff film prototype screened at Mar a Lago. Jake Johnson, a staff writer for *Common Dreams*, wrote the headline: 'Vile and Dangerous': 'Edited Video Showing Trump Gunning Down Media and Political Opponents Shown During Conference at President's Resort.' The film's theatrics would personify the discourse in the Office of the President. This snuff film may indicate how far business insiders are willing to go.

President Trump is willing to go the extra mile to work on behalf of the Good Hitler agenda. There is a list of alternative-right organizations from the infamous White House social media conference. These interveners make millions from "hate clicks," including Bill Mitchell, QAnon, Carpe Donktum, Ali Alexander, Charlie Kirk, Turning Point, Benny Johnson. [196]The social media conference's significance is that previously it was believed that extremists were not permitted into the White House. Now, they are an intricate part of the governmental structure. Through the President of the United States' propagation, former fringe groups were empowered by a coordinated effort where the White House would create incitement. The Alt-Right developed "hate clicks" and conspiracy theories that ultimately made them millions. Recently the 2020 election shows just how many parents are willing to serve as facilitators supporting this plan.

They play mind games with it, pitting one user (teen) against the other, poisoning them over the internet with sexual and violent

---

[196] Darcy, Oliver. "Trump invites right-wing extremists to White House 'social media summit'." *CNN Business.* 11 July 2019.

suggestions. [197] Facebook served as a primary resource for this extreme *marketing*. A sophisticated group experienced in data mining took its access to an entirely different level, one that psychological warfare units would call a cyber assault. Later a rendition of one propagated video was witnessed in plain sight. President Trump sent his unmarked personal militia to Democratic Mayoral cities that evoked this type of graphic violence that Mr. Trump promotes. Many more "hate clicks" for income.

The Mercer family bankrolled an effort, according to Christopher Whylie Cambridge Analytica, knowingly using Russian disinformation to help the Trump campaign win the 2016 election reported by Justin Hendrix of *Just Security Org* on 21 March 2018. Dept. of Defense still returned to their pattern working with Strategic Communication Laboratories/Cambridge Analytica after this.

In 2015, SCL's head of defense business Steve Tatham edited a Stratcom journal on subjects ranging from "Russia's 21st Century Information Warfare" and "Memetic Warfare" to "Narrative and Social Media." That same year SCL was hired by NATO for training services on disinformation, including countering Russian information warfare. The action of hiring a guilty party like Cambridge Analytica that sold out the security of the 2016 elections and then engaging them in 2018 as the top defenders of NATO is a lot like allowing white-collar criminals in the mafia to infiltrate the Dept. of Justice Staff. For example, Mr. Hendrix stated, "The company is currently working with the U.S. State Department on a $500,000 contract for countering ISIS propaganda. [198] Not only were the Dept. of Defense systems used against America in its election of President Trump, but it was about to serve the purpose of a more excellent robbery. One that stole from all the groups, individual supporters in the newly developed Trumpian

---

[197] Plutchik, Robert. *The Emotions*. University Press of America; Revised edition (July 25, 1991). ISBN-10: 0819182869. ISBN-13: 978-0819182869. Chapter 1. "Measuring Emotions and Their Derivatives."

[198] Ramsey, Adam. "Cambridge Analytica is what happens when you privatize military propaganda." *Open Democracy*. 28 Mar. 2018.

sphere. This thieving larceny is the culmination of a true "mining of the miners."

While Breitbart News also used the disinformation platforms to help Russians spread false election reports. The excitement over the hate campaigns led to higher membership roles among Alt-Right groups serving its dual purpose. [199] The Koch brothers' conservative political donor network disconnected formally from Dr. Robert Mercer. "Make America Number 1," which employed both Steve Bannon and Kellyanne Conway at various points during the election cycle, received $15 million of Robert Mercer's disclosed $22 million made in donations during the 2015-2016 primaries and election. Mercer also invested $10 million in Breitbart News, Yiannopoulos's former employer." wrote Matt Guariglia of *Motherboard, Vice News,* on 27 March 2017. [200]

"Human beings seem to have an almost unlimited capacity to deceive themselves and to deceive themselves into taking their own lies for truth." ---R. D. Laing, Psychiatrist

Benjamin Netanyahu's "wonderful friend" of the Jewish people everywhere created a perfect foil for Jews that support him with the Ku Klux Klan and neo-Nazis. The President's Executive Order, 11 December 2019, allegedly reduces discrimination toward Jewish people. It interprets Title VI of the Civil Rights Act of 1964, defining the categories of "race, color, and national origin." Intended to be too highly specific while eradicating the definition of Judaism as a religious practice, it seeks to define it as a race. Dr. Warren J. Blumenfeld, "Geneticists tell us that there is often more variability within a given so-called "race" than between "races." That there are no essential genetic

---

[199] Elsner, Alan. "Neo-Nazis Look for New Home in Trump's Republican Party." *J Street.* 12 Jul. 2018.

[200] Guariglia, Matt. "Billionaire Trump Funder Also Paid for Milo Yiannopoulos' College Speaking Tour." Motherboard, Vice News. 27 March 2017.

markers explicitly linked to "race." They assert, therefore, that "race" is discursively constructed—an historical, "scientific," biological myth, an idea. — that any socially-conceived physical "racial" markers are fictional, and are not concordant with what is beyond or below the surface of the body. Donald Trump uses Jews, and by so doing, he demonstrates his hateful antisemitic bigotry by attempting to weaponize Jewish bodies!" [201]

Q-Anon's Conspiracy Theory

QAnon is a disproven and discredited far-right conspiracy theory alleging that a cabal of Satan-worshipping pedophiles runs a global child sex-trafficking ring and plotting against US President Donald Trump, who is fighting the cabal. ---Wikipedia

The holy church particularly the ecclesiastical body, acknowledges that sin and evil have an ever-presence in society but are not Omnipresent. The community doesn't have the words for the monstrous conditions of the soul's mental illnesses and diseases when they become intertwined as inseparable bodies.

Monsters in and Among Us: Toward a Gothic Criminology by Cecil Greek writes about evil and the gothic in this way. "The Gothic settings and trappings have become such a hallmark of horror that they have become cliché-ic gimmicks. The early Gothic novel's hallmarks included the graveyard and the convent, the moats and the drawbridges, dungeons, towers, mysterious trap doors and corridors, rusty hinges, flickering candles, burial vaults, birthmarks, tolling bells, hidden manuscripts, twilight, ancestral curses. Crucial to the outlines of the Gothic landscape is the concept of extreme contrasts: "the Gothic landscape plunges from extreme to extreme; from the height of an

---

[201] Blumenfeld, Warren J. Donald Trump, the Antisemitic Provocateur. *University of Massachusetts* Amherst Adjunct. Undated paper received 9 Nov. 2020.

airy bell tower to the depth of a dungeon vault; from the mass of heavy stone walls to the delicate illusive spiderweb; from utter darkness to a candle's flicker; or from the hollow silence to a high-pitched squeak."[202]

Among the folklore followers in America in the hollows and rural places, the gothic notion is tied to culture. Bigfoot, the Jersey Devil, and Jung's Wotan inhabit the brain's geography. This is not only true for white people in *The Wizard of Oz* but written about by Maya Angelou in *A Caged Bird Never Sings.* Nature lovers found their folklore in *The Mother Earth News.* The ghost stories of *The Foxfire Magazine* hypnotic folklore that was inscribed, "I shall be telling this with a sigh. Somewhere ages and ages hence. Two roads diverged in a wood, and I—I took the one less traveled by. And that has made all the difference.", Robert Frost. Those not accountable to parents sought out the gothic in the speeches of the hate and horror of Donald J. Trump, who offers a sexual paternalism to Q-Anon.

Vasily Grossman may have been the first writer and chemist (like Fritz Kuhn) to explain alchemy by how the previous generations' submerged thoughts are stored. The mind somehow encompasses the generational memory of the ages of previously submerged memory. The memories from that contain the Gothic of war and barbarism. Those can be gathered and awoken by an evil medium, e.g., the wicked witch and racist. These memories can then be lit in what Melita Maschmann explained: "Something intangible that can awake through superstitious and religious means. Not surprising that the commemoration of World War Two in Eastern Europe would stir the region as these passions rekindle. They start a fire that can quickly get out of control." [203]

---

[202] Greek, Cecil E. *Monsters in and Among Us Toward a Gothic Criminology.* Fairleigh Dickinson University Press. 2007. ISBN: 9780838641590, 0838641598.
[203] Epstein, Helen, "I was a Nazi and here's why." *The New Yorker.* 29 May 2013.

It shouldn't be surprising that since a long repose in Virginia's Cemetery in 2013 and 2020, the inscription on the Confederacy's graves and The Daily Stormers Song's commemoration would show the same configuration of subconscious memory. Then exhibit a similar response through the same evil mediums of this era, i.e., Conservatives of today, Conservatives of the past, and result in a sequence of dark murders—some in churches signifying perhaps the human sacrifices of witchcraft and paganist lore of the fire, stakes, and innocent bodies of women in the subconscious.

Employing the Gothic is a form of language and strikes a chord of the familiar evil of racial, sexual, child-specific violence. One came about from the images of thoughts expressed by a wicked Donald J. Trump at Mar a Lago in the snuff film he acted in. It involved killing democrats, press members, and later reenacted by Border Patrol 10-15 that involved rape by Donald J. Trump against a Congresswoman. Mr. Trump routinely engaged in the Gothic, also associated with his associate Jeffrey Epstein. This hostility was later extended to the Governor of Michigan. These thoughts of sexual perversion and rape of women are fluid in a sense they have become an expected adjunct to Donald J. Trump's histrionics.

Theatre of the absurd. The Conservative body has connected itself to the gothic themes for decades and is inseparable from its origins in the film during the productions by Dr. Joseph Goebbels. Scandal as a social function is part of human life, but it has become something different as it evolved from family and faith politics. Q-Anon chooses to consult their members' childhood taking part in a preview regarding the "pedophile" experience. No one is told from whom. It relates and communicates the bonding between predatory and child victims of sex transgressed images of sexed children collapsing in a political posture of tainted homosexual politicians that they will punish by force.

In the entire conversation, it is difficult on purpose to determine how this gothic-inspired political drama was actually written into a Q-Anon script. Behind the mask, it would have to be someone in a political position, with an altered state of consciousness and a connection to children they want to scare and frighten "out of their minds." So, this is determined by a complete loss of peacefulness in their actions.

"The savage and primitive throb in the very heart of the modern, "civilized" metropolis. These same themes resonate in the second chapter. To Davis Houck, *Dirty Harry* (1971) is not merely a popular and enduring film about a 44-magnum-wielding homicide cop and his extra-legal pursuit of a crazed murderer. He argues that Dirty Harry can be productively read against the backdrop of what he calls the "urban monstrous." Set amid the Haight-Ashbury-addled late '60s, the film functions rhetorically to critique and ultimately dominate the freaks, pimps, swingers, queers, blacks, Hispanics, and other minority groups made to appear monstrous within the cinematic cartography of San Francisco. In asserting his dominance over the urban grotesque, the middle-class, heteronormative white male represented by Harry Callahan is re-masculinized. The process of re- instantiating his phallic authority occurs at several levels, not the least of which involves the ambiguity surrounding his nickname and the metonymic function of his handgun." [204]

This Q-Anon phenomenon coincides with the future in what will be performed by yet another Donald J. Trump monstrosity. One that comes as an enemy online. The other as in-person cruelty, by their supporters, against the children this conspiracy theory wants to protect. Although Q-Anon states they insist on protecting children, they have instigated a gothic crime scene using cages to confine babies. From this messaging, QAnon revealed the identity and author of the conspiracy as the Trump family. When this psychographic pattern is laid bare, the central part has always been a scene with Donald J. Trump and his family on the screen playing himself!

---

[204] Ibid.

Pentagon's Right-wing Extremists

In a short-lived newsreel on the internet, known as the Orion *Solar Winds* hack. A news feed read, "Russia says that they did not hack the United States." The content explained they hypothesized and speculated that the Trump Campaign had but never supplied the information. In 24 hours, the statement was erased by Google.

Facilitated by Facebook and Twitter for profits, the next level of schemes co-occurred, indicating substantial interdependence. This conspiracy to collect and weaponize personal data coincided with Lieutenant General Michael T. Flynn's Trojan Horse called *Flynn Intel Group. In his FBI declarations, he* was financially connected to SCL/Cambridge Analytica, the Mercer family, and Steve Bannon. [205] Lieutenant General Flynn appeared to decipher his role as the "bag man" who could walkthrough security protocols working with SCL/Cambridge Analytica.

Flynn never discussed operating on a whim, he kept within the chain of command, so it can be assumed his actions were directed by some subset of officials in the Pentagon above and below his level. Flynn "provided his counsel and guidance on public sector business opportunities for secure communications technology within the U.S. Department of Defense" and other agencies. [206] He worked on the SCL project. Did he do this with permission from the Department of Defense or as a rogue foreign agent? Public records did not indicate at this point who directed Flynn. —not the last domino within the Pentagon building.

Lieutenant General Michael T. Flynn, with a shared interest in finances while pleasing Trump, was connected to Turkish client Kamil Ekim Alptekin. Mr. Alptekin is the Turkish copy of Andranik Migranyan, Ph.D. Kamil Ekim Alptekin (born 1977), a businessman with real estate, aerospace, and consulting interests. He is Chairman of the Turkey-U.S. Business Council (TAİK), an advocate for improved Turkish-American relations. We can infer, there are ties to the Turkish and an

---

[205] Day, Chad and Stephen Braun. "Flynn files new financial form reporting ties to data firm." *AP News Service.* 04 Aug. 2017.

[206] Ibid.

attempt to influence the United States government and Congress. All of his cast worked directly with Donald J. Trump and his Campaign for President. That continues to operate today. Michael Flynn paid for research and lobbying work against the Gülen movement, central to American politics' ongoing political controversy. The Alptekin indictment of 12 December 2018 included conspiring to act as an agent of a foreign government and making false statements to investigators. [207] It was, operationally speaking, of the same kind of tactics that Trump's employed using foreigners as operatives to infuse money into the Trump Organization. The same goals of making them money while skimming off the top. The Trump family was not indicted.

Christopher Wylie's summation, 'this global behavioral management service continues to recreate programs. Whose full intention is to raise alternative-right and Nazi membership among the youth.' [208] Thus, fulfilling the long-range ideological goals of the Russian state. At no other time in history, the American people felt they lost control over their government. Senator Mitch McConnell refuses to release election interference bills to suppress efforts to stop white supremacist group increases in membership. [209] The first-time observers saw a tangible connection between the psychological campaign, the United States, and a rogue Lieutenant General. With an undercurrent of financial links to a foreign government. The next play in this game requires a reference not from spies but from psychiatry to decipher what is happening—President Vladamir Putin's game of playing an actor in a monstrous movie about Adolph Hitler's Inner Circle.

"They are playing a game. They are playing at not playing a game. If I show them, I see who they are, I shall break the rules and

---

[207] Meyer, Theodoric. "Flynn lobbied for Turkish-linked firm after election, documents show." *Politico*. 08 Mar. 2017.

[208] Whylie, Christopher. *Mindf*ck: Cambridge Analytica and the Plot to Break America*. Random House (October 8, 2019). ISBN-13: 978-1984854636.

[209] Ramsey, Adam. "Cambridge Analytica is what happens when you privatize military propaganda." *Open Democracy*. 28 Mar. 2018.

punish me. I must play their game, of not seeing I see the game."
— R.D. Laing, Psychiatrist

Mr. Putin had (characteristically) taken advantage of these dramatic situations playing a game of Chess master. It would be fair to say he sort of enjoyed his work in some sinister plot with that consistent blank look and smile underneath. While President Boris Yeltsin was calculating moves to decommunize the political structure in the Soviet Union and Russia to build a modern economic nation. Mr. Vladamir Putin castled him, placing these ideas to the periphery of the chessboard. In this elementary, uncomplicated play, timing is more important than anything. The King goes to a corner while the castle takes its place. This appeared satisfactory.

The elites of conservative Russia now had their hero. Just like the one they would create as his American friend, Donald J. Trump. Paraphrasing Alexey Tereshchenko, who lived in Moscow (1979-2003), explains how these theatrics work to a national audience. Later, Tim Dowling, *The Guardian* newspaper, picked up the analogy in a film review on 23 March 2020. Just a note, Americans tend to think of themselves as technologically superior and, therefore, the victor. Harsh as it sounds, technology matters very little, but combined psychology and intelligence hold the most important keys.

"The first popular TV program within the Soviet Union was *Seventeen Minutes of Spring*, including the excellent Soviet on-screen character Vyacheslav Tikhonov. Tikhonov played a high-ranking Nazi official, Max Otto von Stierlitz, who is, in reality, a Soviet spy. Whereas imagining to be a faithful adherent of Hitler and effectively guarding himself when suspected by the Gestapo chief Müller. He moderates down the Nazi A-bomb program. Subverts partitioned peace talks between Nazis and US mystery administrations and saves Warsaw from annihilation. This film made the picture of a spy impressive and prestigious in Russia. Putin was regularly compared with Stierlitz. This comparison played well since Putin was a previous KGB operator who had lived in Germany. And it makes Putin more available, but it moreover secured him from the allegation of complicity with the much-hated Yeltsin. If Stierlitz pretended Nazism to assist the Soviets, at that point, Putin might imagine Yeltsinism to help the Russian people. It worked. The Second Chechen War furthermore boosted Putin's notoriety. Individuals who loathed him got to be less and less numerous. On 31 December 1999, Yeltsin resigned, leaving Putin Acting President. This position was exceptionally profitable to Putin on the eve of the presidential decision. On the same day, Putin signed a decree that ensured Yeltsin and his family are spared from arraignment and gave them material benefits."

Not everyone can imagine and reconcile how the future will look like. Sometimes it's necessary to view it from past examples. Many Europeans viewed Max Otto von Stierlitz as a dark historical period living in their subconscious memories. The road ahead of Mr. Putin is fraught with dark memories but not just his own at the Berlin Wall. Historical periods and subconscious memory belong in what Carl G. Jung, MD called the collective unconscious. The darkness from behind the veil was also felt by the remaining Nazis in Eastern Europe. Such as Melita Maschmann.

"A deft writer and practiced propagandist. Who understood the power of a vivid quote, detail, or anecdote? Melita Maschmann portrayed herself as a girl who came of age. In a culture imbued with the shame of Germany's defeat in the First World War. "Before I understood the meaning of the word 'Germany,' I loved it as something mysteriously overshadowed with grief...," she writes." [210] Something intangible that can awake through superstitious and religious means.

---

[210] Epstein, Helen, "I was a Nazi and here's why." *The New Yorker*. 29 May 2013.

Not surprising that the commemoration of World War Two in Eastern Europe would stir the region as these passions rekindle. They start a fire that can quickly get out of control."

Some comparisons can be made between the traumatic times of Melita Maschmann and those of Mr. Vladamir Putin coming of age as an actor-politician. Taking the above accounts to their conclusion, some would say that the familial history of both has an undercurrent of similarity in experiencing war trauma. One is directly involved, the other a secondary trauma growing up in a setting peripheral to Vladimir Ilyich Ulyanov Lenin's central power through his father. Nikolai Ssorin-Chaikov explains these two sides of Russia as a bi-polar influence quite accurately. Thus, it is surmised that as the plotting, Mr. Vladamir Putin gained his authority at President Boris Yeltsin's expense through acting. It stands to reason that as President that Mr. Putin could gain from his acting in controlling Donald J. Trump.

There is still a great deal of "romance" and "allure" of wartime activity involving the Nazis, often fictionalized and objectified on social media platforms. Often without any relationship to the psychological state of mind, it creates through murderous images. Although we may detail all of the above realities about the United States' weakness and excuses for not prosecuting white-collar crime. The United States desperately holds onto the pre 9-11 myth that the wealthy class is not at the same time undermining democracy by their ideological influences. Neo-liberalism paved the way forward for Conservatives through its 19 and 20th Century ideals.

There is a need to see how overlooking this issue had led to a consolidation of power between the expected benefits between organized white-collar criminals and the political advantage to neo-Nazis and Russia when they use tactics to overthrow democracy. A preview of "Trump's dream and Mr. Putin's dystopia" was choreographed in Slovakia and Slovenia, where the fruits of American extremism coupled with gangsterism, the religious, and the Trump Presidency became a dramatic play of how the United States projects its problems on the world.

Robert Osenenko, Ed.D.

Melania's Ice and Slovenia's Fire

Yugoslavia is crucial because it has been invaded several times, and as a result, its people have been harmed by repeated conflict. Slovenia has learned quite a lot about resistance. The government is resilient and is resistant to the world's ebbs and the flow of trends, particularly with nationalism. There are parallels between policies and social behaviors in the United States. An outbreak and integration of crime and neo-Nazi politics in the United States Presidency came to its shore. I begin by outlining the experience in Yugoslavia with Slobodan Milosevic, the banker, and President. More can be learned about the long-term outcome of his policies in how it impacts the consciousness and psychology of leadership while learning about President Donald J. Trump's impact on foreign policy. Slobodan Milošević is a product of past and future time. His time spent under Yugoslav and Stalinist communism to his genocide. Melania Knavs-Trump's time of visiting the Southern Border reflects her history.

Psychoanalyst Otto Kernberg was an expert in malignant narcissism that he initially thought to be part of Slobodan Milosevic's personality. By the 1950s, the writing about communism's bond with specific individuals is notably a topic in Commonweal but not CIA files in the 1990s, abandoning any such correlation to history. [211] Warren Zimmermann, U.S. ambassador to Yugoslavia from 1989 to 1992, had believed that Slobodan Milosevic's personality shared psychopathic traits "driven by power rather than nationalism," the search and retention of power even when it meant overlooking his supporters was his primary motivation. Zimmermann observes, "Milosevic-style nationalism has proven singularly resistant to economic inducement, penalties, or any other pressures short of force." For narcissistic leaders, this is par for the course: they focus less on threats to their people and their country than on how situations can best be exploited for self-

---

[211] Communism as Unremorseful. *The Washington Post* "Ex-Communists Remain Totalitarian at Heart." 3 May 1953.

preservation, self-promotion, and tightening their grip on the reins of power."

Zimmermann notes that in the late 1980s, Milosevic first tried to consolidate his power by preserving Yugoslav unity but "became the major wrecker of Yugoslavia" when he realized that the strength of the Slovenian and Croatian independence movements could not be checked by military force. [212]He then reverted to "an even more aggressive approach" by sowing ethnic hatred as a ruse to forging a greater Serbia incorporating the Serbian populations of Croatia, Bosnia, Montenegro, and possibly Macedonia." ---*Courtesy of Unit for the Study of Personality in Politics at Saint John's University and the College of Saint Benedict in Collegeville and St. Joseph, Minnesota.* 21 May 1999.

The observation of the development of criminal organizations is crucial to understand the recent expansion of political influence. Its persuasion is used to position itself as an avenue for its own self-generating capitalization. In other words, sophisticated criminal organizations can generate enough income from governmental-corruption. For lack of better terms, these efforts are called mafia, a generic term for underground movements. The mafia may rise in their development stage to challenge the Constitutional government if perceived as weak. In the United States, the white-collar criminal organizations that govern Wall Street have tapped into the populism of hate to profit while protecting their involvement. That is until Mr. Trump exposed their position when he repeatedly prioritized gifts to them. In doing so, white-collar crime organizations realize that the dangerous hate they generated places their interests in greater danger by exposing their previously hidden hand.

The transition from Yugoslavia to Slovenia brought with it the horrors of its past. Vincenzo Scalia witnessed this transformation of crime and ideology partnerships in the Sicilian mafia, the internationalization of the organized criminal merging with politics. The merging of crime interests, business, and violent crime (terrorism) in cases like

---

[212] Hueven, Marten van. "Sense of the Community" Report on Yugoslavia. Declassified. NIC-03236-88. CIA File. 31 Oct. 1988.

Mr. Scarfo. [213] In this expansive view, "Cosa Nostra, unlike the Calabrian 'Ndrangheta and the Neapolitan Camorra, can be considered more akin to white-collar crimes than underworld mobs. Its government of land estates, its constant relation with politics, its relations with finance make the Sicilian Mafia a different criminal actor than the other criminal organizations. Since its beginning, Cosa Nostra is part of a wider power network involving politicians, noblemen, and legal entrepreneurs. It is for this reason that I argue the Sicilian Mafia can be considered more akin to white-collar crimes than to the mobs." [214] With a cover of legitimacy, the mafia wants to elevate its status as a regular partner in the government. This may come from the deal struck after World War II when Allied commanders permitted the mafia to govern regions, particularly in Sicily. However, they facilitated the Nazis and fascists for profit and survival. Organized criminals integrated their need for continuity to the Nazi need for dominance. This also reveals the secret of how different groups adopt certain powerful stigmas to suit their goals.

A timid First Lady who was received well when she returned with her husband in 2017. The reunion she had in Slovenia was remarkably described by some as "everything Melania." Some western influence was noticeable in how she was romanticized as Melania dropping her native name Melanija. Melania has positioned herself importantly as replication in the role previously held by the competitor Ivana Zelníčková-Trump's network, a businesswoman, media personality, author, and former model. This comes at the price of losing some identity. The similarity reflects a cultural view from Eastern Europe's past about America as a land of opportunity where anyone could make good. Slovenia built a statue of Melania that was later torched because of "lies and crime," but Melania has been seen quite the contrary as a captive queen in the United States.

---

[213] Thachuk, Kimberley L and Rollie Lal, eds. *Terrorist criminal enterprises: financing terrorism through organized crime.* Praeger Security International. ISBN: 978-1-4408-6067-6. Copyright 2018.

[214] Ibid.

Outside of this, Slovenian native Melania received a positive reception in a history of a torn-by-wars country grasped by extermination camps and mass killing. People came out to greet her personally with stories and positive memories of her transformation from a businesswoman's model. No one in Slovenia is untouched by this History. Since her marriage to President Donald J. Trump, I wanted to reflect on Mr. Trump's foreign policy. That is an adaptation of author Viktor Mihály Orbán, Prime Minister of Hungary's Zero Tolerance. As well, Mr. Trump's history with organized crime and the neo-Nazi alt-right has undoubtedly been established in numerous media outlets. Is this having an impact on Slovenia? Drawing a parallel in Germany, growing right-wing extremist organizations have pronounced loyalty to Donald J. Trump. Some of them are based on Mr. Trump as a QAnon savior against a pedophile-cannibal "cabal" in the Democratic Party. When has a geriatric political party ever been accused of pedophilia?

Later in Slovenia, the time has been marked by the movement of Holocaust denial in the government. Leon Rupnik (1880-1946), a General and collaborationist found guilty by a military tribunal, was recently determined to be based on a wrong reason to ascertain his guilt. Opponents of the decision that second-guesses the evidence began to form based on no actual evidence. Slovenians are taking a second look at their proceedings. This signifies an undercurrent movement in Slovenia's social structure and assumes a shift in Slovenian's reference to time and current genocide relevance. These events also offer an explanation of Melania Knavs-Trump's change in attitude by her famous gothic inscription, "I Don't Care Do You?"

One can see what has recently happened in these headlines, "*Murder, mafia, and Nazis loom over Slovak election.*" Mr. Gosling explained the background 'On trial, businessman Marian Kocner denies ordering the hit. But Kuciak was investigating a scam involving European Union funds in the east of the country that allegedly linked the powerful oligarch to Italy's notorious 'Ndrangheta mafia clan and the office of the prime minister himself, via a young and glamorous assistant. The trial has shown just how deeply Kocner has become involved in the country's power structures, leading to claims from the opposition that Slovakia has become a "mafia state," in which democracy and the rule of law have been replaced by corruption and cronyism. [215] There are details published reminiscent of President Trump's White House.

The Slovak Spectator on 5 June 2019, Beata Balogová wrote, "Without a fundamental change of the atmosphere in society, it could have been turned into a criminal state. A state where democratically elected representatives adopt a family of power will protect and elevate above the law. The family is granted benefits that come with a specific price tag: loyalty, silence, or protection. "If we look at the dirty links between organized crime and politicians in Slovakia, it might really seem like our country has become a mafia state," the outgoing President Andrej Kiska said in early May for the German daily *Die Welt*. It wasn't the first time he used that label… After the murder, the nation learned the name 'Ndrangheta, as one of the most powerful and richest organized crime groups in the world, and its links with the Slovak government were what Ján Kuciak wrote about in his last, unfinished article. Kočner, whom the police believe in having ordered the murder, built up a criminal organization of his own. Its honorable members were secret service agents, police officers, judges, attorneys, and people with ties to the ruling power… Hungarian sociologist Bálint Magyar says that Viktor Orbán has built a mafia state across our borders. His concept has its critics. Some Russian liberal analysts do not see today's regime in Hungary as a mafia state." [216]

Viktor Orbán is the author of Zero Tolerance. A policy used as the basis for the cruelty of immigrants at the Southern Border in Texas. Including their internment and seizure as though they are

---

[215] Gosling, Tim. "Murder, mafia and Nazis loom over Slovak election." 21 Feb. 2020. *Aljazeera.*

[216] Balogová, Beata. "Is Slovakia a mafia state?" 5 Jun. 2019. *The Slovak Spectator.*

terrorists though this is not substantiated. [217] Not the least of this cruelty was revealed by Mr. Trump in his public rationalization for coexistence between the fine people of the United States with the fine Nazi people. Clarifying his position on Charlottesville, Va. protests. A predictable outcome that potential terrorists will find a way to profit from a relationship of these types of Conservatism since money from criminal endeavors is complicated and sometimes impossible to trace to whom it may benefit. [218]

That is, apparently, much more difficult to prosecute in the United States. *Emerging Europe* reported on 7 April 2020, "Murderer of Ján Kuciak sentenced, but the case that changed Slovakia is far from closed." Writing, "A court in Bratislava sentenced former soldier Miroslav Marček to 23 years prison on April 6 for the murder of journalist Ján Kuciak and his fiancée Martina Kušnírová. Prime minister Robert Fico's party, Smer, continued to govern until two months ago, when it was ousted by a coalition of four other parties, after a general election campaign in which corruption, the rule of law, and the legacy of the Kuciak murder were crucial issues. The Movement of Ordinary People and Independent Personalities (OL'aNO), a center-right populist party led by Igor Matovič, a millionaire and former news business owner, scored a decisive win on a slogan of *Let's Beat the Mafia Together.*"

Slovakia's case is instructive to the European Union and the United States. Its history of invasions by the Soviet Union, Nazis, and experience with Slobodan Milosevic are noteworthy. Each of these regimes introduced legislatures and officials to different, more toxic systemic policies. From a systems analyst's viewpoint, the authorities made available a bank of stored laws and processes awaiting revival from a catalyst-provocateur. The murder of Ján Kuciak revealed the

---

[217] Gosling, Tim. "Murder, mafia and Nazis loom over Slovak election." 21 Feb. 2020. *Aljazeera.*

[218] Thachuk, Kimberley L and Rollie Lal, eds. *Terrorist criminal enterprises : financing terrorism through organized crime.* Praeger Security International. ISBN: 978-1-4408-6067-6. Copyright 2018.

system of past regimes that need to be destroyed. This is evident in the arrest of the infected representatives of the government. Namely, "Prosecutors claim that Kočner paid Marcek 70,000 euros for the killing. Three other people are also charged with aiding the murder. Last month, Slovak police said they had arrested 18 people, including 13 judges, who were accused of obstructing the investigation into the murders. Last year, the deputy speaker of Slovakia's parliament, Martin Glváč, the president of Bratislava's highest court, David Lindtner, and deputy justice minister Monika Jankovská were all forced to resign…"

Speaking of collaboration, silence, one has to raise moral questions of Ms. Melania Knavs-Trump. Ms. Trump has mirrored the Zero Tolerance policy of Viktor Orbán, her indelible words, "I really don't care, do you?" The history of Communist Slovenia was being commemorated to mark the 20th Anniversary of the Srebrenica Genocide in March 2015 when 8,000 Bosniaks, mostly men, and boys, were massacred. This does not compare to the 2007 revelation of an additional 100,000 minimum additional bodies found in the woods, cited by *The New York Times* in "World War II mass graves open a wound in Slovenia." *The Slovenia Times* reported all the details.

Even though one might not know the events that took place there, history and public memory recognize all the people, both present and future, are a part of that place. 'You are from Slovenia, the site of the Srebrenica slaughter.' It will always be a special place and inseparable from Ms. Melania Knavs-Trump more potent than anything else, as though her identity reads, "I am the people from Srebrenica, Slovenia." Slovenian President Borut Pahor illustrated this point, saying it was "our duty to remind one another and ourselves time and again where the slightest of intolerance can lead to "tragedies…closer than we can imagine." Ms. Trump is familiar with this as she carries around past Slovenia in memory.[219] The Soviet invasion,

---

[219] Mimesis is a term with an undeniably classical pedigree. Originally a Greek word, it has been used in aesthetic or artistic theory to refer to the attempt to imitate or reproduce reality since Plato and Aristotle. -Miriam Webster.

the Nazi one, a collapse in the system, innumerable graves some hidden. Spetsnaz retirees recruit "little Green Men" in the Slovenia forests to fight for Mr. Putin in Crimea. Upon her return, her countrywomen and men herald her as the most achieved in her town. Still, Ms. Melania Knavs-Trump has forgotten from where she comes. Slovenian President Borut Pahor's prophetic words follow her on return to the White House as a witness to "tragedies…closer than we can imagine." They also follow Borut Pahor's government, which has been accused of harboring neo-Nazis.

In foreign countries, it is difficult to reconstruct events that may consist of crimes against humanity. Vietnam was a particular war that evoked films, soldier witnesses, and the accusations by locals of unmarked graves, mutilations, and higher commanders' consent that appeared to approve and consent to murderous actions. Any action that does not have a strategic purpose is automatically subject to review if the participants flagged an event where several noncombatants without weapons were killed.

A scenario when it appears likely that some people were found on the Southern Border dead in a truck may have been the work of a guide that did not want to release migrants. So, they were locked in a cargo shipment and suffocated. These acts are considered crimes against humanity and, in some circles, are a moot question. Only due to the murderous intent and evidence of a clear and decisive action would it be considered a homicide.

The topic of murderous consent is meant to be addressed in private meetings. Mainly not do the sensitive nature of planned killing that states sanction or accident inflict on people unknowingly or without receiving the proper order to kill. We could say the vulnerable part of murderous consent was practiced in the United States prolifically pre- and post-World War Two. Industrialists investing in expansion and golden opportunity viewed Adolph Hitler what he was. Early on, he exhibited the perfect man of extreme conservatism. Judith Goldstein has written extensively on American life's attributes and qualities that attracted Adolph Hitler to consider United States industrialists a suitable partner.

When the war progressed, there were many ambiguous and unclear war efforts. These dark data were later learned as the implementation of the Holocaust. That should have symbolized the end of the extremist conservative. Still, for the most part, they escaped prosecution due to weak laws and apathy. Through decades it wasn't until President Bill Clinton and his administration held the investors to account. Much to his own peril. The accommodation of violence in some populations always proceeded in the same way. A group of people portrayed in a distant land, designated as harmless and not a threat, stands in the course of someone's ambitions for expansion.

This practice has evolved in a sinister application. So that murderous consent need not directly be a result of state order. It is sufficient to presume the intent of a state under one's position in society. Mary Jo Kopechne and Senator Edward M. (Ted) Kennedy's incident speaks to this type of consent. Delegated authority is also presumed suitable in the case of mass child murder. The argument goes because they are not rooted in the nation's soil or come from unprivileged bloodlines. They have no individual sovereignty or rights as an individual. Due to their social position, these particular children are valued along the same lines as any commodity. Therefore that can be disposed of and thrown away. It is enough for local citizens to make these judgments on their own. With a little encouragement, the 45th President has delegated his authority. Primarily to monsters in his Cabinet and those in the deserts to carry on this "blood and soil" policy. The result is that people can use this excuse by adhering to the autoimmunity laws that permit them to commit violence and other crimes like terrorism without penalty.

5. Murderous Consent Legal Genocide

"We should not underestimate the capacity of well-run propaganda systems to drive people to irrational, murderous, and suicidal behavior."---
-Noam Chomsky

Recently there is a landslide of discussion about the government's use of murderous consent. The issue is choosing between different moral conduct, person-to-person, or drone warfare. Due to the unfamiliarity most people have in addressing this subject, this chapter illustrates some of the hands-on and some thinking that goes into the ideal way assassination and military targets are carried out by murder. History plays a prominent role in responding to crises and often runs headlong into those forces that wish to erase history and evidence. Propaganda is a tool for erasing personal identity but not more effective than murder and kidnapping. The way laws are written, the provocateur, and incitement for someone else to murder or cause harm to another are forces to consider. States that do this under their rubric are nonetheless subject to the law.

There are differences from the soldier's point of view between human and drone warfare; objectives are derived from necessity and evidence. The shooter, in both cases, is the one living with the result of a gunshot. The reason for this is to initiate lethal force or to disable threats under strict control and responsibility. It must be legally justified; the suspect must be a threat to national or military security. Above this, choosing a specific type of person to kill requires both mental and emotional calculations. In a sense, the shooter has a relationship with his target, studying his behavior, habits, and nuances. The calculus includes wind direction, the air's scent, the sun's warmth, and the sounds of nature imprinted on the central nervous system.

There is also a spiritual component in murder; in fact, each moment is a reenactment of Cain's murder and moral drama. It is addictive and pleasant, like fire. However, it may be state-sanctioned; nevertheless, these decisions result in two simultaneous victims, the murdered and the perpetrator. In this lies the essence of all state-sanctioned murderers and their performance. Man is considered a machine part of a robot with mechanical drone killings, one link in a command chain. Without thoughtfulness state involved murders against innocent non-combatants is regarded as a war crime.

The classification of crimes against humanity may not have an obvious purpose at the outset. It may have been the result of a government-ordered and necessary action. This introduces us to the harsh reality that states may implement consent to their citizens to commit crimes against humanity. Higher echelons of government bureaucracy may assemble decision-makers who conspire around a specific plot to rid itself of individual people. The architects of such a planned scheme usually are not plots by the lower echelons of government, but the ones considered high integrity, culture, and fine breeding with years of trustworthy service. One of the high conspiracies ever perpetrated by humankind were those consented to at the Wannsee Conference and the Khmer Rouge regime during its rule of the country from 1975 to 1979 by the infamous Pol Pot. On a smaller scale, the insidious planning, and the same kind of evil planning, took place by the 45th President's Cabinet, who gave majority consent for "child separation policy." Too grievous than one would expect, given the intelligence of some of the Cabinet members and policy authors. They had a strong connection and full understanding of the two examples I initially gave, including those events at U.S. Attorney General Jeff's authorization Sessions and deputy Rod Rosenstein and Stephen Miller. Were we to gauge the value of human life against their actions. The sacrifice of all of the accrued benefits they receive seems minimal recompense for partaking as the conspirators and perpetrators of what the United Nations Office of Genocide Prevention calls a violation based on the standard.

I. *Wilfully causing great suffering or serious injury to body or health; II. Unlawful deportation or transfer or unlawful confinement; III.inhuman treatment.*

For state-sponsored murder, the individual (s) victims cannot appear innocent as that killing would be deemed publicly repulsive. Using theatrics, governments may try to turn innocents into an enemy of great magnitude. The press might write a fictitious article propagandizing the event. Americans have learned this stream of propaganda, 'The direction of the nation rests on this murder, all future generations the alignment of the cosmos depends on it.' And the people have to be convinced that the murderous intent of that nation is justified. Frequent use of propaganda should not be used to create mental images of an enemy unworthy of killing. One example of illegal and unjustified murders can be seen in the ISIS approach. They may use posters, graphics, and books to justify their targets.

Mass murder is different, so we draw on history for a reference. Members of the Reich are dead, but they're still alive in the minds of believers. The Anschluss is time-significant; some psychological archaeology illustrates the decisions by civilians subjected to mass psychology manipulators. [220] It was a time in Austria when a murder by consent was intimately practiced by the local residents. These events have particular resonance with today's type of men in the White House. The type of supporters who are alienated from themselves and the bloodiness and pain of the policies.

Participants at the Wannsee Conference, like the White House, did not make up an established group. The group was convened only for a particular meeting about murder but hid its objective by stating *the Jewish problem--a* problem defined by someone else. It represented

---

[220] Anschluss the annexation of Austria by Germany in 1938. Hitler had forced the resignation of the Austrian Chancellor by demanding that he admit Nazis into his cabinet. The new Chancellor, a pro-Nazi, invited German troops to enter the country on the pretext of restoring law and order. Political union of Austria with Germany, achieved through annexation by Adolf Hitler in 1938. Mooted in 1919 by Austria, Anschluss with Germany remained a hope (chiefly with Austrian Social Democrats) during 1919–33,

a cross-section of the Conservative elite. This laid out how a "modern division of labor" was assembled, observed Gerald D. Feldman and Wolfgang Seibel. Who were the individuals observed inside the conference? How did they react to the presentation for the mass slaughtering of European Jews? If nothing else, "it allowed the perpetrators to think that they were only one link in a chain of command and, therefore, not individually responsible for their deeds." [221] Remember Peter Viereck, "Political anti-Semitism is no isolated program.", confined to just one individual or group.

The *Wannsee Conference* members, as Hans-Christian Jasch communicated, "Kenneth Branagh's Heydrich, who shows up to have wandered out of a Shakespeare play." These men do not appear up at the start to be monstrous mental cases. As shocking as it sounds, they were "ordinary men." The men's actions were persistently mechanical, like a wheel in machinery that occasionally skipped its cog but proceeded production. How could someone act with indifference to take it on themselves to conduct such cruel acts even when no one asked them to actually commit each murder? The United States parallel to Conservative officials allowed the similarity of planning and convenience of approving the plan to "save America" by President Trump's Cabinet, hand-selected as the most Conservative in American history. This is a prime example of the underlying hostility that centrists pose. The White House rendition of The Wannsee Conference was intimately known by Melania Trump. [222] Attendees were Stephan Miller,

---

[221] Jasch, Hans-Christian and Christoph Kreutzmüller. *The Participants. The Men of the Wannsee Conference.* Berghahn New York and Oxford. 2017.

[222] Walsh, Savannah. "Melania Trump Was Secretly Recorded Addressing Trump's Child Separation Policy, White House Holiday Décor." 2 Oct. 2020. ELLE "They say I'm complicit. I'm the same like him, I support him. I don't say enough I don't do enough where I am," Trump said of criticism she received due to her husband's separation of migrant children at the border. The First Lady added, "I'm working my as_ off on the Christmas stuff, that you know, who gives a fuc_ about the Christmas stuff and decorations? But I need to do it, right?" ---Melania Trump.

a white Jewish supremacist, and Rod Rosenstein with Attorney General Jeff Sessions. [223]

Along the same line of authority, the president exercised a misperceived prerogative in the Iranian Major General's assassination, also related to President Trump's Islamic policy. Finally, the opportunity existed where he could press the button. It should have warned of possibilities to come. [224] This behavior was well documented in military and diplomatic archives. Where it will read, "President Trump killed an Iranian Major General who dedicated himself to destroy ISIS, one of America's goals." In response to the process of murderous consent, Benjamin Ferencz, former Nuremberg Court judge in *Newsweek* 17 Jan. 2020, discussed, "The public is entitled to know the truth. The United Nations Charter, the International Criminal Court, and the International Court of Justice in The Hague are all being bypassed." Pivoting backward, let's return to the Nuremberg period for reference. There was a repetitive and revolving system when murders were conducted summarily, not by courts or judicial reviews. Still, individuals are given authority by Heinrich Himmler, Reichsführer of the Schutzstaffel (Protection Squadron; SS), a prime example of a non-judicial murderer.

Albert Einstein condemned these personality types, "He who joyfully marches to music rank and file has already earned my contempt. He has been given a large brain by mistake since the spinal cord would surely suffice for him. This disgrace to civilization should be done away with at once. Heroism at command, senseless brutality,

---

[223] Ainsley, Julia and Jacob Soboroff and Phil Helsel. "Justice officials drove family separation policy; draft watchdog report says." *National Broadcasting Network.* 6 Oct. 2020.

[224] Blackwater. "We now know that Blackwater was hired as part of the secret CIA assassination program that former Vice President Dick Cheney ordered concealed from Congress and that the company continues to work for the CIA as part of its drone bombing campaign in Pakistan and Afghanistan." In Scahill, Jeremy. "Why Is Obama Still Using Blackwater?" *CBS News.* 17 Sept. 2009.

deplorable love-of-country stance. All the loathsome nonsense that goes by the name of patriotism. How violently I hate all this, how despicable and ignoble war is; I would rather be torn to shreds than be part of such a base an action! It is my conviction that killing under the cloak of war is nothing but an act of murder."

Given the Southern Border's present situation, President Donald J. Trump and his administration enacted the cruelest policy against children. Most people in the United States missed the actual intent of Southern Border activities and their purpose. It wasn't just about *those* Central Americans. It was about all children everywhere, from the wealthiest child in Greenwich, Connecticut, who sipped soup at the Golf Club during brunch to the poorest in Iraq begging for food in a refugee camp two days before its death. Every one of these children was told through social media; they were murderers, rapists, and terrorists to be rounded up and placed behind cages in a military encampment. These psychological detachments establish the rationalization of mass murder and torture.

Americans are always divorced from the reality of the world. They think world events won't touch them. Self-alienation is a poison because it captures all the hate and transforms it by blending itself among the ritual of daily routine regarded as more important. The Wannsee Conference, explained by Kevin Myers in the Irish Times of 18 Jan. 2002, reiterates how educated and business-like the corporate lawyers and experts were. In sync with Hitler's promise three years before threatened a holocaust. Drawing on the usefulness of the prisoners, could they be slaves? Or, in America's case, could they simply be torn away from their mothers, and what did it entail?

For White House staff and the President's Cabinet, this was an economical and efficient way on the hand to shake all the world's children while setting the stage for specific children and their parents, "Why not terrorize all of the children?" Let me show you. Just the details about the cruelty were more satisfying than writing about the system's implementation of it ever was. What's surprising is that the White House Chief of Staff did not request videos of Central Americans being pushed into steel cages, their cries, and baby whimpering---

something all children do when afraid. They simply stood by as the media propagandized it for them. We cannot be content to reside in comfort and call President Trump a devil. While at the same time, we ignore the systems that allowed his behavior, especially the White House Cabinet. Those leaders who believed they were explicitly entitled to undermine their oath of office and custodial responsibilities to pass down such sentences throughout history are known as collaborators in war crimes.

There is one last comparison to be made. The portrayed malevolence and romanticism of the Southern Border era on digital record has grasped the imagination of those that surround the Conservatives. Republican Conservatives, who like Mr. Putin, the actor-KGB agent, try to hide the resonances that reflect the Second World War. Whose actors staunchly reenact their interpretation of a less volatile monarchy, gratuitously setup by Andranik Mygranyan, Ph.D. that reputedly turned Adolph Hitler into a tolerable actor. Compared to the film Slaughterhouse-Five's volatility, Germany and Eastern Europe slowly became populist, a murderous place. Now Mr. Putin and Trump conjointly bring these images directly into every home in the world. They have placed their entire future on the cooperation and compliance of the extremism they have worked so hard to achieve. Tapping into history, we look into the effect of their strange beliefs that what they have done is not cruel but benevolent compared to what they actually wanted to institute.

An eerie cloud of history hangs over the present from a prediction, "Don't you want to play a part in this film, to be brought back to life in a hundred years?" --- Speech to the Propaganda Ministry in Berlin, April 17, 1945, Joseph Goebbels, thirteen days before his suicide.

Blood and Soil the Stormers Sang

Step into history in Austria, where the Reich is just getting started, it is evident that Hitler's presence is everywhere in Austria 1920-1938. His attendance is felt in the United States, where it mobilized thousands of supporters. Adolph Hitler treasured recognition and is given the titles Commander-in-Chief of the German Army, Navy & Air Force, and the Third Reich's Chancellor. *Time* magazine called him Man of the Year. Hitler established himself as a law-and-order Führer by a paternalist approach stating how law and order led to more freedom while eliminating the individual's rights. In the German museum, now a display reads "Hitler and the Germans — Nation and Crime."

Early seeds of Nazism proved it had the best development of its internal structures, communication, sciences, education, and technology. A pathological shift among its founders gravitated to nationalism, the German ego's greatness, which eventually led to others' inferiority and deprivation by malicious use in each of its areas of progress. In the first psychological steps of its birth, the Third Reich spent nearly 20 years establishing the Empire by militarizing civilian life. This helped the propagandists seat the Empire within the psyche. Joseph Goebbels, Ph.D., spent a large portion of his time speaking to political groups about their opinions, slowly and diligently gauging their sentiment. Seizing the time, entering middle age, Goebbels associated militarization with men's strength, the attractiveness of blondes, the ability of Nazism to make civilians more harmonious, healthier, sensual, more virile, and pregnant. Then, the pre-Nazi Party's intellectuals ensured a type of equivalent to social media campaigns, making sure each household had a radio and loudspeakers were posted along the street. Mass communication achievement served as an extension of the Reich media blitz and visual poster campaign.

The pre-Nazi voice is not only in the air, but millions of individuals could see Adolph Hitler in everything. Some of the most militant saw him in themselves and got similar uniforms: literature, theater, military campaign medals, music, poetry, radio. Many of the accouterment of rising Nazism were drawn on government accounts or from National Socialist Party coffers. All these public representations are the body "eyes," "ears," and "arms" of Hitler. So long as they saw the swastika, they looked into the *face* of Adolph Hitler and the body politic. But did he make everyone into a terrorist? Or did the people make him execute for them, from the elderly to babies? Just how close did the people identify with him?

In the next step, Adolph Hitler and Joseph Goebbels intervened with the public through the Reich Church. Enemies of the Reich are defined based on sovereign people's laws. Those worthy of being called German must have blood and genes to prove it. Supporting the progress of freedom against their enemies made it easier for Germans to depart from it. Falling subject to conforming to demands. Christians and other religions who did not serve were beheaded by the Executioner Johann Reichhart. Everyone else was transformed into industrial commodities and some interned as prisoners. Others murdered. It was necessary for followers to vicariously share and, in some instances, enjoy, feel, smell, or expect their ego to gain substantially from their murders. Allen Hall, *Daily Mail Online*, 15 Jun. 2016 reported a trend that 1 in 10 Germans would like the return of a "Führer" perhaps to frighten immigrants, Muslims, Jews, and the "usual subjects" minus themselves that are invading the countryside in 2020 surveys. No mention of what murders they might consent to or already have done during nighttime.

The implementation of the pre-Nazi regime had not (yet) replaced the German government's superstructure. Adolph Hitler was just becoming a citizen of Germany, denouncing his Austrian background. It was a distraction from what went on internally. Inevitably there was the development of threatening SS courts. The functioning bureaucratic framework of the Brigadeführer, police commanders, Common Representative, State Secretary. At that point, various specialist lines that, like cobwebs, went back to the Reich Main Security Office.

People outside the "network authority" wanted to profit and benefit from this establishment in exchange for an "informant and collaborator role." This was also the case with foreign investors who may have read *The New York Times*' Man of the Year 1938 edition. Privately foreign investment was used by the Nazis during the so-called "quiet years" establishing Dachau Camp. To be known as a supporter could mean sustaining a livelihood, protection, food during severe economic distress. Austria was vital to Hitler's emotional wellbeing. Who wanted to walk its streets as a conqueror. Anschluss, this time, the surroundings were already being enveloped in the Empire. A similar arrangement was being made for Czechoslovakia. Preparing the people for Empire, the psychological sense of order and official superiority had to be established first. Supporters were ordered to become mobilized "to serve the Führer." This state of obedience changed the character of the Bohemian National Socialist Party into Adolph Hitler's Nazis. [225]

Philosophers that watched this display of fanaticism referred to the thoughts of Lactantius, an Ante-Nicene theologian. He described in his Divine Institutes demonic purveyors of evils as a kind of global stalker of the soul, serial killers of the spirit, who engage in home invasions. They "... wander over the earth," "seeking the destruction of men" through deceit, "cling[ing] to individuals" and "whole occupying houses..."---Thomas White, *The Hollow Men: Moral Evil as Privatized Self.*

In 1938 Thomas Mann, who ten years before called the fledgling Nazi Party "Swastika nonsense," disembarked New York. He had condemned Neville Chamberlain, British Prime Minister, for laying down with Adolph Hitler that he guaranteed would quickly lead to Austria's annexation. In his book, Mann wrote about Germany stating, "the mystery and precept of our age is not liberation and development of the ego. What our age needs, what it demands, what it will create for itself, is—terror." ----*The National Interest* Jacob Heilbrunn 14 August 2019. By November 1942, American authorities seized the Bush-affiliated Silesian-American Corporation to supply coal to the Nazi

---

[225] Smelser, Von Ronald M. "Hitler and the DNSAP: Between Democracy and Gleichschaltung." This is a revised Version of a paper presented at the annual Convention of the American Historical Association in Dallas/Texas, December 27—30, 1977. 1. Note: Gleichschaltung, the standardization of political, economic, and social institutions as carried out in authoritarian states.

government. [226] This was not the only infraction working for the W.A. Harriman & Co banking George Herbert Walker and his son-in-law Prescott Bush engaged with relationships with Fritz Thyssen, an enthusiastic German financier of the impending takeover by the Nazis. Meanwhile, a severe confrontation was occurring in Austria. Well beyond the reaches of the Wall Street investment markets.

Journalist, Gitta Sereny, wrote in her account, *"My Journey to Speer,"* a visit with the architect of the Nazi regime. [227] The Gitta Sereny account enlightens us to the humanity of the time. Little of it reminds us of anything close to a civilized society and reflects "something" emerging from the ethereal that depicts a man in his primordial and medieval character. Gitta Sereny witnessed 105,000 Nazi storm troopers, many of them singing, marching into the country on 12 March 1938, and formally declaring political union or "Anschluss." "Josef Magnus Wehner gave a speech of dedication at one memorial in 1932: 'The dying sang! The Stormers sang. The young students sang as they were being annihilated: "Deutschland, Deutschland u¨ber alles, u¨ber alles in der Welt" ... The dead heroes became an omen for the German people." --- Nicholas Neocleous.

Her testimony could be spoken like this, 'I Gitta Sereny, when a child in Austria practicing dancing, went to a rally in Austria. I witnessed this unforgettable hollowness that shook me. The visuals of free-flowing flags, banners, music, and parades were filled with joy for children but half-dreaded by some adults by the looks on their faces. When I grew up a little, I realized these rallies were recruitment campaigns for Nazi brownshirts.'[228] Though 70 years later, this scene could

---

[226] Marrs, Jim. *The Rise of the Fourth Reich: The Secret Societies That Threaten to Take Over America.* William Morrow Paperbacks; Reprint edition (June 23, 2009). ISBN-10: 0061245593. ISBN-13: 978-0061245596.

[227] Sereny, Gitta. "My Journey to Speer." *The Independent.* 30 Sept. 1995. (Note, these words are not a direct quote but a summation of what could've been her visualization.)

[228] Ibid.

have been likened to any Trump Racial Rally approximating the similar oration of hate and vicious themes.

Gitta Sereny began her journey to Speer as fond of her neighbors and felt comfortable considering her neighbors as loved ones. When sick and desperate, she often frequented them while they had severe illnesses. She walked down these same streets as a young person offering some assistance. Today it was similar except in one way. Gita Sereny was beginning to feel skittish and uneasy. It felt like an uncanny pull on the subconscious from far away at the site of Third Reich's speeches and Berlin, apart from its charismatic and gravitational pull. [229] Hitler changed from the relatively benign to develop offices in Berlin that were purged of democratic and bureaucratic officials. Replacing these government workers with staff appropriate to the headquarters of Secret State Police, the SS, and the Reich Security Main Office that now hosts the documentation center *Topographie of Terror.*

In *Journey to Speer,* Gita Sereny walked and cautiously stepped to a grouping of frenzied neighbors. They were surrounding a few people handing them toothbrushes, soap, and making jokes. Then without explanation, suddenly, they became stern as she approached. Gitta Sereny's mind began to quickly engage her memories. Are these really my neighbors? By force, making their doctor and his wife go to their knees on the ground, making them clean sidewalks with toothbrushes because they were Jews. She recalled several realities. Her doctor was a Jew when he delivered them as babies. He was a Jew when he sat with them all night, abating their fevers. A soft chubby man and his kindly wife lived among friends like Gitta Sereny, who knew them as loving neighbors. They came over for dumplings in chicken soup. [230] It is too positive to say in retrospect that were it not for the populism, people in the neighborhood would never have turned out. They were the transformed horrific, the disrespectful, and the murderous supporters

---

[229] Gravitational: Referring to what Ian Kershaw described as "moving toward the Führer."

[230] Sereny, Gitta. "My journey to Speer." *The Independent.* 30 Sept. 1995.

of the regime. This gentle part of Gitta Sereny ended soon after that as these once familiar friends and loving neighbors gassed the Jews that helped them so much in Sobibor, Poland, in 1943. [231]

Citizen neighbors that, in their recent past, could still recall the lack of basis on the moral belief that would not have allowed them to collaborate to murder. Given their benefit of the doubt, the guilt, and Scriptures, this could not happen, except the reason for it happening was their misinterpretation of these events. At this point, Gitta Sereny witnessed the Zeitgeist of depersonalization. What makes this visualization so powerful is that civilians in "community life" made decisions on mass murder themselves based on their "Deputization." Individuals seeking favor or acting out their cruelty made the decision to terrorize the Jew that delivered their children, then handed their friends up to be killed exceptionally easily. In this scene, Gitta Sereny's physician warned her she was not safe from intervening. Doing their first war crime as community members of Austria in a famous slogan and propagandized consent-to-kill order, like "I can kill someone on 5th Avenue." Citing presidential status of chief law enforcement officer in the U.S. and his perceived "qualified immunity." In similarity, the system allowed for it.

There is still the question of what reasoning was used that justified the neighborhood people to target the doctor and his wife then rationalize their death. Perhaps this should be flipped, and should be; what made it so easy? It all had to do with under what identity they acted and whether they were vicariously working as Hitler, the Master choreographer. Although in modern society, we like to think of ourselves as beyond the point of criminality, denying we could be manipulated by Ted Bundy, Charlie Manson, or Donald J. Trump. Similar events occur in American society. A paramilitary leader sent his forces to the border, encouraged by the President. [232] The designation of who should be fearful was publicized nationally by the FOX News

---

[231] Ibid.

[232] Papenfuss, Mary "GOP Rep Slams Trump's Quoting of Pastor's 'Civil War' Warning As 'Beyond Repugnant'," *Huffington Post.* 30 Sept. 2019.

network attacking the Pope. [233] There were also the two most appealing "lock her up" and "shoot them at the Southern Border." These orders became popular in humor, addictive, and obsessions of pleasing President Trump.

State consent is a critical feature in culture. It also defines who in the neighborhood is worthy of killing. In the transformative year of 1938, not only had a demi-god cloaked himself in patriotism, but a majority of the people identified themselves on equal par with this theme. It must have been good because the system permitted it. Yes, they like to think of themselves as accomplished individuals suitable to belong in a community and obey the rule of law. Civilians were fused to the psyche of what would later be known as the *Hitler mentality*. One of the most mentally intrusive beliefs in modern society.

"We can recognize this logic as being applied all the time when determining who is the legitimate target of war and state violence. Discussions about "collateral damage," the killing of civilians versus armed combatants, all hinge on the idea of consent. It's OK to murder soldiers; this logic goes because they have consented to fight for the state. But this argument can be flipped around: it's OK to kill civilians. Some groups avow because they have consented to be in a hostile group as citizens of this or that nation or polity. Hence are our legitimate target. Either way, the notion of consent itself is a complete fabrication (based on hypotheticals dreamed up by social contract theorists) that serves its murderous purpose."

Modern man likes to think of himself as not the same feral creature of his past. Turn on the radio. Vicarious violence is heard every day as political extremists identify a state's legitimate target. Accommodation to destructive ideologies and their exhibition is a result

---

[233] Media Matters Staff, "Anti-Semitic Fox News contributor Robert Jeffress attacks the Pope as a 'globalist' who wants 'a one-world government,'" *Media Matters*, 02, Nov. 2018.

of long-held resentments. Their message expands with their influence, making it more evident that it hinges on old fascist forms of designating to the population who the state's enemies are. In the mouths of extremists, this extends to who the enemy of an individual is. Thereby justifying the death of their opposition. William C. Langer, MD Hitler profiler, thought that the people's madness flowed between them and the leader. To what extent do civilized people allow themselves to consent to murder children? Then what extend will they go to terrorize them?

The *Wannsee Conference* members marked a concerted effort of the German state, the army, and big business to exterminate European Jews. The core of the policy initiative was to define who was a Jew. Therefore, who needed to be captured, enslaved, and murdered. A bit of background to the recorded interview altered how we discuss Holocaust children today. Early on, it was planned at The *Wannsee Conference* that Heinrich Himmler would be authorized in SS thefts and Lebensborn children's relocation. Stealing them away from Poland to become children of Nazi mothers. The Reichsführer (national leader) of the SS said in a speech to officers in Posen in October 1943, "It is our duty to take their children with us, to remove them from their environment, if necessary, by robbing or stealing them." and send them to Germany.

For Gitta Sereny, the Holocaust years past, what could only be described as a confrontation Gitta Sereny was called for interview. In this bizarre and strange yet royal opportunity, an arrangement that only could be described as a spiritual encounter, Gitta Sereny conducted a meeting with Commandant Franz Stangl. The previous Austrian police officer with no particular skills advanced to the SS T-4 Killing Program. He was in charge of the killing regime at Camp Sobibor, Poland, in 1943. Stangl trained Gustav Franz Wagner, an Austrian member of the SS and Staff Sergeant, who was also captured in South America and committed suicide in 1980. What follows is the Gitta Sereny sit-down interview with Commandant Stangl, who transformed a train station in Potemkin Village architecture, complete with fake facilities and flowerbeds to reduce the shock of arrivals. This was to hide the execution and burnt bodies. Sereny's questions are italicized. [234]

Interview about Sobibor, Poland Extermination Camp. [235]

'There were so many children; did they ever make you think of your children, of how you would feel in the position of those parents?' "No," he said slowly, "I can't say I ever thought that way. You see," he then continued, still speaking with this extreme seriousness and obvious intent of finding the truth within himself, "I rarely saw them as individuals. It was always a huge mass. I sometimes stood on the wall and saw them in the 'tube'" (the path to the gas chambers, which was surrounded by a high brick wall – the Germans called it the *Road to Heaven*). "How can I explain it? – They were… they were naked, packed together, running, being driven with whips, like…" Like cattle, he meant but stopped short of saying it.

'Could you not have changed that?' I asked. *'In your position, could you not at least have stopped the nakedness, the whips, the horror of the cattle pens?'* Commandant Franz Stangl, "No, no, no. That was the system. Wirth had invented it. It worked. And because it worked, it was irreversible."

---

[234] Gitta Sereny's presentation, near the beginning of the Inner Circle Seminar, *'Into That Darkness 30 Years On: The Psychology of Extermination'*, conducted by Gitta Sereny, Michael Tregenza, and Anthony Stadlen, on Sunday 10 October 2004 in the Herringham Hall, Regent's College, London. Reproduced with the permission of Jeffrey A. Schaler. All rights reserved.

[235] Sobibor, Poland Death Camp was created by order. Wannsee Conference on Jan. 20, 1942. The conference began with a recap of all past efforts that had been aimed "to cleanse German living space of Jews in a legal manner." See Jasch, Hans-Christian and Christoph Kreutzmüller. *The Participants*. The Men of the Wannsee Conference. Berghahn New York and Oxford. 2017.

Gena Turgel's camp experience: [236]

"I wear a lot of perfume," she whispers. "The stench of the camps will always stay with me, and I try to block it out." It's not the only physical reaction she has to her ordeal. Her 17-year-old sister Miriam used to sleep with her on her left side. Miriam was shot by the Germans for smuggling food into Plaszov. She says she still feels a constant chill along her left arm. The ghosts of the camp and her family — she lost seven siblings and her father — still haunt her. As we talk, tears come to her eyes, but she doesn't let them fall."

American racial rallies are indoctrination; statistics show they are larger by several thousand than Hitler and Goebbels's. Speakers often say who it is appropriate to kill, seeking to gain broad consent and normalization. It is supported by the media because it operates within a vast system of a Velvet Genocide. They saw themselves and their actions as patriots. For many Americans, state-organized violence is a problem only for barbaric countries seen on evening television. Americans believe they could never condone such distinct criminality and grief. Yet thousands not only fully participate in overt racial and political attacks in the United States but often incite it.

They fantasize about it, heavily finance it, bring it into their neighborhoods, and teach it to their children. Americans often disguise themselves as innocent bystanders to murderous events. Lieutenant William Calley of My Lai applied this logic to his actions. Still, clearly, most people in Vietnam were faced with similar situations and did not elect to kill civilians and children. Most Vietnam veterans still recall the My Lai Massacre circumstances in equally vivid terms as those of other mass murders. These experiences' universality is carefully taught to protect soldiers in the field from the madness of war

---

[236] NBC News London. "Auschwitz Survivor Gena Turgel Walked Out of Gas Chamber Alive." 26 Jan. 2015.

and guard against the values people use that justify random and planned civilian killing. [237]

Americans often rely on a nonverbal social contract with the military that has recently been extended to the Southern Border. The agreement says civilians will turn away from convicting them of their heinous acts as long as soldiers defend the country. Meanwhile, society is slowly eaten away by these crimes. Thus, collaborating to continue the behavior. This account could be of every combat soldier's nightmare that haunts the military judiciary and the issue of immunity based on the social contract.

The Private First-Class Paul Meadlo witness testimony: [238]

"At Calley's order, Meadlo and others had fired round after round into the ditch and tossed in a few grenades. Then came a high-pitched whining, which grew louder as a two- or three-year-old boy, covered with mud and blood, crawled his way among the bodies and scrambled toward the rice paddy. His mother had likely protected him with her body. Calley saw what was happening and, according to the witnesses, ran after the child, dragged him back to the ditch, threw him in, and shot him."

Declaring the necessity of military force at the American Southern Border, which most people knew had such reduced crossings rates. Individuals residing along the fence questioned the legitimacy of a "Cold War propaganda" effort by the President Trump administration. These attitudes were preemptive to a series of cruelties to those

---

[237] Ackerman, Spencer and Asawin Suebsaeng, White House Reporter. "Trump Tells Allies He Wants Absolved War Criminals to Campaign for Him." *The Daily Beast*. 25 Nov. 2019.

[238] Hersh, Seymour N. "The Scene of the Crime A reporter's journey to My Lai and the secrets of the past." *The New Yorker Magazine*. 30 Mar. 1968.

in United States custody. This was typical of extreme Conservatism seeking an excuse to clamp down, a solution searching for a problem. What was implemented was the deployment of militia in Border Patrol fatigues. ----a disguise and an image from the theatrics of war. President Trump also demanded immediate justice by the private militia to hunt down migrants in the desert and laughed over it. According to William Cummings of *USA Today* 9 May 2019, "'Only in the Panhandle': Trump chuckles when audience member suggests shooting migrants.", giving the go-ahead to commit murder.

Deployment of Southern Border security is the intersection of national anxiety, residual fears from 9-11 during the lowest immigration influx. When President Trump took office, the Southern Border crossings were at their lowest. In a year, he aggravated the situation citing an "invasion." The Presidential administration of Trump has blown the issue totally into a surrealist view of the problem. Fear and expectation of inadequate identification of "threat" have encouraged labeling anyone seeking entry as a suspected terrorist. Wall Street, Conservatives, and President Trump have changed the focus of economic difficulty Americans feel on Central Americans' problems along the Southern Border. Migrant workers are now depicted by the administration as equivalent to terrorists transforming them into enemies of the state—an enemy of economy, the neighbor's economy, the fault of economic prosperity, individual failure, sexual frigidity, and impotence.

Switching this around, the immigrant, migrant worker, and refugee fleeing violence view it from a different framework. It's a victim of a poisonous system of belief so real it can be touched. They see death hanging, like an act of strangulation, waiting for the congestion to attach itself to their outside and inside clothing. Then anxiety permeates all the hairs on the body and follicles. A smell soon follows them around; it haunts them. The sun will make the skin feel slippery, and it smells distinctly like rice. Closer, the scent has materialized as a fine yellow mist under the arms and legs that hardens into a crust. This unforgotten sweating, after five years, the smells arise again in memory of the confinement. Pets that pick up this scent may growl and run away. Babies may cry in your arms. Horses whine and show their teeth, then leap down a field. The entire "smell" of border security should be more of a relief effort while clearing people medically for farm labor and other work they have been recruited for.

Homeland Security and Border Patrol are viewed as militia or a well-organized gang. 'Considering immigrants as terrorists, no matter how much they assimilate into American society, no matter what secular employment they have, no matter who they socialize with, no matter how well they speak English, the Central and African Americans will always never be American.' ----Adapted from Sarah Coates, "The Poisonous Mushroom."

After Trump's family separation policy went into action, immigrant Marco Antonio Muñoz had his family taken away. [239] Then he killed himself. A father separated from his wife and child under Trump's harsh new border separation policy. Marco Antonio Muñoz killed himself while in custody in a Texas jail, days after the Trump administration activated its "Zero tolerance" approach to border crossings. Under this new policy, families crossing the border are prosecuted, which triggers families' separation. Only a few people know what Marco Antonio Muñoz was thinking, but his observations were similar to what the overall experience is for survivors. U.S. District Judge Micaela Alvarez ruled that the U.S. government could not be held accountable for Marco Antonio Muñoz, discovered dead in his jail cell after being apprehended at the border. With his wife and their then-3-year-old son. [240]

---

[239] *(After) Trump's family separation policy went into action, immigrant Marco Antonio Muñoz had his family taken away. Then he killed himself.* A father separated from his wife and child under Trump's harsh new border separation policy. Marco Antonio Muñoz killed himself while in custody in a Texas jail, days after the Trump administration activated its "zero tolerance" approach to border crossings. Under this new policy, families crossing the border are prosecuted, which triggers the separation of those families.

[240] Garcia, Berenice. "Judge partially dismisses lawsuit in Honduran man's suicide." *The Monitor.* 03 Jul. 2020.

The court decision was seen as justification for Zero Tolerance's White House policy that was recommended and implemented by Stephen Miller, a white Jewish supremacist, and ideologue. [241] Maybe, for this reason, his moral center, the human experience of Stephen Miller's proposed process, was approved by the White House Cabinet because it worked, and it worked because it was a mechanical industrial-military process. [242] Therefore, it was found acceptable to 11 out of 18 in the Conference. The immigrant experience may be the first time post-traumatic stress is deliberately induced due to a White House policy? Confinement is a physical constraint as well as psychological punishment akin to torture in many countries. Additionally, this may be a trend as people see how punishing it can be in healthy, well-adjusted children who react violently to being home alone due to the Covid-19 pandemic. What is the experience of confinement like?

Imagining, during national anxiety, it does take a certain kind of police enforcement to initiate the cold cruelty exacted in such domestic policies set aside for infants. Political violence, no doubt, has the distinctive scents and smells that float in the air. Of no concern to the baby is the nurturing smell of breast milk around the nipple. Were the nipple and breast not feel there would be no possibility of bonding and intimacy as the baby identifies the mother lovingly by this texture. The smells confirm the bond that, in the course of a lifetime, without doubt, we could say she is needed to identify what is love. This scent of honey, nurturance, and affection lasts an entire lifetime. The nurturance cannot be duplicated. There is no proxy or stand-in for a woman that could produce this kind of love and bonding. In related experiences of the confinement process as inmates, fathers, and other

---

[241] Garcia-Navarro, Lulu. "'Hatemonger' Tracks How Right-Wing Media Shaped Trump Policy Architect Stephen Miller." *National Public Radio*. 16 Aug. 2020.

[242] Ainsley, Julia and Soboroff, Jacob. "Trump Cabinet officials voted in 2018 White House meeting to separate migrant children, say officials." *NBC News*. 20 Aug. 2020.

women are distanced from these close quarters. They are barred from detecting scents and fragrances associated with confinement. [243]

The officer enters the room of glistening steel cages and feels the warmth generated by so many bodies. They are not alone, accompanied by those that watch 70 years former. It is difficult to identify them as individuals covered in aluminum sheets on the floor, others huddled on benches, some standing up under the bright industrial lights. The orders are explicit, the door must be opened, and mothers separated from their babies no matter what ages. Due to the *specific command orders*, the person's values are pushed deep within them, and their hands grab the nearest detainee starting the process of removal. This is what happens next.

When bonding is interrupted by separation, like in Marco Antonio Muñoz's and his 2-3-year-old child's situation, a series of nurturance and grief events follow not from "natural" fear but something artificial. It is similar to the therapy called (implosive) "flooding," an entirely experimental artificially induced anxiety. It signals a life-and-death situation that has taken place. The bonding link is broken, and the trauma of induced feelings of shock at being abandoned begins. It is an emotionally powerful approach that allows the person to relive the traumatic experience. Because these emotions are induced and artificial, they have an industrial quality---something like an assembly line approach, not one used on an individual, but large groups. The same emotions are invoked in concentration camps. It sets off a sequence of psychological and biological events that marks the cruelty that mother-child separations cause. The closest way to describe it is when a death has occurred in the mother or baby, and they must be abandoned in an open field.

---

[243] Pascoe, Carla. "Silence and the History of Menstruation." *Oral History Association of Australia Journal* No. 29, 200728.

Their mother's breast milk provides the necessary antibodies to help the baby grow through this early stage.[244] For 120 days, real effort must be made to ensure regular feedings and sanitary conditions occur so that the child's antibodies can resist disease. This natural feature is disrupted by the lack of sterile conditions, long-term and long-distance confinement. The purposeful degradation of immunity may be calculated in premeditation to spawn grief events—early death or disability of children by physical, emotional, and sensory deprivation. A problematic prospect since anxiety militates against immunity. A similar denial/deficiency of social access tactic was used in Guantanamo Bay Detention Camp by the military and CIA for hardened ISIS fighters and terrorist detainees.

The minds of children at this early stage are also imprinted with memories of their environment. Like any recording, the initial trauma of separation, even when disguised by other interactions, does not resolve the initial loss. Maternal bonding cannot be substituted. Nature purposefully imprints the central nervous system's damage, and it becomes part of a person's identity. In the interim, of childhood and adult, mental pictures of militarization are recorded. When the child becomes an adult, severe psychological effects can be repeated as attachment and nurturance disorder.[245] Everyone has seen the drastic steps taken by adults to find their mother after 40+ years. This drive is unconsciously indicative of those that wander until reunification. There is so much emotional distance meeting a woman at a reunion whom they never knew was their mother can also be like suffocating as the world seems to close into focus. [246] We can see beyond any doubt

---

[244] Cerini, Chiara; Grace M. Alddrovani. "Breast Milk: Proactive Immunomodulation and Mucosal Protection Against Viruses and Other Pathogens." *Future Virology.* 2013;8(11):1127-1134. Source: Department of Pediatrics & Molecular Microbiology & Immunology, Children's Hospital Los Angeles, University of Southern California, Los Angeles, CA, USA.

[245] Dyck, Brendt Douglass. "The Terrifying Story of Hitler's Stolen Children." *Warfare History Network.* 24 Nov. 2018.

[246] Cazzoli, Lise. "An Uncomfortable Truth: Democratic Culture and The New Left-Behinds." *M.A. Candidate from the Graduate School of Public and*

that such acts came as a substitute for a plan for more physical severe brutality, perhaps actions that were considered but not implemented for fear of condemnation.

Using the highest law enforcement officer in the United States to pursue this policy was the yes-men Jeff Sessions and William P. Barr, U.S. Attorney Generals. Their office masked the underlying nihilism in the psychopathology of these men. Like the men of Wannsee, Conservative extremism, not to mention that its implemented action was by a series of men and women performing their duties under the Presidency and Congress's official seal. It occurred not only in full view of the Congress but provoked their silence. This is another instance where Congressional members failed again in preventing cruelty because, to do so, legislators must acknowledge the systemic policies that permit it.

I underscore, their actions are considered war crime and psychological torture. This hatred and spite for humanity were meted out and carefully calculated so that its implementation went half to women the remainder to the baby. The child separation policy plot never mentioned racial purity tests for fear of the populace and fears of being called anti-Semitic. Considering this, it tried to avoid comparisons to Germany's events planned to separate children from mothers. It was more diplomatic and insidious in the United States, as the baby separated ceased to become a terrorist through adoption. By implementing baby separation as a solution to the President Obama Magnitsky Act through adoption. There would now be plenty of babies for white mothers to raise as their own. President Barack Obama endorsed the practice that led to adoption by FOX News' Laura Ingraham. [247]

Conservative individuals often state that Central American refugees and immigrants are the sources of their own cruelty. Republicans

------

International Affairs, University of Ottawa. She currently attends the M.A. in International Development, Sciences Paris, and researches on global politics theory, sustainable development and human rights. June 2017.

[247] Joyce, Kathryn. "The Threat of International Adoption for Migrant Children Separated from Their Families." *The Intercept.* 1 Jul. 2018.

and conservatives alike have repeatedly charged this since the Southern Strategy. That minorities are the victims of their own evil, and their presence on the earth violates "preventive security." It is the same aggressive justification that psychologically led Commandant Franz Stangl, "…That was the system. Wirth had invented it. It worked. And because it worked, it was irreversible." [248] Therefore, infant separation policy solves the immigration problem by harming them by a method of choice called deterrence. It not only applies to the United States but to foreign nations. The United States military was used to construct the caged detention facilities for babies due to a distant "security threat."

With an eye on the 20th Century involving children, separations reveal a sadistic character of extreme Conservatives who created the system. Capturing mothers with babies as terrorists. Joyce Sparer Adler states her autopsy of this type of situation. She asks, the logical, is there any precedent in the world that can be cited in choosing a people considered wronged in history as a symbol of Evil in work devoted to that history? [249] Even in compliant soldiers, anything can happen in this blurred breakdown of morality. When officers confuse their military thinking of "protect and serve" mottos to thinking political, there are appalling outcomes. Police institutions cease to be of service to individuals when they become protectors of state interests alone, such as America First. [250]

---

[248] Sobibor, Poland Death Camp was created by order. Wannsee Conference on Jan. 20, 1942. The conference began with a recap of all past efforts that had been aimed "to cleanse German living space of Jews in a legal manner." See Jasch, Hans-Christian and Christoph Kreutzmüller. *The Participants*. The Men of the Wannsee Conference. Berghahn New York and Oxford. 2017.

[249] Sparer Adler, Joyce. *War in Melville's: Imagination* (N.Y.U. Press, 1981): 127, defending Melville's Indian-hater episode in "The Confidence-Man" from charges of racism.

[250] Snow, Shawn. "16 Camp Pendleton Marines arrested by NCIS for alleged human smuggling and drug offenses." *Marine Corps Times*. 26 July 2019.

"Both Marines face federal charges for allegedly smuggling three undocumented immigrants near the U.S.-Mexico border for financial gain, court documents detail. The Marine Corps said in Thursday's press release, the 16 Thursday arrests were based on information learned during a previous investigation. Marine officials with the 1st Marine Division worked alongside NCIS during the arrests, the release said. "Any Marines found to be connected with these alleged activities will be questioned and handled accordingly concerning due process," the Corps said."

Once a respected military service, the U.S. Marine Corps did not hesitate to participate in the actions leading to what amounted to slave trading and smuggling. These judgments and distortions occur when people are compromised by allures and impossible promises. It is indicative of crimes against humanity and conscience. The "most loyal believers" may otherwise kill the victims openly instead of by diseases like scurvy. [251] Seeing the Central American condition from the inside, most people would attempt to flee. Major Fitzpatrick draws from his field experience describing the truth about an ongoing Central American tragedy Americans have ignored. [252]

Witness --Maj. Derek Fitzpatrick U.S. Army:

"On the morning of January 2, 2016, Mexican cartel hitmen stormed into the home of Gisela Mota Ocampo. After beating her, the men dragged Ms. Mota outside her home. With her family looking on from the doorway of her house, they shot and killed her. The day prior, Gisela Mota had been sworn in as the mayor of Temixco, Mexico, a small town roughly an hour's drive from Mexico City. She used her inauguration speech to further advocate for judicial reform and

---

[251] Carroll, Linda. "U.S. authorities confiscate migrant kids' medications at the southern border." *Reuters*. 03 Dec. 2019.

[252] Fitzpatrick, Derek Maj. "Greed and Grievance and Drug Cartels: Mexico's Commercial Insurgency." Master's Thesis. *U.S. Army Command and General Staff College*. 25 May 2017.

speak out against Mexican cartels' growing power and influence. The governor of Ms. Mota's home state of Morelos, Graco Ramírez, speaking at a news conference following the attack, stated it was a "deliberate and premeditated action that aimed to sow an environment of terror, both among authorities and citizens." He also revealed that thirteen other mayors within the state were recently threatened with a similar fate. Gisela Mota Ocampo is one of the nearly 100 Mexican mayors assassinated by the cartels since 2006."

The cynical use of humor alongside words acknowledged with the audience's support of this incredible cruelty during the campaign was conceded. Their Conservative resolution in a policy call for Central Americans who, after work as adults that leave Conservatives with "a bad taste, a bad smell." There is no other conclusion that the result of border captures by far was envisioned as a method to gain white supremacist support while creating/forcing the legal situation to place the courts to offer the stolen and separated children for adoption. Preferably, non-Hispanic mothers would have otherwise sought adoptions in Russia before President Obama instituted the Magnitsky Act. Mothers who wanted anonymous children to raise as white. It was also the opportunity for influential individuals to act on their cruel beliefs as psychic terrorism. [253]

"The investigation comes after a ProPublica report exposing the secret three-year-old Facebook group called "I'm 10-15" and has some 9,500 members. Group members posted offensive graphics. Including a photo illustration of Democratic Rep. Alexandria Ocasio-Cortez being sexually assaulted by President Donald Trump; discussed plans to disrupt a congressional visit to a Border Patrol facility; joked about the deaths of migrants."

---

[253] Thompson, A.C. and Dara Lind. "Patrol Group Launched as New Degrading Facebook Posts Surface." *Propublica.* 01 Jul. 2019.

Medical evidence suggested residents of the area where children are crossing have been identified as having parasite disease from the desert. [254] Delivering the necessary treatment may be stopped not by clinicians but by political need or social control. The highly regulated aspects of medical screening are intended for the treatment, not for identifying political contagion. [255] Compared to Coronavirus's response, this was also declared a political disease showing continuity of depraved behavior, not just directed at the Democrats but everyone. Both aspects contributed to risking patients needing treatment. The same scenario the White House used in privatizing the delivery of supplies for Covid-19 life support.

U.S. District Judge Micaela Alvarez or any other judge could not protect those that viewed Central Americans as 9-11 terrorists. In an example of violent social control, one rape was discovered that warrants examination. The rape appeared politically activated, imitating the 10-15 Facebook example. Evidence that the death of Marco Antonio Muñoz was indicative of a series of worse, more illegal events that occurred in Pennsylvania. It involved the rape-abuse of a mother with her 3-year-old baby in Pennsylvania. Paid staff charmed and lured the young mother, at that point, threatened and raped her over and over. They intentionally kept the mother holding her infant in her arms amid the assault. In effect, the baby was intimately part of the rape as the baby saw the mother's face, looked into her eyes and those of the perpetrator. Such was the intent, so the perpetrator's precise positioning and timing deliberately looked into the faces of their helpless victims.

Between 2012 and March 2018, 1,448 allegations of sexual abuse were filed with ICE. There was an issue of assaultive consent by Berks County Family Residential Center. They stated that although

---

[254] Carroll, Linda. "U.S. authorities confiscate migrant kids' medications at the southern border." *Reuters*. 03 Dec. 2019.

[255] Nolan MS, Aguilar D, Brown EL, Gunter SM, Ronca SE, et al. (2018) Continuing evidence of Chagas disease along the Texas-Mexico border. *PLOS Neglected Tropical Diseases* 12(11): e0006899.

they had complete institutional control over residents, they were not responsible for the staff's nefarious intent. The complaint read, "ICE Detention Center Says It's Not Responsible for Staff's Sexual Abuse of Detainees." [256] This statement might be translated as a posture that communicates the staff's use of torture, sadism by authorities, and violent acts. Though there are 1,448 allegations that Congress could have hired more investigators, they did not. [257]

These conditions were compounded in President Trump's administration of the Velvet Genocide. Eugene Jarecki of *The Washington Post* 6 May 2020 reported," Leading epidemiologists have put a finer point on this, estimating that 50 to 80 percent of COVID-19 deaths in New York and approximately 90 percent of all American COVID-19 deaths can now be attributed to the administration's delay between March 2 and 16."

Presidential Terror

When the Vietnam War ended, it was a surprise and the rapidity to wit the declarations of withdrawal. On land, the ground soldier witnessed a significant change in the villages after the historic Tet Offensive that was supposedly won by Americans and its allies. A dramatic difference in the landscape showed that the enemy fighters' average age shifted from middle-age and elderly to children, adolescents, and young men and women. The war in this regard became the first teenage war for both sides. To avoid the killing of children, the general's sought to end this conflict and determined privately never to repeat this sort of killing. Because of American arrogance and institutional forgetfulness, there was no public acknowledgment, so the risk of its repetition increased with time.

---

[256] Ibid.

[257] López, Victoria. Senior Staff Attorney, ACLU National Prison Project & Sandra Parc, Senior Staff Attorney, ACLU Women's Rights Project. "ICE Detention Center Says It's Not Responsible for Staff's Sexual Abuse of Detainees." *American Civil Liberties Union.* Report. 06 Nov. 2018.

The United States alone cannot bear the responsibility for assessing all the actions at the Southern Border. International Criminal Court would be useful. The High Commissioner for Refugees has not toured border installations. Still, the former was banned from the United States based on the political stance that partially involves Israel's conflict with the ICC concerning Palestinians. President Dwight D. Eisenhower developed the domino theory of collapsing events seen in domestic warfare policy. The idea that a political event in one country will cause similar events in neighboring states, like a falling domino causing an entire row of upended dominoes to fall. This theory can also be used in a corresponding moral crisis and gauge the extent of systemic corruption and the Dept. of Defense. Think of Cambridge Analytica's issues and the intrusion into the 2016 elections by Steve Bannon and Dr. Robert Mercer. One can hear the voices of these two men behind the following narrative.

Richard H. Walker, in 2000, testified before the Securities Exchange Commission "the depth and breadth and to what extent of corruption." During President Barack Obama's administration, it was not widely publicized that Wall Street had any connection to private armies and mercenaries. By 2009, Erik Dean Prince's investment in Blackwater (Academi) led to a significant private equity firm named Frontier Resource Group. He is chairman of Hong Kong-listed Frontier Services Group Ltd. Erik Dean Prince knew Russian banker and UAE ruler Mohammed bin Zayed since 2009. Mr. Prince latched onto the Trump administration for profits and, in 2017, had years working in the Middle-East conflict zones. The Blackwater (Academi) training centers try to train local police academies, militarize them, reap a distinctly military and Middle-East posture, and teach them to determine who a terrorist is. Domestically one can see the results where African Americans, Central Americans, and their sympathizers were labeled the state's enemies, thereby appropriate targets.

President Bill Clinton conducted a United States strategy as Commander in Chief that helped propel the mercenary military image, Blackwater USA (Academi). Another creation to appease Wall Street and help generate investment. Wall Street investors funded a private organization using a high-yield Cambridge Analytical and Strategic Communication Laboratories formula to obtain beyond-lucrative federal Dept. of Defense contracts. Relocating near the Southern Border to provide some military intervention ultimately led to border patrol and domestic police militarization. Blackwater USA (Academi) deployment to train local police authority complements the United States' trend to militarize its police departments. In dictatorships, Blackwater, Inc. (Academi) would be classified as a government-sponsored mercenary group.

Although people associate the United States government as a democratic country, it might surprise them that a group of white supremacist motivated groups emanating from Wall Street and those friendly to Republican and Democratic party investment firms that want to terminate the military establishment. Effectively this would remove the military command's answerability to Congress and the American people in favor of financial returns. This would effectively lay bare the motivation to declare war and conflict based on financial investments. Casualties and lives saved and destroyed singled out to meet these insidious purposes.

Erik Prince, the founder, for example, is well-known as a manager of this privatized army. Some associate him with the mafia. The former U.S. Navy SEAL officer founded Blackwater (Academi), the USA branch in 1997, a so-called "private military company." He is the brother of the Secretary of Education, Betsy DeVos. During the George H.W. Bush, Presidency Erik Prince served as an intern to be reward by relationships from Presidents Clinton, George W. Bush, and Barack Obama. The United States placed no restriction on him and his rumored intent on developing an army strategy for China. Under a military contractors' guise, Erik Prince and his anti-democratic forces and militias operate a shadow presence in every military theater near our regular soldiers. They are permitted to wear uniforms in similarity to the United States ordinary Army soldier. Their actions are in line with gangsterism.

The financial investor on Wall Street could expand its portfolio. This was an acceptance by the Pentagon of Blackwater USA by

Sheik Mohamed bin Zayed al-Nahyan of Abu Dhabi, who hired Erik Prince to build a fighting force without the U.S. approvals. Peter W. Singer of Brookings Institution 2 Oct. 2007 warned of Blackwater writing *The Dark Truth about Blackwater*. That was followed by Joseph Stiglitz, the Nobel Prize-winning economist, co-author of *The Three Trillion Dollar War* professor at Columbia University. He states direct government spending on those wars amounts to roughly $2 trillion--$17,000 for every U.S. household--with bills yet to be received, increasing this amount by more than 50%. How is it that a Blackwater mercenary gets a $20,000 per month salary for its soldier, and a regular U.S. Army soldier gets a fraction of that? In 2007, private security guards working for Blackwater and Dyncorp were earning up to $1,222 a day, most in noncompetitive contracts amounting to $445,000 a year.

Representing the United States military, they are similar to the military gangster factions of the U.S. Marines along the Southern Border, Homeland Security, and Border Patrol. Once intended to be of high character to counteract the "Abu Ghraib mentality." In 2007, Blackwater (Academi) threatened to kill a State Dept. Official conducting inspections. Riddled with fraud and misconduct, in 2008, the organization's chain of command permitted its "soldiers" to shoot into a crowd of civilians, killing 17 people, including a child. Military officials called the incident "Worse Than Abu Ghraib." Numerous complaints have followed, including evidence of the random shooting of civilians.

Blackwater (Academi) is the product of hedge fund investors and part of Jason De Yonker's portfolio, Managing Partner of Forté, who protects Wall Street firms while receiving approval from The State Dept. Add Dean Bosacki, Managing Partner of Manhattan Investors, also a Blackwater financial backer (Academi). The infiltration of white-collar crime mafia operation in Wall Street, financial regulation leniency, as previously documented, does not instill confidence in national security and transparency. New militarization efforts in police departments, driven by profit incentives, establishing the basis for suspicions that consensus of who is a terrorist is more a product of profit than national security. Total State Dept. and Dept. of Defense contracts with Blackwater (Academi) have been as high as 1 billion dollars--- a boon for Wall Street investors and the military-industrial complex that supplies Blackwater.

CBS News, "A former Blackwater employee, known as John Doe #2, recently alleged in a sworn statement originally obtained by *The Nation.* That Erik Prince "views himself as a Christian crusader tasked with eliminating Muslims and the Islamic faith from the globe," and that Prince's companies "encouraged and rewarded the destruction of Iraqi life." Prince, the former employee, charged, "intentionally deployed to Iraq certain men who shared his vision of Christian supremacy, knowing and wanting these men to take every available opportunity to murder Iraqis. Many of these men used call signs based on the Templar Knights, the warriors who fought the Crusades... Prince's executives would openly speak about going over to Iraq to 'lay Hajiis out on cardboard.' Going to Iraq to shoot and kill Iraqis was viewed as a sport or game. Mr. Prince's employees openly and consistently used racist and derogatory terms for Iraqis and other Arabs, such as 'ragheads' or 'hajiis.' Another former Blackwater employee, an ex-US Marine, charged in a sworn statement that "Blackwater was smuggling weapons into Iraq. This 'night hunting' entailed Mr. Prince's men, armed with night goggles and riding in Mr. Prince's wholly-owned helicopters after 10 pm over the streets of Baghdad, killing at random." [258] Prince's fundamental beliefs are modeled from the gangs in Central America, "Los Caballeros Templarios De Michoacán." [259]

In summary, this happens when political parties fail to separate themselves from gangsters with an ideological purpose, e.g., such as

---

[258] Scahill, Jeremy. "Why Is Obama Still Using Blackwater?" *CBS News.* 17 Sept. 2009.

[259] Bunker, Robert et al. "Los Caballeros Templarios De Michoacán: Imagery, Symbolism, and Narratives." Los Caballeros Templarios de Michoacán: Imagery, Symbolism, and Narratives (2019). April 2019 *Small Wars Foundation.* Bethesda, Maryland.

gangsterism. Congress cannot be defined as undermining law and elevating privilege, developing secret armies, and torturing children. No matter how much Wall Street consensus says otherwise. The calls for civilized discourse and elimination of conspiracy theories of Knights of the Templar, the warriors who fought the Crusades, are ignored by both major political parties. The magnitude of this damaging foreign policy has no discernable place on the battlefield. The United States' Presidency has become a residence of what began the Iraq war-- a Royal Guard.

The world has seen inside the life of a democracy. In many ways, the United States has handled the seizure of power by the Republican Party poorly. It certainly does not compare to how the nation managed the last insurgency of extreme Conservatism in the 1930s. One crucial comparison was the use of Washington, D.C. city jail. Concluding that the present system has been too dependent on its past virtues, not enough action. Turning the world upside down, the Republican Party had resorted to its early years when it was inseparable from Germany's spawning of extreme conservatism. Throwing itself to its past, contemporary Conservatism has enlisted the assistance of the Democratic Party, who seems thoroughly convinced there must always be a Republican Party to ensure American system survival. "The Republican Party is fighting for a freer and stronger America, where everyone has the opportunity to achieve the American Dream." according to its platform, every statement must include a terror word such as "fight."

Donald J. Trump's history, FBI record, and sundry manner of corruption were already known. Specifically, the Republican Party and conservatives in authority were seeking a Presidential continuity of Reagan. There is sufficient reason to believe President Obama had this information, Walter Reed Army Medical Center, the Democratic Party, and Secretary of State. None of which was functional to protect the American people from what had become a personal economy of death, a blend of "new" fascism, hypomania in the populace. An indication of the first alert came out in Secretary Hillary Clinton, then a hard copy of reactionary conservatism in Madeline Albright's book Fascism A Warning. Both have avoided describing what they knew. So, I have done this work for the reader, including new developments.

Readers may be reminded of how a Trump family developed a life of fraud and criminal conduct by reading my first book, subtitled When the Daily Stormers Sang. The complete history is compatible with how the American system selects its politicians. President Trump is a second Ronald Reagan with just his negative attributes and no moral personality. Still, the disastrous plan they had to turn over the government has evolved in full force. Both major parties that include Conservatives and Reagan Democrats are presently a coalition bound together with the alt-right, neo-Nazis, and the mafia. The effect of this was exported and encouraged in formerly war-torn Slovakia and Slovenia. The poisonous ideology was immediately recognized throughout Eastern Europe by its racial principles and Wall Street supremacy.

Peppered with appearances by Paul Manafort, Roger Stone (starting their careers in the Nixon and Reagan White House), Donald J. Trump, and Dr. Armand Hammer's Russian participation arranged by the President Reagan White House dinner programs to meet Secretary General Gorbachev and the usual pawns that once surrounded and operated the Reagan White House. These political operatives led each one except Mueller to seek-out relationships with the type of dictators following Dr. Hammers *modus operandi* of profiting and privatizing terroristic, dictatorial, and communist regimes in an expanding circle of influence, financing, and maintaining their tyrannical and murderous power structures.

The underlying belief among this "cartel of robbing the thieves" is central to what American character became—namely, the above operatives who were once the most respected in White House history by 2020 were exposed as maintaining some of the worst political criminals the world ever imagined. The United States became a haven for their activities. According to Michael Schmidt, 3 Nov. 2020, and New York Times, under secret orders from a mysterious unpublished source, it blocked and evaded all investigation into President Trump's ties to a financial arrangement to a foreign government as Russia. This is the same "remediation" received by Lt. Gen. Micheal Flynn in which no one knows of his contacts in the Pentagon when he made arrangements for Strategic Communication Laboratories.

President Trump, under the Civil Rights Act, altered nationality to race. This is while participating with Jewish staff to perpetrate Zero Tolerance. This sets up a high potential of fiery anti-Semitism between his other loyalists. However, his diplomatic and untactful use and manipulation of others reveal Mr. Trump is not always in control of his long-term intentions of minimizing violence. But, shows a willingness to use violent measures for his gratification despite the resentment and death this may cause. Breeding anger, unfocused resentment, the seeds of totalitarianism. In Origins, Hannah Arendt writes, "The social resentment of the lower middle classes against the Jews turned into a highly explosive political element because these bitterly hated Jews were thought to be well on their way to political power." Here resentment refers to the mobilization of mass antisemitism and the driving force behind the scapegoating of Jews."

Domineering the courts' Conservative appointments and vastly empowering his Cabinet, Senator Mitch McConnell's Wannsee Conference began. Complete with reenacting World War Two's war crimes cited by former Nuremberg Trials Judge Ben Ferencz. [260] The Judge made reference to the Nazi illegal use of armed forces against humanity "other inhumane acts committed against any civilian population." President Trump continued to develop resources and funding for the future by way of excessive tax cuts for the elite that supported the Conservatives throughout his administration, allowing this group to distantly participate in the family cruelty. Presidential terror comports to this image.

From arrest records far away as Greece, also made headlines with *National Public Radio*. The world's greatest criminology minds have worked overtime to solve the mafia-neo-Nazi relationship. It was, without a doubt, the work of organized crime. Reporting on the incident of 14 October 2020, 'A Greek court has sentenced Nikos Michaloliakos, the far-right anti-immigrant Golden Dawn party, to 13 years in prison. Presiding Judge Maria Lepenioti read the sentences less than a week after the court's landmark ruling that Golden Dawn lawmakers had run a criminal organization under the guise of being a democratically elected party. On Tuesday, a prosecutor proposed long prison terms for 57 of the 68 original defendants convicted of murder,

---

[260] Sampathkumar, Mythili. "Last surviving prosecutor at Nuremberg trials says Trump's family separation policy is 'crime against humanity.'" *Independent*. 16 October 2018.

assault, possession of weapons, and leading or participating in a criminal gang. Last week, a leaked police report revealed that up to 16 far-right groups are trying to fill the void left by Golden Dawn. Among them is Greek Solution, a nationalist party led by Kyriakos Velopoulos, an ardent admirer of Hungarian Prime Minister Viktor Orbán, who has 10 deputies in the Athens parliament in July 2019.' [261]

A mystery continues to exist of how Rod Rosenstein, U.S. Attorney General's office, ended up approving a family separation policy that had its roots in the offices of Hungarian Prime Minister Viktor Orbán. Rosenstein hand-picked William P. Barr's friend Robert C. Mueller III as special counsel to the Russia Investigation while banning him from any Trump family's crimes they committed.

The brandishing of threats against the mafia and neo-Nazi organized crime effort was made public by France 24 media reported on 13 March 2019, Otari Arshba, a lawmaker with the pro-Kremlin United Russia party and the prominent supporter of the bill amending Russia's criminal code. [262]Arshba, a Soviet-era KGB officer who worked organized crime cases, said the law's critical change will be a provision making the event "the simple fact of being in charge of a criminal organization is enough" to convict crime bosses. No acceptable outcome for the people who have been harmed can be anything less than to witness the perpetrators' trial behind the injustice. So, what did they achieve?

Long as millions are collected, fraud schemes to be perpetrated, and societies that harbor the criminals of this scope and magnitude, there will always be men with identities that are not correctly fit for the Nazi meritocracy. Though the corresponding features are inexact, the goals remained the same. Right, this is not the Weimar Republic. Still, organized crime has its cultural ambitions that remain succinctly in tempo to the past history of the 1900s-1930s. Foreign governments

---

[261] Chappell, Bill and Joanna Kakissis. "Golden Dawn: Leader Of Greek Neo-Nazi Party Sentenced To 13 Years In Prison." *NPR*. 14 October 2020.

[262] Lapenkova, Marina. "Russia's powerful 'Thieves in Law' face reckoning under Putin." *Agence-France Presse*. 12 March 2019.

want to create civil unrest in exchange for capitalization, oil, resources, gas. About fascism, the neo-Nazi meritocracy behind the planning of riots and unrest remains an excited audience of reactionaries. —conservatives, who are paying tributes to criminal enterprises.

In the neo-Nazi system of beliefs, the Trump alternative right politics supporters are considered in a similar vein of the folkish European. They attend to mystical theatrics, are easily convinced, and mostly ignorant of their use as pawns in the drama. Mr. Rocky Suhayda has complicated politics to accept and is connected to the Third Reich inner circle's death fantasy. Mr. Suhayda accurately said Trump's improbable presidential run "confirmed the suspicion that more Americans share his party's views than many would have thought." [263]

The National Socialist is an inseparable religion from its counterpart of civil cruelty and deaths. The Republican Party and Democrats may long for President Ronald Reagan's days and his open door of political perverseness at the White House that encouraged men like Donald J. Trump. The Donald J. Trump that arrived at his inauguration with Reagan hacks. Namely William P. Barr, Roger Stone, Paul Manafort, and a slew of Reagan-recruited Eastern European's with ideas that Hannah Arendt credited as the remaining sediment and collaborators of neo-Nazidom. Though the Republican Party renamed all of the Nazi features on its platform, they find it impossible to challenge men like Harold Keith Thompson, an SS officer that supported their thinking for decades. We know that the Wannsee Conference participants were alive in the 1980s during President Reagan's administration.

One of the most critical features of the Trump family was their heresy of the Christian and Judaic faiths by incorporating them into a racial category while reducing their message of salvation and deliverance. This pagan allegory appeared in *Christianity Daily* on 9 November 2020. They reported, "…the rabbi recounted how he previously

---

[263] Cortellessa, Eric. "American Nazi Party: Trump victory would be 'a real opportunity'." *Times of Israel.* 7 Aug. 2016.

predicted that Trump would be given four more years as US president so that he could "complete the mission given him by God" and related it with the final vision described in the book of Daniel. Weisberg is a rabbi at Machon Mishne Torah belonging to Chabad, which is one of the most prominent Hasidic groups…" [264]The Rabbi may not have read David's Psalms 115 about idolatry and riches. The inseparable reality in today's world about idolatry and treasure, where "Those who make them become like them; so, do all who trust in them." Chabad continues ties to Putin-Trump-Netanyahu. What is this crime? Weisberg should explain the role of Jewry in the Trump administration.

Donald J. Trump does not seem to understand he is a *nom de plume,* the figurehead of a global order researchers first learned about when Dr. Armand Hammer revealed himself in much the same manner. With backing from heads of state in the West and in the East, Vladamir Lenin and Russian statesmen took totalitarian-minded world leaders that went deep into the areas of dictators and tyrants. Dr. Hammer became a wealthy man even to the extent that Adolph Hitler allowed him to fly into Berlin during the Second World War. Dr. Hammer was a dedicated Republican Party participant in rearranging the global world order relative to nuclear warfare. No such empathy exists in Mr. Trump's personality, as this character analysis shows. It appears not just as a present problem but an intergenerational trait.

Once we decipher the criminal plots and those on the borderline, it often reflected a catch-and-kill story whose authors are never discovered and alleged truths no one can verify. Except in rare instances when illegal acts occur, it seems from out of nowhere Conservative legal defense funds are organized, the best legal scholars assemble, the Congress suddenly bows under pressure and release said, criminals. Pardoning individuals who committed crimes against the United States and its people further clarified the Republican Party's intent, then the velvet genocide and tragedy. The plot is abrupt but

---

[264] Chachila, Julio. "Rabbi Stands By Prediction Trump Will Have 4 More Years To Complete 'Mission' God Gave Him." *Christianity Daily.*" 9 Nov. 2020.

simple-minded; it was what they had done in other countries when freedom-loving people got out of line and wanted to break away. The following paragraphs outline how the fascist influence over the Republican Party specifically and conservatives conducted a "cooperative" plan with the Alt-Right in its Russia and American sphere.

The malpractice of conservatives is not because they had chosen President Trump. Given the conservative history and the collapse of both major political parties, it is expected. Like, a strong-arm government delays their inevitable demise while enriching the wealthy elite. It surprises no economist that the immensely wealthy Wall Street continuously benefits as a selective group who glean the best policies, health care, and trade. It takes no mysterious turn to learn that the fascist economies of the plantations reassert their dominance. After all, it attracted Adolph Hitler and his American fascists to incorporate the plans of what he identified as the "American union" of highly organized separate and racialized economies.

In parallel to the Third Reich development and its early thinking in America, the Trump family began their legacy. Readers will recall Friedrich's 1900s arrival from Bavaria, deported him for lack of moral character and disloyalty to Germany. Friedrich was an accused fraud and con artist in Alaska who stole mining rights from gold miners, fooling them into making him a justice of the peace. To wit, he used his office to extract mining rights to their property while operating a brothel. In Congressional hearings, his son Frederick made his public debut stealing from the government in taxes and mortgage interest rates from returning World War veterans. This ultimately forces him into the Ku Klux Klan's general view, a Congressional investigation worthy of President Dwight D. Eisenhower's focus.

The Trump family's legacy appears as though it was initially intended for Fred Trump Jr. to inherit but unintentionally went to Donald. The latter tried to con Fred Sr. out of his Will and Testament. The odd man out from his father's intentions, Donald's behavior is imitative of Friedrich's actions and his father's style. One exception is the cultural preference of Eastern European culture,

Russophilia, sexual exploitation to which he goes to a great extent to not just imitate but incorporate into his business and political economy.

There was a strange self-defeating similarity of Fred's past when he lost his business then rebuilt. The hereditary and intergenerational line of conduct is evident throughout the family members. All the features of authoritarianism in the family hierarchy exist except that occasionally, women play an increased role to temporarily dominate when an interruption in the order occurs. This was evident when Friedrich died, and his wife dominated Fred until he came of business age.

Donald's propensity of purposely and routinely destroying his wealth then built it back may exhibit a learned trait from his experience. This would indicate a mental block, but this may be too rational a view. It could be that Donald simply enjoys being self-destructive. His behavior proves little indication of conformity to the prevailing laws. This reveals a legal fracture his supporters find enjoyable to watch machismo and sadism unfold. Mr. Trump and Sen. McConnell realize they operate within a privileged arena with "autoimmunity" laws permitting them to do almost everything for any purpose. Mr. Trump's remarkable statement, "I am the state." In other words, I get my identity in how the family reflects the states' condition. This personality type may imitate others' appearances and behavior that match his evil and mental makeup to conduct the monstrous and the death he perpetrated on 6 Jan. 2021. American society's condition and its platform excuse all elites promising to repeat the above incidences.

These profound and similar behaviors unfold across time in the criminal spectrums from New York to Siberia and Peking's Hidden City. The expanse of societal fractures in the United States pit the unreasonable and irresponsible market approach versus an actual need of populations who freeze and get infected due to the "unresponsive tyrant." The middle ground controlled by thieves/conspiratorialists a mirror product of societies like the Trump types, which emerge in different scenarios to ravage everyday citizens' wealth.

Appendix A: War Crimes and Propaganda

War Crimes and Propaganda in "Analysis of Nazi Propaganda A Behavioral Study" by Dr. Karthik Narayanaswami, Holocaust in History, Literature, and Film Harvard University. *Excerpt.*

As we examine the chronology of events leading up to the Holocaust, it becomes vital to understand propaganda's role in perpetuating this proportion's crime. To this end, this paper will analyze the fundamental tenets of Nazi propaganda and the role that they played in not just the genocide of Jews, Romani peoples, homosexuals, and other undesirables but also in helping turn Germany into an aggressor nation. We will look at the calculation methodology adopted by the Nazi party under the guidance of both Adolf Hitler and Joseph Goebbels and analyze the underlying techniques used. However, while the breadth and scope of Nazi propaganda were quite exhaustive and included posters, movies, radio, and the press, this paper will focus on the primary method of rallying the German people – the creative use of signs to serve malignant ends. These posters will be analyzed through a behavioral lens to understand and identify critical cognitive and psychological drivers that created them and their role in instigating social and other cognitive biases in the German population. This analysis will primarily be visual in nature and will look for behavioral cues that trigger bias responses.

Finally, this paper will provide an overview of the critical set of behavioral manipulations and provide a framework to help identify such propaganda attempts wherever they may appear. Furthermore, this paper will also provide a list of elements for the "ideal" Nazi poster, with critical details borrowed from the various other signs. Cognitive Biases are situational instances of deviation in judgment, usually stemming from a stimulus. Typically, cognitive biases are triggered for various reasons, and their origins can be traced to evolved mental behavior to cope with new situations and make quick decisions. However, they can also be manipulated by providing an artificial stimulus to induce specific target populations' responses. We will be analyzing Nazi propaganda with this lens to better understand how they could manipulate an entire nation-state.

Appendix B: Reactionary, Conservative, to Nazi

Arthur Moeller van den Bruck: The Man & His Thought. *Excerpt.*

Reactionaries and Conservatives are often seen as interchangeable, but Moeller emphasized that there are essential differences between them. A reactionary is essentially someone who believes in a total reinstitution of a past form. He seeks to reverse history and bring back into being all old practices, regardless of whether they are actually good or bad, because he believes that everything of the past was good. Moeller thus distinguished the conservative's reactionary: —The reactionary's reading of history is as superficial as the conservatives are profound. The reactionary sees the world as he has known it; the conservative sees it as it has been and will always be. He distinguishes the transitory from the eternal. Precisely what has been can never be again. But what the world has once brought forth, she can bring forth also. This means that while a reactionary seeks to completely revive past forms, the conservative understands how the world actually functions. Societies evolve, and therefore, some values and traditions change, but at the same time, specific values and traditions do not change or should not change. The conservative tries to preserve the values and customs that are good for the nation or are eternal in nature while simultaneously accepting new values and practices when they are helpful for the country or replacing older ones that were negative in effect. Therefore, [the conservative] has no ambition to see the world as a museum; he prefers it as a workshop to create things that will serve as new foundations. His thought differs from the revolutionary. It does not trust something that was hastily begotten in the chaos of upheaval; things have a value for him only when they possess specific stability. Stable values spring from tradition.

What, then, is a —Revolutionary Conservative or —Conservative Revolutionary? In many ways, Moeller's conservative definition is equivalent to revolutionary conservative, one who values eternal or good while leaving behind what is no longer tenable or bad. However, strictly speaking, for Moeller, the extreme conservative is a conservative who merges conservative and revolutionary ideas for its benefit. Moeller wrote that —conservative-revolutionary thought‖ is the —only one that is a time of upheaval guarantees the continuity of history and preserves it alike from reaction and chaos. Thus, it is a necessary development that recognizes and reconciles —all the antitheses that are historically alive amongst us. Conservative Nationalism and the Third Empire According to Moeller, conservatism, and nationalism are linked, meaning that a conservative is now a nationalist. But how does he define —nationalism, a term which often has contradictory definitions? Nationality (or alternatively, ethnicity) is not based merely on being born in a specific country and speaking its language, as has often been assumed in the past; a nation is defined by —its own peculiar character from how the men of its blood value life.

Thus, Moeller wrote: —Consciousness of nationhood means the consciousness of a nation's living values. Those are Germans who speak German, or were born in Germany, or possess her civil rights. Conservatism seeks to preserve a nation's values by conserving traditional values. These still have the power of growth and assimilate all new values that increase a nation's vitality. A country is a community of values, and nationalism is a consciousness of values. It is interesting to note here that liberal-egalitarian intellectuals frequently claim that nationalists believe that a nation is a totally unchanging entity in terms of character. Simultaneously, Moeller's concept of conservatism and nationalism, as explained above, entirely defies these anti-nationalist prejudices.

Similarly, Moeller's associate, the influential völkisch (—Folkish) thinker Max Hildebert Boehm, held that a Volk was not an unchanging organism but always in a state of flux. Finally, Moeller declared that —The crumbling state threatened to bury the nation in its ruins. But there has arisen a hope of salvation: a conservative-revolutionary movement of nationalism. It will establish a —Third Empire, a new and final Empire that would unite the German people as a whole, be founded upon conservative values and country's love, and resolve

Germany's economic and population problems. However, Moeller emphasized that the aim was not to fight only for Germany's sake. Still, in fact —at the same time, the German nationalist is fighting for Europe's cause, for every European influence that radiates from Germany as the center of Europe. Thus, the fulfillment of German destiny would mean the salvation of Europe.

Influence and Death. Moeller's grand vision for the future of German nationalism and conservatism had much impact among right-wing groups in Germany. They were critical in the development of —revolutionary conservatism. However, his most prominent influence was on Hitler's National Socialist movement, even to the extent that Moeller is repeatedly said to be a precursor of National Socialism. Although the term —Third Reich‖ did not originate with him, he popularized it during the Weimar Republic and was the source from which the National Socialists adopted it.

Furthermore, Moeller's concept of a Leader who identifies with the nation, the idea of a —national socialism, his anti-liberalism, and his belief in the importance of nationality all bear an apparent relationship to Hitler's National Socialism. However, on the other hand, these ideas are certainly not unique to either Moeller or Hitler and predate them. There are also apparent differences between Moeller's worldview and Hitler's. Moeller did not share Hitler's anti-Slavism or his particular racial views, nor was his anti-Jewish attitudes as strong as Hitler's, even though he recognized Jews as a problem. When Hitler visited the June Club in 1922 and had a discussion with Moeller, Moeller believed that while Hitler clearly was fighting for German interests, he did not have the right personal qualities or tendencies: —Hitler was wrecked by his proletarian primitivism. He did not understand how to give his national socialism any intellectual basis. He was passion incarnate but entirely without measure or sense of proportion. According to Otto Strasser, another associate of Moeller, Hitler also did not understand Moeller's phrase —We were Teutons, we are Germans, we shall be Europeans, which meant that Germany should become —a member of the great European family. Yet despite all this, Hitler still admired Moeller, and a signed copy of his Das Dritte Reich was found in Hitler's bunker in 1945. By the year 1925, Moeller began to despair over Germany's political situation and various adverse developments. He did not have any confidence in the right-wing political forces which emerged, and it has also been suggested that he had feared that the National Socialists abused or distorted his ideas.

As he began to withdraw from political activism, Moeller became lonelier and more depressed and was finally struck by a nervous breakdown, after which he committed suicide on May 30, 1925. But as Arthur Moeller van den Bruck passed from this world, he left behind his imposing vision: —" German nationalism fights for the possible Empire . . .. We are not thinking of the Europe of Today, which is too obnoxious to have any value. We are thinking of the Europe of Yesterday and whatever thereof may be salvaged for Tomorrow. We are thinking of the Germany of All Time, the Germany of a two-thousand-year past, the Germany of an eternal present which dwells in the spirit, but must be secured in reality and can only so be politically secured . . .. The ape and tiger in man are threatening. The shadow of Africa falls across Europe. It is our task to be guardians on the threshold of values."

Appendix C: Mafia Like Corporations, Government

"The financial mafia. The illegal accumulation of wealth and the financial-industrial complex." By Umberto Santino in Crime, Law, and Social Change. Volume 12, issue 3, September 1988. *Excerpt.*

The contemporary scene. Organized crime has entered a new era. The presence of large criminal organizations in many parts of the world is a historical reality that has been developing over more than a century. But it is only during recent years that we have been observing the growth of a 'world mafia market' whose two essential characteristics are the extension on a world scale of the trafficking of various goods (not only confined to drugs and weapons) and the gradual transformation of this traffic into a mass commodities market. This is where the new mafia exercises hegemony over vast segments of the 'Black Economy.' These mass-market characteristics imply that although criminal organizations persist in having their own specific cultural aspects connected with various traditions, they are becoming more and more alike in structure and international connections, taking on multinational corporations' characteristics cooperation-competition-rivalry within a global division of criminal-legal work.

During recent years, at the same time as the Sicilian-American mafia has expanded in scope and economic significance, other kinds of organized crime have also grown, such as the Columbian and Bolivian mafias, the Chinese 'Triads,' and the Japanese Yakuza. The same type of development can also be seen among Puerto Rican mobsters and Australian racketeers (2). All this is part of developing an international financial network consisting of systems for recycling illegal capital and providing investment outlets. This, therefore, allows for the merging of 'legitimate' and 'illegitimate' capital within international financial markets, and thus also for the development of an identification process between criminal syndicates and the military-political power in many parts of the world. Such basic standard features conclude that various criminal organizations are becoming increasingly 'mafia-like,' vertically integrated with national and political systems.

Among the consequences of these processes are bewilderment, political indifference ('qualunquismo'), the extension of mysticism as an escape from reality, intolerance, and terrorism. The 'new era' of organized criminality is embedded in this context, whose specific features explain the development of world criminality itself.

Abou-Sabe, Kenzi and Tom Winter, and Max Tucker. "What Did Ex-Trump Aide Paul Manafort Really Do in Ukraine?" *NBC News*. 27 Jun. 2017.

Ackerman, Spencer, and Asawin Suebsaeng, White House Reporter. "Trump Tells Allies He Wants Absolved War Criminals to Campaign for Him." *The Daily Beast*. 25 Nov. 2019.

Adelman, Jonathan. "Russians and Jews: The Odd Couple." *The Jerusalem Post*. 11 Oct. 2018.

Adler, David. "Centrists Are the Most Hostile to Democracy, Not Extremists." *The New York Times*. 23 May 2018.

Ainsley, Julia, and Jacob Soboroff, and Phil Helsel. "Justice officials drove family separation policy; draft watchdog report says." *National Broadcasting Network*. 6 Oct. 2020.

Aked, Hillary. "The undeniable overlap: right-wing Zionism and Islamophobia." *Open Democracy Report*. 29 Sept. 2015.

Akerlof, George A. and Romer, Paul M. "Looting: The Economic Underworld of Bankruptcy for Profit." *Brookings Papers on Economic Activity*, 1993, No. 2.

Akhtiorskaya, Yelena. "Welcome to Брайтон Бич, Brooklyn." *The New York Times*. 14 Dec. 2018.

Alesci, Cristina. "Armed authorities enter Trump hotel in Panama amid standoff over a legal dispute." *CNN*. 28 Feb. 2018.

Alexievich, Svetlana "On the Battle Lost." Nobel Laureate in Literature 2015. The Nobel Foundation in 2015.

Associated Press. "The white-collar mafia: From the back alley to the boardroom, mobsters take over the family company." *Daily Mail*. 01 Nov. 2011.

Altemeyer, Bob. *The Authoritarians*. Cherry Hill Publishing; Unabridged edition ISBN-10: 0972329889. 27 Nov. 2008.

Alter Ego. A doctrine used by the courts to ignore the corporate status of a group of stockholders, officers, and directors of a corporation about their limited liability. So that they may be held personally liable for their actions when they have acted fraudulently or unjustly or when to refuse to do so would deprive an innocent victim of redress for an injury caused by them. –Legal Dictionary.

Alternative Right. The alt-right had various ideological forebears. The idea of white supremacy had been dominant across U.S. political discourse throughout the 19th and early 20th centuries. After World War II, it was increasingly repudiated and relegated to the far-right of the country's political spectrum. Far-right groups retaining such ideas—such as George Lincoln Rockwell's American Nazi Party and William Luther Pierce's National Alliance—remained marginal. –Wikipedia

Anschluss. The annexation of Austria by Germany in 1938. Hitler had forced the resignation of the Austrian Chancellor by demanding that he admit Nazis into his cabinet. The new Chancellor, a pro-Nazi, invited German troops to enter the country on restoring law and order. The political union of Austria with Germany was achieved through annexation by Adolf Hitler in 1938. Mooted in 1919 by Austria, Anschluss with Germany remained a hope (chiefly with Austrian Social Democrats) during 1919–33).

Applebaum, Anne. "100 years later, Bolshevism is back. And we should be worried." *The Washington Post.* 06 Nov. 2017.

Arreguín-Toft, Ivan. How the Weak Win Wars: A Theory of Asymmetric Conflict. Cambridge Studies in International Relations. Cambridge University Press. 08 Dec. 2005. ISBN-13: 978-0521839761.

Artemiw, David. "Towards a Definition of Fascism." Fourth Year Paper. Address: 319-1544 Dundas Street West Toronto, ON M6K 0C2 CANADA.

Associated Press. "U.S. Military Used Nerve Gas to Kill Vietnam War Defectors, Report Says." *Los Angeles Times.* 08 June 1998.

Associated Press. "Trump pardons former US soldier convicted of killing Iraqi prisoner." *The Guardian.* 07 May 2019.

Attorney Mitchell Palmer. (Attorney General of the United States). "The Case Against the "Reds." The Forum, Feb. 1920, v. 63, pp. 173-180. The plans for fomenting a nation-wide revolution in this country, prepared by Trotsky in Moscow, are in the Attorney-General's office files. Upon these proofs, the Attorney-General has decided upon a vigorous system of arrest and deportation of radical aliens, which he says he will pursue until the United States is purged of Bolshevism. In this article, the Attorney-General sets forth his legal authority for whole-sale arrests and deportation, revealing the Department of Justice against Radicalism.

Austin, John. *How to Do Things with Words*. New York: Oxford University Press, 1962. John Austin's theory of speech-acts, whereby in "the act of saying something, utterances or locutions can be invested with an illocutionary force designed to have an effect" (p. 76).

BBC. "Russia profile – Timeline." 26 Apr. 2019.

Baehr, Peter. "The informers: Hannah Arendt's appraisal of Whittaker Chambers and the ex-Communists." *European Journal of Cultural and Political Sociology*, 2014 Vol. 1, No. 1, 35 –66.

Baker J., Graham. "Christianity and Eugenics: The Place of Religion in the British Eugenics Education Society and the American Eugenics Society c.1907–1940." *Soc Hist Med*. May 2014; 27(2): pp. 281–302.

Balogová, Beata. "Is Slovakia a mafia state?" 5 Jun. 2019. *The Slovak Spectator*.

Barnett, Errol. "Immigrant children with life-threatening illnesses facing possible deportation." *CBS News*. 29 Aug. 2019.

Bastone, William. "The Last Jewish Gangster." *The Village Voice* online. 26 Jun 2019.

Beckett, Lois. "My six years covering neo-Nazis: 'They're all vying for the affections of Russia'." *The Guardian*. 17 Feb. 2018.

Behrmann, Savannah. "Advocacy group releases leaked emails from White House adviser Stephen Miller to Breitbart." *USA Today*. 12 Nov. 2019.

Beiner, Ronald. Univ. of Toronto. "The Conservative Revolution of the 21st Century: The Curious Case of Jason Jorjani." *Kellogg Institute for International Studies*. Taking Radical New-Right Thinkers Seriously: Perspectives on Europe, Russia, and the US. 01 May 2019.

Bellant, Russ. *Old Nazis, the new right, and the Republican Party: domestic fascist networks and U.S. cold war politics.* Copyright© by Russ Bellant 1988, 1989, 1999. ISBN 0-89608--41 9. Political Research Associates, 678 Massachusetts Avenue, Suite 205, Cambridge, MA 02139. South End Press.

Benjamin, Walter. 1996a. *One-Way Street* in *Selected Writings Volume I: 1913-1926*, Marcus Bullock and Michael W. Jennings (eds.) (Cambridge, Mass.: Belnap Press): 444-488.

Berlusconi G, Calderoni F, Parolini N, Verani M, Piccardi C (2016) Link Prediction in Criminal Networks: A Tool for Criminal Intelligence Analysis. LoS ONE 11 (4): e0154244.

Berlin, Isaiah, and Henry Hardy. *From Hope and Fear Set Free.* Oxford Scholarship Online. Nov. 2003. ISBN-13: 9780199249893. In Sora, Alina. "Freedom a Way of Surviving in the Novel Everything Flows." *Linguistic and Literary Broad Research and Innovation*. Volume 5, Issue 2, 2016.

Bertrand, Natasha." A model for civilization': Putin's Russia has emerged as 'a beacon for nationalists' and the American alt-right." *Business Insider*. 10 Dec. 2016.

Bevensee, Emmi, and Alexander Reid Ross. "Alt-Right and Global Information Warfare." Instructor, *Department of Geography, Portland State University*. Portland, Oregon, USA. May 2019.

Biddle, Sam. "The Time Donald Trump's Ex-Wife Accused Him of Brutally Raping Her." *Gawker*. 30 Jul. 2015.

Bideleaux, Robert. *Leon Trotsky*. The Wiley-Blackwell Encyclopedia of Social Theory. 04 December 2017.

Billington, James H. *Fire in the minds of men*, Transaction Publishers, 1999, p. 455, ISBN 978-0-7658-0471-6.

BIBLIOGRAPHY

Birnbaum, Emily. "Trump rails against 'terrible bias's at social media summit." *The Hill.* 11 July 2019.

Blackwater. "We now know that Blackwater was hired as part of the secret CIA assassination program that former Vice President Dick Cheney ordered concealed from Congress and that the company continues to work for the CIA as part of its drone bombing campaign in Pakistan and Afghanistan." In Scahill, Jeremy. "Why Is Obama Still Using Blackwater?" *CBS News.* 17 Sept. 2009.

Blair, Gwenda. "Fred Trump Slays the King of Cooperative Housing." *The Gotham Center For New York City History.* 08 Feb. 2018.

Blee, Kathleen M., and Kimberly A. Creasap. Conservative and Right-Wing Movements. Department of Sociology, University of Pittsburgh, Pittsburgh, Pennsylvania 15260.

Bloche, Gary. "Law, Theory, and Politics: The Dilemma of Soviet Psychiatry." *The Yale Journal of International Law.* Volume 11, Number 2, Spring 1986. Author: Columbia Presbyterian Medical Center, New York; J.D. Candidate, Yale University, 1986.

Blumenfeld, Warren J. Ph.D. "Donald Trump, the Antisemitic Provocateur." University of Massachusetts Amherst Adjunct. Undated paper received 9 Nov. 2020.

Blumenthal, Ralph, and Celestine Bohlen. "Soviet Emigre Mob Outgrows Brooklyn, and Fear Spreads." *The New York Times.* 04 Jun. 1989.

Blunt, Katherine. "Unrecognized Potential: Media Framing of Hitler's Rise to Power, 1930-1933." Elon Journal of Undergraduate Research in Communications, Vol. 6, No. 2. Fall of 2015.

Bobrovnikov, Vladimir. "The Islamic Discourse of Visual Propaganda in the Soviet East Between the Two World Wars (1918-1940)." Islam Perspectives Org. *Russian Perspectives on Islam* is made possible through funding from the Henry Luce Foundation, the National Endowment for the Humanities, and the Mardjani Foundation's support.

Bois, Marcel, Joe Sabatini translator. "The KPD and the United Front during the Weimar Republic." *Marx 21 USA.* 19 May 2017.

Boland, Stephanie. "This 2014 Donald Trump interview hints at a new kind of special relationship." *New Statesman America.* 17 Nov. 2016.

Bolstad, Richard, Ph.D. "The Day the Tide Went Out: Using Neuro-Linguistics on a Global Scale." Transformations International Consulting & Training Ltd. Browns Bay, North Shore, Auckland, New Zealand.

Bolton, Kerry R. "H. Keith Thompson Jr." Profiles in History. *Inconvenient History.* Committee for Open Debate on the Holocaust. Vol. 6 (2014) No.2. See the Hoover Institution Archives for the complete file. See also *Appendix to The Congressional Record*: There Must Not Be a Third World War. Hon. Arthur G. Klein. Weds. Aug. 19, 1949. Congressional Record: Proceedings and Debates..., Volume 95, Part 16.

Bonapartism. Actively participates in or advocated conservative, monarchist, and imperial political faction in 19th century France.

Bonneuil, Christophe and Jean-Baptiste Fressoz. *The Shock of the Anthropocene.* Translated by David Fernbach. London: Verso, 2016.

Brown, Sherri. "What Is Truth? Jesus, Pilate, and the Staging of the Dialogue of the Cross in John 18:28-19:1 6a." *Creighton University.* Omaha, NE. THE CATHOLIC BIBLICAL QUARTERLY. 77, 2015.

Browning, Christopher. 2018. "The Suffocation of Democracy," *New York Review of Books* In Gandesha, Samir. The Spectre of the 1930s. See also: Adorno, T.W. 1982. "Freudian Theory and the Pattern of Fascist Propaganda," *Essential Frankfurt School Reader*, Andrew Arato and Eike Gebhardt (eds.) (New York: Continuum): 118-137.

Bump, Phillip. "In 1927, Donald Trump's father was arrested after a Klan riot in Queens." *The Washington Post.* 29 Feb. 2016. See Wikipedia under the *New York World Expose of the Ku Klux Klan.*

Bunker, Robert et al. "Los Caballeros Templarios De Michoacán: Imagery, Symbolism, and Narratives." April 2019 *Small Wars Foundation.* Bethesda, Maryland.

BIBLIOGRAPHY

Burkett, Paul. *Marx and Nature: A Red and Green Perspective.* Chicago: Haymarket Books, 2014.

Burton, Tara Isabella. "The biblical story the Christian right uses to defend Trump." *VOX.* 05 Mar. 2018.

Callahan, Maureen. "'1000s' of Russian spies in the U.S., surpassing Cold War record." *New York Post.* 04 Jul 2010.

Carlson, John Roy. *UnderCover: My Four Years in the Nazi Underworld of America.* Blakiston Company and Dutton and Company Publishers. December 1943.

Camp of the Saint's Worldview" combines moral conflict and physical combat to illuminate the ideological and religious roots and deadly consequences of Jean Raspail's French fantasy novel Camp of the Saints and the Eurabia Project writings Egyptian Jewish exile writer Bat Ye'or. They are, respectively, the "intellectual forefather" and the "matriarch" of the counter-jihad or "rising Muslim tide" movement.

Carney, Timothy. "It's Time to Create a Conservative Ecosystem That Doesn't Welcome Racists." *Washington Examiner.* 04 Sept. 2019.

Carpenter, Michael. "Russia Is Co-opting Angry Young Men." The Atlantic. 29 Aug. 2018. in "Mobilizing 'uncivil society': how Russia's 21st Century 'active measures' actually work." *Democracy Digest.* National Endowment for Democracy. 29 Aug. 2018.

Carroll, Linda. "U.S. authorities confiscate migrant kids' medications at the southern border." *Reuters.* 03 Dec. 2019.

Cazzoli, Lise. "An Uncomfortable Truth: Democratic Culture and The New Left-Behinds." *M.A. Candidate from the Graduate School of Public and International Affairs, University of Ottawa. She currently attends the M.A. in International Development, Sciences Po Paris. She researches global political theory, sustainable development, and human rights.* June 2017.

Greek, Cecil E. *Monsters in and Among Us Toward a Gothic Criminology.* Fairleigh Dickinson University Press. 2007. ISBN: 97808386 41590, 0838641598.

Cerini, Chiara; Grace M. Alddrovani. "Breast Milk: Proactive Immunomodulation and Mucosal Protection Against Viruses and Other Pathogens." *Future Virology.* 2013;8(11):1127-1134. Source: Department of Pediatrics & Molecular Microbiology & Immunology, Children's Hospital Los Angeles, University of Southern California, Los Angeles, CA, USA.

Chachila, Julio. "Rabbi Stands by Prediction Trump Will Have 4 More Years to Complete 'Mission' God Gave Him." *Christianity Daily.*" 9 Nov. 2020.

Chappell, Bill, and Joanna Kakissis. "Golden Dawn: Leader of Greek Neo-Nazi Party Sentenced To 13 Years in Prison." *NPR.* 14 October 2020.

Cherep-Spiridovich, Maj.-Gen., Count. *The Secret World Government* or "The Hidden Hand." *The Anti-Bolshevist Publishing Association.* 1926.

Chládková, Lucie. "The Far Right in Slovenia." Supervisor Master's Thesis Miroslav Mareš, Ph.D. *Masaryk Univ. Faculty of Social Studies Dept. of Political Science.* Security and Strategic Studies, 2012.

Cheney-Rice, Zak. "Bernie Sanders and the Lies We Tell White Voters." *Intelligencer.* New York: 11 Nov. 2018.

Clark, Emma. "A Psychological Analysis of Adolf Hitler." *Univ. of Mary Washington.* 03 Dec. 2012.

Coates, Sarah. "The Poisonous Mushroom: Indoctrinating antisemitism into the Nazi youth." *The Department of Religions and Theology Trinity College, Dublin.* Dr. Zuleika Rodgers. 19 March 2013.

Cole, Devan. "Chris Christie: Jared Kushner's father committed 'one of the most loathsome, disgusting crimes' I prosecuted." *CNN.* 30 Jan. 2019.

Communism as Unremorseful. *The Washington Post* "Ex-Communists Remain Totalitarian at Heart." 3 May 1953.

Complacency is doom: The principal diagnosis is that many are complacent. To be complacent means to feel satisfied with the current state and to be disinclined to try to make things better. It is self-satisfaction accompanied by a lack of awareness of dangers or deficiencies. It is a kind of myopic condition in which one cannot see beyond one's own situation to recognize others' plight. It is like the rich man who could not see beyond his feast to the starving Lazarus at his very door. Perhaps the meats were piled too high, or the wine blurred his vision. All of this is a form of denial. Lazarus was still there even if the rich man couldn't or wouldn't see him.

Condon, Richard. *The Manchurian Candidate*. McGraw-Hill. 27 Apr. 1959.

C-O-Two Fire Equipment Co. v. The United States, 197 F. 2d 489, 494 (9th Cir. 1952), cert. denied, 344 U.S. 892 (1952). "Conspiracy: Evidentiary Value of Conscious Parallelism." Doyle explains," The difficulty arises determining what sufficient truth of the existence of a conspiracy is and then actually obtaining the necessary quantum of proof. It is not essential to prove a conspiracy by direct evidence of an express agreement, written or oral. Circumstantial evidence has always been enough. Evidence of a formal contract is unnecessary and was the law; otherwise, such conspiracies would flourish...." See Twombly et al. v. Bell Atlantic et al., 425 F.3d 99 (2d. Cir. 2005) briefed, argued, and submitted to the Supreme Court in November 2006.

Cordero, Carrie. "How to Understand Kushner's Back-Channel." *Politico Magazine*. 06 June 2017.

Corrigan, John. "Visual Culture and the Holocaust: Nazi Anti-Semitic Propaganda. Historical Visual Survey." *Professor at the University of Wisconsin – Stout*. 23 Jul 2013.

Cortellessa, Eric. "American Nazi Party: Trump victory would be 'a real opportunity'." *Times of Israel*. 7 Aug. 2016.

Cotter, Phil. Managing Director, Risk, Refinitiv. "Revealing the true cost of financial crime" 2018. Publication No. RE903599/12-19.

Crepon, Marc. *Murderous Consent on the Accommodation of Violent Death*. Translated by Michael Loriaux and Jacob Levi Foreword by James Martel. *Fordham University Press*. New York: 2019. Library of Congress Control Number: 2019935377.

Criminal Insurgency: Describes an insurgency movement whose political motivation has been perverted by criminal interests. It hasn't necessarily become a criminal organization itself, but it has become impossible to determine if its objectives are purely political or criminal.

Criss, Doug. "This is the 30-year-old Willie Horton ad everybody is talking about today." *CNN*. 01 Nov. 2018.

Curtis. Charlotte. "Dr. Hammer's Real Concern." *The New York Times*. 19 Nov. 1985.

Darcy, Oliver. "Trump invites right-wing extremists to White House 'social media summit'." *CNN Business*. 11 July 2019.

Davis, Deryl. "Affluent Terrorists Challenge Narrative that Poverty Drives Extremism." The Washington Diplomat. 31 May 2019.

Day, Chad, and Stephen Braun. "Flynn files new financial form reporting ties to the data firm." *AP News Service*. 04 Aug. 2017.

Deconstructivism is a movement of postmodern architecture that appeared in the 1980s. It gives the impression of the fragmentation of the constructed building. It is characterized by an absence of harmony, continuity, or symmetry. Its name comes from the idea of "Deconstruction," a form of semiotic analysis developed by the French philosopher Jacques Derrida. -Wikipedia.

de la Cruz Díaz-Valdés, Daniel. "A study of political manipulation in discourse: Comparing Hitler and Trump's speeches." Thesis. Degree in English Studies TFG Supervised by Dr. Elena Martínez Caro Universidad Complutense, Madrid. June 2017.

DePass, Dee. "Apprenticeship programs abound as labor shortage deepens in Minnesota." *Star Tribune*. 11 Jan. 2019.

Derrida, Jacques. (1930 - 2004). Although Derrida himself denied that it was a method or school or doctrine of philosophy (or indeed anything outside of reading the text itself), the term has been used by others to describe Derrida's particular methods of textual criticism, which involved discovering, recognizing, and understanding the underlying assumptions (unspoken and implicit), ideas and frameworks that form the basis for thought and belief. Philosophy basics.

DeSimone, Daniel. "Neo-Nazi Rinaldo Nazzaro running US militant group The Base from Russia." *BBC*. 24 Jan. 2020

Di Antonio, Michael. "The Men Who Gave Trump His Brutal Worldview." *Politico*. 29 Mar. 2016.

DLA Piper Law Firm. "Concession law in Russia." *Lexology*. 03 Sept. 2014. See also: World Bank Group. "Public-Private Partnerships Laws / Concession Laws." Public-Private Partnership Legal Resources Center.

Dobrovolskaya, Lily, and Nicholas Nehamas. "Russian official linked to South Florida biker club spent millions on Trump condos." *Miami Herald*. 28 Jun. 2017.

Donovan, Stewart. *Not Built for Peacetime*. A review of Secondhand Time by Svetlana Alexievich London: Fitzcarraldo Editions, 2016, pp. 694.

Duffy, Peter. "" The Congressman Who Spied for Russia." *Politico Magazine*, History Dept. 06 Oct. 2014.

Duma. The State Duma (Russian: Государственная дума, Gosudarstvennaya Duma, common abbreviation: Госдума, Gosduma) in Russia is the lower house of the Federal Assembly of Russia (parliament), the upper house being the Federation Council of Russia. Under Russia's 1993 constitution, there are 450 deputies of the State Duma (Article 95), each elected to four years (Article 96); this was changed to a five-year term in late 2008.

Dyck, Brendt Douglass. "The Terrifying Story of Hitler's Stolen Children." *Warfare History Network*. 24 Nov. 2018.

Early, Pete. "Interview with The Spy Master." *The Washington Post*. 23 Apr. 1995.

Eisenhower, Dwight D (1958). *"Public Papers of the Presidents of the United States: Dwight D. Eisenhower, 1956", p.281.*

Elsner, Alan. "Neo-Nazis Look for New Home in Trump's Republican Party." *J Street*. 12 Jul. 2018.

Epstein, Edward J. "The Riddle of Armand Hammer." *The New York Times*. 29 Nov. 1981. See FOIA Request.

Epstein, Helen, "I was a Nazi, and here's why." *The New Yorker*. 29 May 2013.

Epstein, Edward. J. *DOSSIER: The Secret History of Armand Hammer*. Random House. 1996.

Epstein, Jay. "The Andropov File: How a short, burly thug became a tall Chubby Checkers fan." *The New Republic*. 26 Nov. 2007.

Epstein, Jay. "The Andropov Hoax." *The New Republic*. 07 Fed. 1983.

Erdman, D. *The Complete Poetry and Prose of William Blake*. Anchor; Revised edition (April 16, 1982) p. 944 and p. 926.

Erickson, Edward, Jr. "Discretion Advised: Trump's mob and Russia ties could prove embarrassing for the Donald, and the FBI as investigations heat up." *City Paper*. 27 June 2017.

Erdmeli, Melis. "Dropping the Mask of Duality: Criminality in The Strange Case of Dr. Jekyll and Mr. Hyde." See also Stevenson, Robert Louis. *The Strange Case of Dr. Jekyll and Mr. Hyde and Other Tales of Terror*. London: Penguin, 2003. Print.

Etter Sr., Gregg W. Ed. D., and Ms. Stacia Pottorff. "The Russian Mafia: Examining the Thieves World from Thieves-In Law to Thieves in Authority" *Journal of Gang Research*. Volume 23 Number 4, Summer, 2016.

Farber, David. *The Sixties: From Memory to History*. Univ. South Carolina. 1994.

Field, Henry. "Biographical Sketches of Hitler and Himmler." Memorandum. *Office of Strategic Services (OSS)*. 03 Dec. 1943.

FBI Files. February 2, 1980. Famous Cases and Criminals. Abscam.

Fearnow, Benjamin. "Viral 'Crime Infested' Trump Organization Thread Details Convicted Criminals, Russian Mobster Tenants Over the Years." *Newsweek*. 01 Aug. 2019.

Federal Bureau of Investigation. Subject: Armand Hammer/Occidental Petroleum. File No. 61-280. 14 June 1921.

FHA Investigation. Hearings Before the Committee on Banking and Currency. United States Senate. 83rd Congress. 2nd Session. According to S. Resolution 229. Gov't Printing Office 1954. pp. 395-420.

Fitzpatrick, Derek Maj. "Greed and Grievance and Drug Cartels: Mexico's Commercial Insurgency." Master's Thesis. *U.S. Army Command and General Staff College.* 25 May 2017.

Flood, Alison. "Hitler speeches published with Donald Trump as cover illustration." *The Guardian.* 03 Oct. 2016.

Folsom, Riley. "In the Land of Gods and Monsters." In Hoy, Pat C. 2013. *Mercer Street 2013-2014: a collection of essays from the expository writing program.* New York: Expository Writing Program, New York University College of Arts and Sciences.

Forum Daily. "Former Kiev resident earned millions of dollars on insurance fraud in the USA." *Voice of Russian Speaking America.* 17 Nov. 2017.

Forrest, Adam. "Trump suggested 'black vs. whites' games in The Apprentice." *The Independent.* 22 Jul. 2019.

Foucault, Michel. *Du gouvernement des vivants.* Cours au Collège de France 1979–1980, ed. M. Senellart, Paris: Seuil/Gallimard 2012, pp. 92–94.

FOX News. "Trump Declines to Run for President, Cites 'Passion' for Business." *FOX News Network.* 16 May 2011.

France-Presse. Agency. "White supremacists and neo-Nazis: 'We need to have Donald Trump's back.'" *The Telegraph News.* 16 Aug. 2017.

Franz Kafka. "In it, a protagonist known only as "K." arrives in a village and struggles to access the mysterious authorities who govern it from a castle. Kafka died before he could finish the work, but suggested it would end with K. dying in the village. The castle notifying him on his death bed that his "legal claim to live in the village was not valid, yet, taking certain auxiliary circumstances into account, he was permitted to live and work there." Dark and at times surreal, *The Castle* is often understood to be about alienation, unresponsive bureaucracy, the frustration of trying to conduct business with non-transparent, seemingly arbitrary controlling systems, and the futile pursuit of an unobtainable goal." ---Wikipedia

Freud, Sigmund. "The Uncanny" First published in Imago, Bd. V., 1919; reprinted in Sammlung, Fünfte Folge. [Translated by Alix Strachey.]

Fryer, Roland G., and Levitt, Steven D. "Hatred and Profits: Under the Hood of the Ku Klux Klan.", *The Quarterly Journal of Economics*, Volume 127, Issue 4, November 2012, Pages 1883–1925.

Gais, Hannah. "Leaked Emails Show How White Nationalists Have Infiltrated Conservative Media." *Splinter.* 29 Aug. 2019.

Galeotti, Mark. "Gangster's paradise: how the organized crime took over Russia." *The Guardian.* 23 Mar. 2018.

Galstyan, Areg. "Third Rome Rising: The Ideologues Calling for a New Russian Empire: The neo-Byzantines believe Moscow will save Christendom." *The National Interest.* 27 Jun. 2016.

Gandesha, Samir. "The Spectre of the 1930s." Undated Paper. Samir Gandesha is an Associate Professor in the Department of the Humanities and the Director of the Institute for the Humanities at Simon Fraser University. See also: Adorno, T.W. 1982. "Freudian Theory and the Pattern of Fascist Propaganda," *Essential Frankfurt School Reader*, Andrew Arato and Eike Gebhardt (eds.) (New York: Continuum): p.118-137.

Garcia, Berenice. "Judge partially dismisses lawsuit in Honduran man's suicide." *The Monitor.* 03 Jul. 2020.

Garcia-Navarro, Lulu. "'Hatemonger' Tracks How Right-Wing Media Shaped Trump Policy Architect Stephen Miller." *National Public Radio.* 16 Aug. 2020.

Gardner, Timothy. "U.S. approved secret nuclear power work for Saudi Arabia." *Reuters.* 27 Mar. 2019.

Goebbels, Joseph. "Der Führer als Redner," *Adolf Hitler. Bilder aus dem Leben des Führers* (Hamburg: Cigaretten/Bilderdienst Hamburg/Bahrenfeld, 1936, pp. 27-34.

Gilman, Nils. "The Twin Insurgencies: Plutocrats and Criminals Challenge the Westphalian State." PRISM. *National Defense University*. 25 Oct. 2016.

Gitta Sereny's presentation, near the beginning of the Inner Circle Seminar, '*Into That Darkness 30 Years On: The Psychology of Extermination*', conducted by Gitta Sereny, Michael Tregenza, and Anthony Stadlen, on Sunday 10 October 2004 in the Herringham Hall, Regent's College, London. Reproduced with the permission of Jeffrey A. Schaler. All rights reserved.

Glasser, Susan B. "Mike Pompeo, the Secretary of Trump." *The New Yorker*. 26 Aug. 2019.

Goldberg, Michelle. "Norway Massacre: Anders Breivik's Deadly Attack Fueled by Hatred of Women." *The Daily Beast*. 24 Jul. 2011.

Gordon, Michael R., and Timothy Puko. "Trump Calls for Control, Use of Syrian Oil Fields." *Wall Street Journal*. 22 Oct. 2019.

Gornick, Vivian. "When Communism Inspired Americans." *The New York Times*. 29 April 2017.

Gosling, Tim. "Murder, mafia, and Nazis loom over Slovak election." *Aljazeera*. 21 Feb. 2020.

Gravitational: Referring to what Ian Kershaw described as "moving toward the Führer."

Gowen, Annie. "Trump Organization's real estate partner in India accused of $147 million fraud." *The Washington Post*. 19 Mar. 2018.

Gozman, Leonid, and Paul A. Goble. "With his changes to Russian Constitution, Putin has suffered a serious defeat, Gozman says." Euromaidan 22 Jan. 2020 International, Op-ed.

Gray, Emma. "The History of Using White Female Sexuality to Justify Racist Violence." *HuffPost*. 19 Jun. 2015.Greek, Cecil E. *Monsters in and Among Us Toward a Gothic Criminology*. Fairleigh Dickinson University Press. 2007. ISBN: 97808386 41590, 0838641598.

Green, B. David. "1990: Armand Hammer, Who Was Named for the Symbol of Socialism, Dies." *Haartz*. 10 Dec. 2015.

Gregg, Aaron. "Trump administration won't say who got $511 billion in taxpayer-backed coronavirus loans." 11 Jun. 2020. *The Washington Post*.

Gross, J. Samantha, and David Smiley. "Pardoned soldiers are Trump's special guests at a closed-door fundraiser in Aventura." *Miami Herald*. 07 Dec. 2019.

Grossman, Vasily. Robert Chadler Ed. *The Road: Journalism and Essays*. NYRB Classics; 1st edition (September 28, 2010) ISBN-10: 1590173619.

Gruenberg, Mark. "Historians find parallels between Hitler's Nazis and today's "alt-right." *The Daily World*. A publication associated with the Communist Party USA. 11 Jan. 2018.

Guariglia, Matt. "Billionaire Trump Funder Also Paid for Milo Yiannopoulos' College Speaking Tour." *Motherboard, Vice News*. 27 March 2017.

Gubenko, Igors. "Haunting futures: the disjointed temporality of collective memory." *HCAS, University of Helsinki/University of Latvia*. Undated.

Gustav von Kahr (November 29, 1862 – June 30, 1934) was a German right-wing conservative politician, active in Bavaria. He was instrumental in Adolf Hitler's Beer Hall Putsch's failure in 1923 and was subsequently put to death more than ten years later in the Night of the Long Knives.

Hans Fritzsche (1900–1953) was head of the radio division of the German propaganda ministry. A relatively minor propaganda ministry official who had not held a policy-making position, Fritzsche was included in the dock at Nuremberg in the absence of the deceased Joseph Goebbels and to mollify Soviet authorities, who held him in their custody.

Harding, Luke. "Marina Salye obituary." *Guardian*. 28 Mar. 2012.

Harding, Luke. "The hidden history of Trump's first trip to Moscow." *Politico*. 22 Nov. 2017.

Havel, Václav. *The Power of the Powerless*. October 1978. Original rough essay. Author deceased 18 Dec. 2011.

Hedges, Chris. *American Fascists: The Christian Right and the War on America*. Free Press. 2006.

Heim, Joe. "National Archives exhibit blurs images critical of President Trump." *The Washington Post*. 18 Jan. 2020.

Heller, Kevin, and Gerry Simpson. *The Hidden Histories of War Crimes Trials*. Oxford University Press; 1 edition. Oxford University Press. 30 Dec. 2013. Also, read Oxford University Online "Capitalism's Victor's Justice? The Hidden Stories Behind the Prosecution of Industrialists Post-WWII." by Grietje Baars.

Hersh, Seymour N. "The Scene of the Crime A reporter's journey to My Lai and the secrets of the past." *The New Yorker Magazine*. 30 Mar. 1968.

Hill, Fiona, and Clifford G. Gaddy. *Mr. Putin: Operative in the Kremlin*. Brookings Institution Press (November 27, 2012).

Hiram Wesley Evans, "The Klan's Fight for Americanism," *The North American Review* (March-April-May 1926).

Hitler, Adolf. *Public Speech. Munich, November 1941*. Cited in The Bulletin of International News, Royal Institute of International Affairs, XVIII, No 5, 1941, p 269.

Hitler's Table Talk, 1941-1944: His Private Conversations, 39.

Hoke, Henry. *Black Mail*. Reader's Book Service, Inc., July 1944.

Holley, Peter. "KKK's official newspaper supports Donald Trump for president." *The Washington Post*. 02 Nov. 2016.

Holocaust denial in Trump seems to derive from conspiracy theory websites: The Unz Review is a "mix of far-right and far-left anti-Semitic crackpottery, from 9/11 'truther' and conspiracy theorist Paul Craig Roberts to 'Holocaust industry' critic Norman Finkelstein, who believes Jews exploit the Holocaust to justify oppressing Palestinians." In Bevensee, Emmi, and Alexander Reid Ross. "Alt-Right and Global Information Warfare." Instructor, *Department of Geography, Portland State University*. Portland, Oregon, USA. aross@pdx.edu. Undated.

Holmes, Steven A., "A Drug Dealer, Finds Many Eager to Launder His Drug Money." *The New York Times*. 24 Jan. 1990.

Holodny, Elena. "Exxon got stuck in the middle as Russia-US relations broke down — and needs a solution soon." *Business Insider*. 05 July 2017.

Horrock, Nicholas, and Lynette Myers. "Extradition Target Says His Real Crime Is Success." *Chicago Tribune*. 03 Apr. 1992.

Hudson, G.F. "Khrushchev's Visit: The German Problem Remains Possibilities for a Settlement." *Commentary*. Oct. 1959.

Hudson, Michael, et al. "How New York Real Estate Became a Dumping Ground for the World's Dirty Money." *The Nation*. 03 Jul. 2014.

Hueven, Marten van. "Sense of the Community" Report on Yugoslavia. Declassified. NIC-03236-88. CIA File. 31 Oct. 1988.

Hundal, Sunny. "White people don't seem to realize that eventually, the far-right will come for them too." *The Independent*. 06 Mar. 2018.

Hunter, Edward. *Testimony*. Committee on Un-American Activities, House of Representatives, Eighty-Fifth Congress, Second Session, 13 Mar. 1958, Printed for the use of the Committee on Un-American Activities United States Government Printing Office, Washington 1958.

Hrabovsky, Serhii. "Lenin. Money. Revolution: The shady side of the Bolshevik activities." УкраїнськаРусский English. *The Day*. Ukraine. Issue: №24 (2010). 22 April 2010.

Ingraham, Christopher. "U.S. lawmakers are redistributing income from the poor to the rich, according to a massive new study." *The Washington Post*. 15 Dec. 2017.

Intermarriage. The use of marriage to form strong bonds across cultures in crime families is suspected to be taken from the Bible, "Some parts of it will be as strong as iron, and others as weak as clay. This mixture of iron and clay also shows that these kingdoms will strengthen themselves by forming alliances with each other through intermarriage.

But this will not succeed, just as iron and clay do not mix."-- Daniel 2:38-43.

Israel, Josh. "20,000 Republicans just voted for an actual Nazi." *ThinkProgress*. 21 Mar. 2018.

Jackson-Vanik Amendment to the U.S.-Soviet Trade Bill, which became law in 1974, was to play a significant role in Soviet-American relations until the collapse of the Soviet Union in 1991. The Jackson-Vanik Amendment had its origins in 1972. In response to the sharp increase in the number of Soviet Jews seeking to leave the Soviet Union, primarily because of rising Soviet anti-Semitism, the Brezhnev regime imposed a prohibitively expensive exit tax on educated Jews who wanted to go. –Encyclopedia.com.

Jasch, Hans-Christian, and Christoph Kreutzmüller. *The Participants*. The Men of the Wannsee Conference. Berghahn New York and Oxford. 2017.

Jewish Telegraph Agency. "Viereck Called Chief Nazi Propagandist in U.S." 17 Dec. 1933.

Johnston, David Cay. "Just What Were Donald Trump's Ties to the Mob?" *POLITICO*. 22 May 2016.

Johnston, David Cay. "The Drug Trafficker Donald Trump Risked His Casino Empire to Protect." *The Daily Beast*. 16 Oct. 2016.

Joyce, Kathryn. "The Threat of International Adoption for Migrant Children Separated from Their Families." *The Intercept*. 1 Jul. 2018.

Julius Streicher, the publisher of *Der Stürmer*, was executed as a war criminal in 1946.

Jung, G. Carl. "Essay on Wotan." WOTAN, Neue Schweizer Rundschau (Zurich). N .s., III (March 1936), 657-69. Republished in AUFSATZE ZURZEITGESCHICHTE (Zurich, 1946), 1-23. Trans. by Barbara Hannah in ESSAYS ON CONTEMPORARY EVENTS (London, 1947), 1-16; this version has been consulted. Motto, trans. By H.C. Roberts:].

Kalinichenko, Dmitry. "Grandmaster Putin's Golden Trap." *Information Clearinghouse*. 25 Dec. 2014.

Kaplan, J. (2001) The post-war paths of occult national socialism: from Rockwell and Madole to Manson, Patterns of Prejudice, 35:3, 41-67.

Kaplan, Sophie. "Trump raised more dollars from small donations." *Politifact*. 13 Nov. 2017.

Kara-Murza, Vladamir. "John McCain saw through Vladimir Putin better than anyone." *The Washington Post*. Opinion. 27 Aug. 2018.

Kaufman, Will. *Woody Guthry American Radical*. Univ. of Illinois. 2011.

Kekes, John. "What Is Conservatism?" *Philosophy*, vol. 72, no. 281, 1997, pp. 351–374. *JSTOR*.

Kennard, Matt. "The modern US Army: unfit for service?" *The Guardian*. 31 Aug. 2012.

Khiterer, Victoria, and Abigail S Gruber. *Holocaust Resistance in Europe and America: New Aspects and Dilemmas*. Cambridge Scholars Publishing. 2017.

Kirillova, Kseniya. "I was told we should work with fascists: former KGB officer Zhirnov." *Euromaidan Press*. 03 Dec. 2018.

Kirillova, Kseniya. Hybrid War. "The hard fate of foreign Russia-lovers: Ksenia Kirillova on the Paul Whelan case." *Euromaidan Press*. 17 Feb. 2017.

"Khrushchev's Secret Speech, 'On the Cult of Personality and Its Consequences,' Delivered at the Twentieth Party Congress of the Communist Party of the Soviet Union," February 25, 1956, History and Public Policy Program Digital Archive, From the Congressional Record: Proceedings and Debates of the 84th Congress, 2nd Session (May 22, 1956-June 11, 1956), C11, Part 7 (June 4, 1956), pp. 9389-9403. Wilson Center Archive.

Kleptocracy, or "rule by thieves," arises when a country's elite begin to systematically steal from public funds on a vast scale. They do so by undermining democracy and the legal system, gaining control over vital economic assets (usually the banking and natural-resource sectors), and ultimately amassing unimaginable wealth.

Kramer, Andrew E. "Gorbachev Calls Trump's Nuclear Treaty Withdrawal 'Not the Work of a Great Mind.'" *The New York Times*. 21 Oct. 2018.

Kubizek, August. *The Young Hitler I Knew: The Definitive Inside Look at the Artist Who Became a Monster*. Arcade; Reprint edition 13 July 2011. See Murray, Henry. "Subject: Adolph Hitler" CIA File. Central Intelligence Agency. Declassified. 18 May 2000.

Kumar, Anita. "Buyers tied to Russia; former Soviet republics paid $109 million in cash for Trump properties." *McClatchy Reports, D.C.* 19 Jun. 2019.

Kunst, Jonas R., and John F. Dovidio, Lotte Thomsen. "Fusion with political leaders predicts willingness to persecute immigrants and political opponents." *Nature of Human Behavior*. 02 Sept. 2019.

Ladd, Christopher. "Pastors, Not Politicians, Turned Dixie Republican." *Forbes*. 27 Mar. 2017.

Laing, R.D. *Politics of the Family*. Vintage Books Edition Sept. 1972.

Lamothe, Dan. "Trump issues pardons in war crimes cases, despite Pentagon opposition to the move." *The Washington Post*. 19 Nov. 2019.

Langer, Walter C. Psychological Analysis of Adolph Hitler. CIA File. *Central Intelligence Agency*. Declassified August 1999.

Lapenkova, Marina. "Russia's powerful 'Thieves in Law' face reckoning under Putin." *Agence-France Presse*. 12 March 2019.

Laub, D. (1998)." The empty circle. Children of survivors and the limits of reconstruction." *Journal of the American Psychoanalytic Association*. 46 (2), 508–529. In Laub, Dori. "Testimonies in the Treatment of Genocidal Trauma." *Journal of Applied Psychoanalytic Studies* (2002).

Layne, Nathan and Ned Parker, Svetlana Reiter, Stephen Grey, and Ryan McNeill. "Russian elite invested nearly $100 million in Trump buildings." *Reuters News Agency*. 17 Mar. 2017.

Lebenswelt. Noun. *Philosophy*. The totality of a person's or society's immediate or everyday experiences, interactions, etc., is mostly considered to underlie a subconscious, presupposed, or unreflective understanding of the nature of human knowledge and existence.

Lebourg, N. "Arriba Eurasia?" in Eurasianism and the European Far Right: Reshaping the Europe-Russia Relationship, M. Laruelle, Ed. Boulder, CO: Lexington Books, 2015, pp. 125–142.

Lee, Martin A. (1997). *The Beast Reawakens*. Little, Brown, and Company. ISBN 9780316519595.

Lengyel, Emil. "The Battlecries of Hitlerism Modified as Election Nears." *The New York Times*. 10 July 1932.

LeTourneau, Nancy. "'Evidence of the President's Mental Incapacity is Overwhelming." *Washington Monthly*. 10 Jun. 2019.

Laruelle, Marlene. *Eurasianism and the European Far Right: Reshaping the Europe–Russia Relationship*. ISBN-13: 978-1498510707. Lexington Books (March 24, 2017).

Levi, Mark, and Michael Rothberg. "Memory studies in a moment of danger: Fascism, post-fascism, and the contemporary political imaginary." *Sage Publications*. Memory Studies 2018, Vol. 11(3) 355 – 367.

Lewis, Matt. "The Last Trump Defense: Attacking Him Is Attacking America." *The Daily Beast*. 24 Aug. 2019.

Liu, Jinyuan. "Correlation and agreement: overview and clarification of competing concepts and measures." Shanghai Archive of Psychiatry. 2016 Apr 25; 28(2): 115–120.

Lindisfarne, Nancy, and Jonathan Neale. "Pence, Trump and Evangelicals." *Cumhuriyet*. E-Newspaper. Turkish. 12 August 2018.

Liptak, Kevin, Daniella Diaz, and Sophie Tatum. "Trump pardons former Sheriff Joe Arpaio." *CNN Broadcasting*. 27 Aug. 2017.

Lockett, Jon. "Lord of The World. Psychic Baba Vanga, who predicted the 9/11 terror attacks, also foretold 'unstoppable' Vladimir Putin will one day rule Earth." *The Sun*. 19 March 2018.

Longhurst, John. "Trump's presidency, 'Christian supremacism' criticized at Parliament of World Religion." *Religious News Service*. 06 Nov. 2018.

Longman, Martin. "Bannon and Breitbart's Nazi Ties." *Washington Monthly*. 06 Oct. 2017.

López, Victoria. Senior Staff Attorney, ACLU National Prison Project & Sandra Park, Senior Staff Attorney, ACLU Women's Rights Project. "ICE Detention Center Says It's Not Responsible for Staff's Sexual Abuse of Detainees." *American Civil Liberties Union*. Report. 06 Nov. 2018.

Lorenzini, Daniele. "What is a 'Regime of Truth'?", in: *Le foucaldien*, 1/1 (2015).

Luhn, Alec. "International Russian Organized Crime Ring Does Old-School Gambling in a New Way." *The Organized Crime and Corruption Reporting Project* (OCCRP); is a global network of investigative journalists. 13 May 2013.

Lungren, Daniel E., and Cowart, Gregory G. *Russian Organized Crime*. State of California Office of the Attorney General, Attorney General, March 1996. P.O. Box 163020, Sacramento, CA 95816-3029.

Lustig, Doreen. "The Nature of the Nazi State and the Question of International Criminal Responsibility of Corporate Officials at Nuremberg: Revisiting Franz Neumann's Concept of Behemoth at the Industrialist Trials." J.S.D Candidate, IILJ Scholar, NYU School of Law. INTERNATIONAL LAW AND POLITICS [Vol. 43:965}.

Macapagal, Katrina Angela R. "HERE LIES LOVE Notes on Fetishizing History." Review of Women's Studies 21 (1): 38-53. Center for Women's Studies, University of the Philippines ISSN 0117-9489.

MacAskill, Ewen. "Donald Trump bows out of the 2012 US presidential election race." *The Guardian*. 16 May 2011.

Machiavelli, The Prince. (XVIII, 3).

Maddow, Rachel. *Blowout: Corrupted Democracy, Rogue State Russia, and the Richest, Most Destructive Industry on Earth*. Crown; First Edition (October 1, 2019). ISBN-10: 0525575472.

Magnitsky Act: The Magnitsky Act, formally known as the Russia and Moldova Jackson–Vanik Repeal and Sergei Magnitsky Rule of Law Accountability Act of 2012, is a bipartisan bill passed by the U.S. Congress and signed into law by President Barack Obama in December

2012, intending to punish Russian officials responsible for the death of Russian tax accountant Sergei Magnitsky in a Moscow prison in 2009.-Wikipedia.

Mallin, Alexander. "I am talking directly to you': US attorney delivers powerful rebuke to white nationalists." *ABC News*. 29 Aug. 2019.

Maan, Ajit. "Narratives are about 'meaning,' not 'truth," *Foreign Policy*, December 3, 2015. Jan H. Kalvik, "Interview with Dr. Ajit Maan, Narrative Strategies," Defense and Intelligence Norway, March 17, 2018. And Ajit Maan, "Plato's Fear: The Power of Poetry Over National Security," *Homeland Security Today*, 1 March, 2019.

Mann, Brian. "Opioid-Makers Face Wave of Lawsuits in 2019." *NPR*. 31 Dec. 2018.

Mansoor, Sanya. "Johnson & Johnson Was Ordered to Pay $572 Million for Its Role in the Opioid Crisis. With Similar Lawsuits Across the Country, That Could Be Just the Beginning." *Time*. 28 Aug. 2019.

Marritz, Ilyaya. WNYC and Justin Elliott, "Trump's Inauguration Paid Trump's Company — With Ivanka in the Middle." *ProPublica*. 14 Dec. 2018.

Marrs, Jim. *The Rise of the Fourth Reich: The Secret Societies That Threaten to Take Over America*. William Morrow Paperbacks; Reprint edition (June 23, 2009). ISBN-10: 0061245593. ISBN-13: 978-0061245596.

Marx, Karl. *The Eighteenth Brumaire of Louis Bonaparte*. (1852) International Publishers. June 1994. ISBN-13: 978-0717800568. Note: Bonapartism has been used more generally for a political movement that advocated a dictatorship or authoritarian centralized state, with a charismatic strongman leader based on anti-elitist rhetoric, army support, and conservatism. Marx argued that in the process, Bonapartists preserve and mask the power of a narrower ruling class. See the Free Dictionary.

May, Ruth. "How Putin's Oligarch's Funneled Millions into GOP Campaigns." *The Dallas Morning News*. 08 May 2018.

McAllister. Margaret and Donna Lee Brien. "Haunted: Exploring Representations of Mental Health Through the Lens of the Gothic." *Central Queensland Univ.* July 2015.

Media Matters Staff, "Anti-Semitic Fox News contributor Robert Jeffress attacks the Pope as a 'globalist' who wants 'a one-world government,'" *Media Matters*, 02, Nov. 2018.

Mehta, Vinita (Ph.D.) "Why Liberals and Conservatives Think so Differently." *Psychology Today*. 17 Feb. 2017.

Meyer, Theodoric. "Flynn lobbied for Turkish-linked firm after election, documents show." *Politico*. 08 Mar. 2017.

Michel, Casey. "Russian attempts to woo American white supremacists have backfired." *Think Progress*. 20 April 2017.

Michael, Robert; Rosen, Philip (2007). *Dictionary of Antisemitism from the Earliest Times to the Present*. Lanham, Maryland: Scarecrow Press. ISBN 978-0-8108-5868-8. Positive Christianity is in the Nazi Party platform Article 24 1920 that dictates Christianity must be favorable toward the Nazi racial purity and German nationalist goals.

Milbank. Dana. "Holy Moses. Mike Pompeo thinks Trump is Queen Esther." *The Washington Post*. 27 Mar. 2019.

Milton, Michael A. Ph.D. "What Are "Sins of the Father"? Understanding Generational Consequences." *James Ragsdale Chair of Missions at Erskine Theological Seminary. He is the President of Faith for Living and the D. James Kennedy Institute*. 17 Feb. 2020.

Mimesis is a term with an undeniably classical pedigree. Originally a Greek word, it has been used in aesthetic or artistic theory to refer to the attempt to imitate or reproduce reality since Plato and Aristotle. -Miriam Webster.

Moran, Lee. "Donald Trump Lied About Almost Dying in Helicopter Crash, Ex-Employee Says." *Huffington Post*. 31 Jul. 2019.

Moore, Jack. "Surprise! Exxon Wants a Waiver to Work in Russia Despite Sanctions." *GQ*. 20 Apr. 2017.

Morgan, Windsor. "Officer who walked into the wrong apartment and killed man faces arrest: Authorities." *ABC News*. 07 Sept. 2017.

Mortimer, Caroline. "Donald Trump's mother asked: 'What kind of son have I created?'." *The Independent*. 04 Nov. 2017.

Mosse, George L. The Fascist Revolution: Toward a General Theory of Fascism (New York: H. Fertig, 1999). Saul Friedländer, Reflections of Nazism: An Essay on Kitsch and Death (Bloomington: Indiana University Press, 1993).

Murphy, Bruce. "City a Leader in White Nationalism: New Berlin is headquarters for a neo-Nazi party founded by George Lincoln Rockwell." *Urban Milwaukee*. 01 Nov. 2018.

Murray, Henry A. "Analysis of The Personality of Adolph Hitler." *Office of Strategic Services (OSS)*. Central Intelligence Agency Archive. Copy No. 14 of 30. Harvard Psychological Clinic. October 1943.

National Republican. A member of a political party formed in opposition to the Jacksonian Democrats. After being decisively defeated in the presidential election of 1832 fused with other elements to create the Whig party. –Miriam Webster. President Donald J. Trump announced he was a nationalist. 24 Oct. 2018.

Nazaryan, Alexander. "Trump is Leading the Most Corrupt Administration in U.S. History, One of First Class Kleptocrats." *Newsweek*. 02 Nov. 2017.

NBC News London. "Auschwitz Survivor Gena Turgel Walked Out of Gas Chamber Alive." 26 Jan. 2015.

Nedelkoff, Robert. "The Last of The Watergate Cubans Speaks." *Nixon Foundation Governing Documents*. 31 Oct. 2009.

Nelson, J.S. "Paper Dragon Thieves." *The Georgetown Law Review*. [Vol. 105:87 2017} B.A. Yale University; J.D. Harvard Law School; Advisor, Center for Entrepreneurial Studies, Stanford Graduate School of Business; and Senior Fellow, The Carol and Lawrence Zicklin Center for Business Ethics Research, The Wharton School, University of Pennsylvania.

New Statesman. "What does entryism mean?" *The New Statesman.* 10 August 2016.

Nihilism. The doctrine of an extreme Russian revolutionary party c.1900 found nothing to approve of in the established social order. Politically it leaned toward knowledge is not possible, or reality does not actually exist.

Nippert, Regina, "Mixing Christianity and Politics Is Killing the Church." *The Hill.* 29 May 2015.

Nisbet, Eric C., and Olga Kamenchuk. "3 charts explain how Russians see Trump and US." *The Conversation.* 13 July 2018.

Nixon, Rob. *Slow Violence and the Environmentalism of the Poor.* Cambridge: Harvard University Press, 2011.

Nolan MS, Aguilar D, Brown EL, Gunter SM, Ronca SE, et al. (2018) *Continuing evidence of Chagas disease along the Texas-Mexico border.* PLOS Neglected Tropical Diseases 12(11): e0006899.

Nuccitelli, Dana. "Trump and the Republican Party Are Dong Big Oil's Bidding." *The Guardian.* 14 Sept. 2016.

Odessa Code Name for 'Organisation der Ehemaligen SS-Angehörigen', in English — 'Organisation of Former SS Members.' Seeking escape from Nazi territory to escape to South America and the Middle East.

O'Malley, JP. "Trotsky's day out: How a visit to NYC influenced the Bolshevik revolution." *The Times of Israel.* 19 Sept. 2016.

Osenenko, Robert (Ed.D.) *Donald J. Trump, An American Dilemma.* Independent Publisher and Amazon. 01 June 2019. ISBN-13: 978-1096064473.

Overby, Peter. "Trump's Cabinet Scandals: Is Abuse of Office Contagious?" *NPR.* 08 Mar. 2018.

Pach, Chester J., Jr. Associate Professor of History Ohio University "Dwight D. Eisenhower: Domestic Affairs." Miller Center. The University of Virginia. Undated.

Palma, Oscar. "Criminal Interests within Political Insurgencies: The Case for Development-Centred Counterinsurgency." In *Handbook of Research on Transitional Justice and Peace Building in Turbulent*

Regions. Universidad del Rosario, Colombia. 2016. ISBN13: 9781466696754.

Papenfuss, Mary "GOP Rep Slams Trump's Quoting of Pastor's 'Civil War' Warning As 'Beyond Repugnant,'" *Huffington Post*, 30 Sept. 2019.

Parvus, Alexander. Russian Revolutionaries: 1914-20. Sparticus Educational.

Pascoe, Carla. "Silence and the History of Menstruation." *Oral History Association of Australia Journal* No. 29, 200728.

Patrick J. Buchanan, "A fire bell in the night for Norway," *World Net Daily*, July 25, 2011, See In "The Camp of the Saints Worldview" essay by James Scaminaci III, Ph.D. Copyright: CC BY 4.0.

Payne, Robert. *The Life and Death of Adolf Hitler.* (New York, New York: Praeger Publishers, 1973).

Pearce, Matt. "Stephen Bannon found inspiration in ancient thinkers, Ronald Reagan and Nazi propaganda." *Los Angeles Times.* 09 Dec. 2016.

Pearson, Jake. "Notorious Russian Mobster Says He Just Wants to Go Home." *NBC Universal Media, LLC.* 27 Jan. 2018.

Percy, Martyn. "To know Donald Trump's faith is to understand his politics." *Guardian.* 06 Feb. 2018.

Persona: the psychic interface between the individual and society that makes up a Person's social identity. It is the person we become due to acculturation, education, and adaptation to our physical and social environments.

Piaget, J. (1969). Piaget's theory. In P. H. Mussen (ed.) *Carmichael's manual of child psychology.* New York, John Wiley.

Picciolini, Christian. House Committee on Foreign Affairs Subcommittee on the Middle East, North Africa, and International Terrorism. House Committee on Homeland Security Subcommittee on Intelligence and Terrorism. 18 Spt. 2019.

Pierce, P. Charles. "Surely It's a Coincidence That a Firm Tied to a Russian Oligarch Is Pouring Millions into Kentucky." *Esquire*. 24 April 2019.

Pierce, P. Charles. "The Russia Scandal Was Desperately Missing a Biker Gang Subplot. Well, Here It Is." *Esquire*. 26 Jun. 2017.

Plutchik, Robert. *The Emotions*. University Press of America; Revised edition (July 25, 1991). ISBN-10: 0819182869. ISBN-13: 978-0819182869. Chapter 1. "Measuring Emotions and Their Derivatives."

Political Architecture: "Firstly, the architecture supports the system with a structural model used by society to conceptualize the world, making it connected with political power, as Mitchell Kapor "Architecture is politics." Hence there is a structural relationship between the social and political sides. Architecture reveals the power that is embodied in it and specifically the monumental architecture that is formed by the political powers." In "Relationship Between Architecture and Politics." UKEssays.com. 11, 2018. All Answers Ltd. 11 2019

Polyakova, Alina. "How Russia Meddled in its Own Elections." *The Atlantic*. 18 Mar. 2018.

Prados, John. "The John Walker Spy Ring and The U.S. Navy's Biggest Betrayal." *US Naval Institute News*. 02 Sept. 2014.

President George H. W. Bush - Nuclear Events. A project of the Nuclear Age Peace Foundation. Nuclear Files.Org. Note President Mikhail Gorbachev.

Prestigiacomo, Amanda. "Both Trump and Clinton Went to Jeffrey Epstein's Sex Slave Island." *The Daily Wire*. 16 May 2016.

Price, Ned. "Good Riddance to CIA Director Pompeo." *Foreign Policy*. 16 Mar. 2018.

Psy-Ops. Psychological warfare, or the fundamental aspects of modern psychological operations, has been known by many other names or terms, including MISO, Psy Ops, political conflict, "Hearts and Minds," and propaganda. The term is used "to denote any action which is practiced mainly by psychological methods to evoke a planned psychological reaction in other people." Wikipedia.

Pynchon, Thomas. *Inherent Vice Quotes*. Published August 4th, 2009 by The Penguin Press.

Radford, Michael. Directed the movie. 1984. A book was written by George Orwell. *Secker & Warburg*, United Kingdom publishers. 08 June 1949.

Radical Republicans. In December 1861, frustrated at the poor showing of the Union Army and the lack of progress toward emancipation, the Radicals formed the Joint Committee on the Conduct of the War. They agitated for the dismissal of Gen. George B. McClellan, and they favored the enlistment of black troops. For his reluctance to move toward speedy abolition, Angry at Lincoln broke with him entirely over Reconstruction policy. —Encyclopedia Britannica

Ramsey, Adam. "Cambridge Analytica is what happens when you privatize military propaganda. " *Open Democracy*. 28 Mar. 2018.

Rauschning, Hermann. *Hitler Speaks A Series of Political Conversations with Adolf Hitler on His Real Aims*. Kessinger Publishing, LLC (September 10, 2010). ISBN-13: 978-1162934914.

Reed, Charles. "Charles Reed, guest columnist: Courts must decide if our presidents are truly above the people's law." *Waco Tribune-Herald*. 08 June 2019.

Riebling, Mark. "Chomsky is a Conservative - CIA author confusion." Conservatism Turned Upside Down, Sam Tanenhaus.s articulate and timely critique of conservative reason. 16 Oct. 2009.

Reich, Walter. "The World View of Soviet Psychiatry." *The New York Times*. 30 Jan. 1983.

Reich, Wilhelm. *The Mass Psychology of Fascism*. Third Edition. Translator Theodore P. Wolfe. Orgone Institute Press. 1946.

Reich, Wilhelm. William Steig, Ralph Manheim. *Listen, Little Man*. Published in 1946. Noonday/Farrar, Straus & Giroux (NYC).

Reiss, Tom. "The First Conservative: How Peter Viereck inspired-and lost-a movement." *The New Yorker*. 24 Oct. 2005.

Rejection. This continuity over time of beliefs rejected by the mainstream is called the "underground of rejected knowledge" in his 1976 book, *The Occult Establishment*, James Webb. Those who find themselves alienated from society are likely to identify established knowledge with the established social order. Therefore, turn to "rejected knowledge" as a basis of their rejection of the mainstream. See American Council on Science and Health. 13 Sept. 2002.

Republicanism. Modern republicanism is a guiding political philosophy of the United States that has been part of American civic thought since its founding. It stresses liberty and unalienable individual rights as central. Making people sovereign as a whole; rejects monarchy, aristocracy, and hereditary political power, rejects direct democracy, expects citizens to be virtuous and faithful in their civic duties, and vilifies corruption. –Wikipedia.

Research Brief. START. National Consortium for The Study of Terrorism and Responses to Terrorism. 2018. See Jensen, Michael A., Patrick A. James, Gary LaFree, Anita Atwell-Seate, Daniela Pisoiu, and John Stevenson. 2016. Empirical Assessment of Domestic Radicalization (EADR). Final Report. National Institute of Justice, Award Number 2012–ZA–BX–0005. National Consortium for the Study of Terrorism and Responses to Terrorism (START), College Park, MD.

Rice, Boyd. "Cold War Cocktails: Last call at Checkpoint Charlie." Blog. Dec. 06.

Ripley, Anthony. "Guilt Admitted by A Nixon Donor." *The New York Times*. Archive. 11 Dec. 1974.

Roberts, James M. "Citgo and Joseph P. Kennedy: Hugo Chavez's Agents of Influence." *The Heritage Foundation*. 23 Jan. 2008.

Robertson, Campbell. "Unpaid Miners Blocked a Coal Train in Protest. Weeks Later, They're Still There." *The New York Times*. 19 Aug. 2019.

Rocchi, Tony. "The Myth of Fascism: misuse of a political construct." The author is a librarian in the Business, Science, and Technology Department of the Toronto Reference Library in Toronto, Ontario, Canada. This work was an unpublished paper. 09 Sept. 2019.

Rodriguez, Adrianna. "Texas' lieutenant governor suggests grandparents are willing to die for the US economy." *USA Today.* 24 Mar. 2020.

Romanticism (Huckleberry Finn) was characterized by emphasizing emotion and individualism and glorification of all the past and nature, preferring the medieval rather than the classical. ... It also promoted the individual imagination as a critical authority that allowed for freedom from traditional notions of form in art. *Realism* is intended to portray the lives of the common man, the ethical struggles, and the social issues of real-life situations. Credits: Britannica Encyclopedia, Mary Dorene Erickson The University of Montana.

Rosenberg, Alfred and Wilhelm Weib, Reichsparteitag der NSDAP Nürnberg 19. /21. Munich: Verlag Frz. Eher. August 1927. pp. 30-32.

Rothfeld, Michael, and Alexandra Berzon. "Donald Trump and the Mob." *The Wall Street Journal.* 01 Sept. 2016.

Rupar, Aaron. "Trump's push to hold the G7 at a resort he still owns and profits from explained." *Vox.* 26 Aug. 2019.

Russia Mania on Lenin Monuments. 2019. Rusmania.com.

Ryback, Timothy W. "Hitler's Forgotten Library: You can tell a lot about a person from what he reads. The surviving—and largely ignored—remnants of Adolf Hitler's personal library reveal a deep but erratic interest in religion and theology." *The Atlantic.* May 2003.

Sabbagh, Dan. "Cambridge Analytica parent company had access to secret MoD information." *Guardian.* 29 Mar. 2018.

Sampathkumar, Mythili. "Last surviving prosecutor at Nuremberg trials says Trump's family separation policy is 'crime against humanity.'" *Independent.* 16 October 2018.

Samuels, Brett, "Backlash erupts at video depicting Trump killing media, critics." *CNN.* 14 Oct. 2019.

Santino, Umberto. "The financial mafia. The illegal accumulation of wealth and the financial-industrial complex." Centro Siciliano di Documentazione "Giuseppe Impastato." Undated.

Scahill, Jeremy. "Why Is Obama Still Using Blackwater?" *CBS News*. 17 Sept. 2009.

Scales-Trent, Judy. "Racial Purity Laws in the United States and Nazi Germany: The Targeting Process.", 23Hum. Rts. Q.259 (2001). University at Buffalo School of Law Digital Commons @ University at Buffalo School of Law. Human Rights Quarterly. 23 (2001) 259-307 © 2001 by The Johns Hopkins University Press.

Scalia V. (2016) *Organised Crime or White-Collar Crime? The Case of the Sicilian Mafia.* In: Crime, Networks, and Power. Palgrave Macmillan, Cham.

Shannon, Don. "Reagan Defends Cemetery Visit: Says German Dead Are Also Victims of Nazis." *Los Angeles Times*. 19 Apr. 1986.

Schmidt, Mike. "Justice Dept. Never Fully Examined Trump's Ties to Russia, Ex-Officials Say. The New York Times. 3 Nov. 2020.

Schreckinger, Ben. "The Happy-Go-Lucky Jewish Group That Connects Trump and Putin: Where Trump's real estate world meets a top religious ally of the Kremlin." *Politico*. 09 Apr. 2017.

Schwaab, Edleff H. *Hitler's Mind, A Plunge into Madness.* (New York: Greenwood Publishing Group, Inc., 1992), xxxvii.

Schwartz, Brian. "GOP megadonor Mercer family donated to a nonprofit conservative group that focuses on historical values of 'English-speaking peoples.'" *CNBC, Inc.* 13 Mar. 2019.

Schwartzman, Paul. and Michael E. Miller. "Confident. Incorrigible. Bully: Little Donny was a lot like candidate Donald Trump." *The Washington Post*. 22 June 2016.

Scrivner, Coltan et al. "Gruesomeness convey formidability: Perpetrators of gratuitously grisly acts are conceptualized as larger, stronger, and more likely to win." Department of Comparative Human Development, The University of Chicago; Chicago, Illinois.

Secret Report. "Five Ideological Tools." Declassified. CIA Report: RPD 80-01065A000200080053-0. Released *Central Intelligence Agency*. 30 Aug. 2000.

Seldes, George. *Witch Hunt: The Technique and Profits of Redbaiting.* Author. Publisher: Modern Age Books. Place of publication: New York. Publication year: 1940.

Sereny, Gitta. "My Journey to Speer." *Independent.* 30 Sept. 1995.

Sergi, Anna. "New York crime families survive and collaborate." Dr. Anna Sergi is a criminology lecturer at the Department of Sociology, University of Essex, United Kingdom, and Deputy Director of the Centre for Criminology.

Shadow (psychology) Carl Jung stated the shadow to be the unknown dark side of the personality. According to Jung, in being instinctive and irrational, the shadow is prone to psychological projection, in which perceived personal inferiority is recognized as a perceived moral deficiency in someone else. -Wikipedia.

Shapiro, Sasha. "Medicine Standing on Its Head." *Geohistory.* 23 Jan. 2018.

Shahak, Israel, and Prof. Michel Chossudovsky, "Greater Israel": The Zionist Plan for the Middle East." *Global Research.* 28 Dec. 2019.

Sherman P. Stratford. "Donald Trump Just Won't Die: By rights, this overextended erstwhile billionaire should be bankrupt by now, but his artful deal with his banks -- 70 of them -- makes the Donald look like a survivor." *CNN Money.* 13 Aug. 1990.

Shevchenko, Vitaly. "Little green men" or "Russian invaders"? *BBC News.* 11 Mar. 2014.

Shreck, Adam. "Iraq suggests Exxon deals with Kurds could stand." *AP Business Writer.* In *Boston.Com/Radio BDC.* 12 Apr. 2012.

Sieradzka, Monika. "Poland plans to tear down hundreds of Soviet memorials." *DW News.* 13 Apr. 2016.

Simonov, Konstantin. "Russia 2006 Report on transformation." President the Center for Current Politics in Russa, (Moscow). III EUROPE–RUSSIA ECONOMIC FORUM Vienna, April 23–24, 2007. Publisher *Fundacja Instytut Studiów Wschodnich Foundation Institute for Eastern Studies ul.* Solec 85 00–382 Warszawa. ISBN 83–60172–01–3.

BIBLIOGRAPHY

Skull and Bones, a secret society of senior (fourth-year undergraduate) students at Yale University, New Haven, Connecticut, was founded in 1832. Male society members are called Bonesmen, and many have ascended after graduation to business or government prominence. Three of them—William Howard Taft, George H.W. Bush, and George W. Bush—became U.S. presidents. The emblem of the society is skull and crossbones with the number "322" beneath it. The name is generally taken to refer to the year (322 BCE) of the Greek orator Demosthenes' death, a turning point in transforming ancient Athens from democracy to plutocracy. -- Editors of Encyclopedia Britannica.

Smelser, Von Ronald M. "Hitler and the DNSAP: Between Democracy and Gleichschaltung." This is a revised version of a paper presented at the American Historical Association's annual Convention in Dallas/Texas, December 27—30, 1977. 1. Note: Gleichschaltung, the standardization of political, economic, and social institutions as carried out in authoritarian states.

Smith, Chris. "Jared Kushner and Donald Trump: Like Father, Like Son-in-Law." *Vanity Fair.* 26 May 2017.

Smith, Greg B. "Mob Looted Tax-Break Towers Rising Along the High Line: Feds." *The City.* 09 Dec. 2019.

Snow, Shawn. "16 Camp Pendleton Marines arrested by NCIS for alleged human smuggling and drug offenses." *Marine Corps Times.* 26 July 2019.

Social Network Analysis (SNA) Examples of social structures commonly visualized through social network analysis include social media networks, memes spread, information circulation, friendship and acquaintance networks, business networks, knowledge networks, complicated working relationships, social networks, collaboration graphs, kinship, disease transmission, and sexual relations. These networks are often visualized through sociograms in which nodes are represented as points, and ties are represented as lines. These visualizations provide a means of qualitatively assessing systems by varying their nodes and edges' visual representation to reflect interest attributes.

Sonne, Paul. "Trump poised to get new low-yield nuclear weapons." *The Washington Post.* 13 Jun. 2018.

Sobibor, Poland, Death Camp was created by order. Wannsee Conference on Jan. 20, 1942. The conference began with a recap of all past efforts aimed "to cleanse German living space of Jews legally." See Jasch, Hans-Christian, and Christoph Kreutzmüller. *The Participants. The Men of the Wannsee Conference.* Berghahn, New York and Oxford. 2017.

Social Pathology in Theory In biology or medicine, when a living organism contracts an illness or virus, it may severely weaken or die. In social pathology, psychologists and sociologists think of societies as living organisms that need a specific function correctly. From their perspective, when a community contracts an illness or pathology, society can weaken or collapse if the cause cannot be discovered.

Soldatov, Andrei, and Irina Borogan. *The Compatriots: The Brutal and Chaotic History of Russia's Exiles, Émigrés, and Agents Abroad.* Public Affairs (October 8, 2019) ISBN-13: 978-1541730168.

Sorluca, Daniel. "The Annexation of National Socialism by Hilterism." *The University of Sidney.* Masters Government and International Relations. 24 Oct. 2014.

Sparer Adler, Joyce. *War in Melville's: Imagination* (N.Y.U. Press, 1981): p. 127, defending Melville's Indian-hater episode in "The Confidence-Man" from charges of racism.

Spark, L. Clara. "Klara Hitler's Son: Reading the Langer Report on Hitler's Mind." *Social Thought and Research, Volume 22, Number 1&2* (1999), pp. 113-137.

Speech and pictorialism. In the history of photography, the term "pictorialism" refers to an international style and aesthetic movement that flourished in particular between 1885 and 1915. Involving some of the most outstanding photographers of the time, pictorialism was a refined art photography style. The camera artist manipulates a stock photo to create an "artistic" image. Speech can also transmit emotional and mental imagery.

Speer, Albert. "His final statement to the Nuremberg court." 31 Aug. 1946. Trials of The Major War Criminals. Before the International Military Tribunal. 14 November 1944- 01 October 1946. Published Nuremberg, Germany 1947. See Khoshkish, A. *The Socio-Political Complex: An Interdisciplinary Approach to Political Life* (Pergamon international library of science, technology, engineering, and social studies). Pergamon; 1st edition 22 Oct. 2013.

Spencer, Keith A. "Jared Kushner wanted to use the Russian embassy to make secure phone calls to Kremlin." *Salon,* 17 May 2017.

Spotts, Frederic. *Hitler and the Power of Aesthetics.* Harry N. Abrams; 1 edition (January 6, 2003). ISBN-13: 978-1585673452.

Ssorin-Chaikov, Nikolai. *Two Lenins: A Brief Anthropology of Time.* 2017 Hau Books, Chicago. ISBN: 978-0-9973675-3-9 LCCN: 2017934091.

State of New Jersey, "Executive Summary, The Tri-State Joint Soviet-Émigré Organized Crime Project, The Nature of Russian-Émigré Crime."

Steorts, Jason Lee. "Alan Dershowitz's Standard for Impeachment Would Make the Constitution Self-Undermining." *National Review.* 31 Jan. 2020.

Strenger, Carlo. "Netanyahu and the Mystics of Safed." *Haaretz.* 17 June 2011.

Steve Bannon's fascism. This fascism is presented as a strong arm. Still, closer scrutiny shows it's closer to neofascism blending with white-collar mafias, components of alternative right ideologies, of the post-Soviet era.

Strickland, Ronald. "The Western Marxist Concept of Ideology Critique." *Michigan Technological University Department of Humanities.* VNU Journal of Social Sciences and Humanities 28, No.5E (2012) 47-56.

Stone, Tobias. "The Trump Kleptocracy: The presidency is officially a cash grab — and a pitstop on the way to autocracy." *Medium Corporation.* 22 Oct. 2018.

Sudakov, Dimitri. "The Soviet Union that Hammer built." *Pravda.* 23 May 2012.

Surkes, Sue. "Oligarchs are pumping money into Elkin Jerusalem mayoral campaign, filing shows." The *Times of Israel*. 24 Oct. 2018.

Surrealism. *Surrealism* indicates a specific thought and movement in literature, the arts, and theatre, which tries to integrate the confused realms of imagination and reality. The proponents of surrealism endeavor to mix up the differences of conscious and unconscious thought through writing and painting by using the irrational juxtaposition of images. A 20th-century avant-garde movement in art and literature sought to release the unconscious mind's creative potential.

Sutherland, Edwin H. "White-Collar Criminality." *American Sociological Review*. Volume 5 February 1940 Number 1.

Suvin, Darko. Emeritus. "To Explain Fascism Today." *McGill University, Montréal QC, Canada* 05 July 2017. Contributing editor *Dichtungsring* (Germany, 1988--). Member of Management Comm. of Literary Research Foundation of Canada; Advisory Board, Utopian *Studies, Conflitti globali, UBIQ* [Zagreb}.

Sutton, Antony C. *Wall Street and the Rise of Hitler*. Studies in Reformed Theology 2000. Also, see Carroll Quigley's *Tragedy and Hope*.

Synovitz, Ron, and Sirojiddin Tolibov. "'Thieves-In-Law' Syndicate Crowns New Crime Boss From Uzbekistan." Radio Free Europe. 18 Apr. 2019.

Szabo, Bernadette. "Hungary's Orban vows defense of 'Christian' Europe." *Reuters and Al-Jazeera*. 10 Feb. 2019.

Tevzadze, Gigi. "Thieves-in-law: New Facts for the History of Social Control." *Ilia State University*. Die Idee der Freiheit in Philosophie und Sozialwissenschaften, Benjamin Verlag, Amsterdam 2009.

Thachuk, Kimberley L and Rollie Lal, eds. *Terrorist criminal enterprises: financing terrorism through organized crime.* Praeger Security International. ISBN: 978-1-4408-6067-6. Copyright 2018.

The Economist. "Come and be an Israeli!" 10 Sept. 2011.

Thieves-in-law: The notion itself is a construct of two terms: the THIEF, in public perception, clearly indicating the criminal sphere, and the LAW, which refers to concepts, such as justice, the state, legislation, legitimization, etc. Thus, the Thief-in-law is a notion that reflects a specific social reality, which is understandable for society and represents a part of a social structure regardless of its inner structural controversy. It needs explanation, which involves understanding historical roots and research of the current state of affairs. A **thief-in-law** (Wikipedia):(Russian: вор в зако́не, tr. *vor v zakone*) in the Soviet Union, the post-Soviet states, and respective diasporas abroad is an expressly granted formal and special status of "criminal dignitary" (kriminalny avtoritet), a professional criminal who enjoys a privileged position among other notified mobsters within the organized crime environment and employs informal authority over its lower-status members. The phrase "Thief-in-law" is a rudimentary, word-by-word translation of the Russian slang phrase "вор в зако́не," literally translated as "a thief in [a position of] the law," that can have two meanings in Russian: "a legalized thief" and "a thief who is the law." ---Gigi Tevzadze.

Thieves-in-law, formed as a society for ruling the criminal underworld within the prison camps, governs the dark gaps in Soviet life beyond the KGB's reach. 29 Jul. 2019 –Wikipedia.

Third Rome refers to Russia's doctrine or, precisely, Moscow succeeded Rome and Byzantium Rome as the ultimate center of true Christianity and the Roman Empire. This is the most generally misunderstood and abused of the several expressions of Russia's new place in the world resulting from domestic and international events of the 1430s and 1520s. –Encyclopedia.

Thompson, A. C. (2001, January 6). "Ex-Klansman David Duke Sets Sights on Russian Anti-Semites." *Los Angeles Times.*

Thompson, A.C., and Dara Lind. "Patrol Group Launched as New Degrading Facebook Posts Surface." *ProPublica.* 01 Jul. 2019.

Thompson, Scott. "Soviet Fixer from Lenin to the Present." *EIR* Volume 12, Number 35, 06 Sept. 1985. EIR News Service, P.O. Box 17390 Washington, D.C. 20041-0390 Order #85006.

Tombazos, Stavros. *Time in Marx: The Categories of Time in Marx's Capital.* Translated by Christakis Georgiou. Chicago: Haymarket Books, 2014.

Tooze, Adam. *The Wages of Destruction: The Making and Breaking of the Nazi Economy.* Penguin Books; Reprint edition (February 26, 2008). See *the Deluge: The Great War, America and the Remaking of the Global Order, 1916-1931. Viking; 2nd Printing edition (November 13, 2014)*

Torok, Robyn. "Symbiotic radicalization strategies: Propaganda tools and neuro-linguistic programming." Edith Cowan University. Australian Security and Intelligence Conference. The Proceedings of [the] 8th Australian Security and Intelligence Conference, held from 30 November – 2 December 2015 (pp. 58-65), Edith Cowan University Joondalup Campus, Perth, Western Australia.

Trevor-Roper, H.R. "The Phenomenon of Fascism." European Fascism. Edited by S.J. Woolf. London: Weidenfeld and Nicolson, 1968.

Trotsky, Leon. "My Life: An Attempt at an Autobiography." Chapter XXIV, In Petrograd. Dover Publications; Dover Ed edition (April 5, 2012).

Trump: (*After) Trump's family separation policy went into action, immigrant Marco Antonio Muñoz had his family taken away. Then he killed himself.* A father separated from his wife and child under Trump's harsh new border separation policy. Marco Antonio Muñoz killed himself while in custody in a Texas jail, days after the Trump administration activated its "zero tolerance" approach to border crossings. Under this new policy, families crossing the border are prosecuted, which triggers families' separation.

Tuohy, John William. "John Tuohy Russian Mafia Gangster Blog." My Writer's Site. Bloglapedia Family of Blogs. John William Tuohy lives in Washington, DC. Accessed 05 Oct. 2019.

Unger, Craig. "Trump's Russian Laundromat." *The New Republic.* 13 Jul. 2017.

US History. "Radical Republicans." *Online Highways*, 4969 Hwy 101, Florence, OR 97439. 1 (800) 348-8401.

Vanden-Heuvel, Katrina. "Trump's Most Dangerous Betrayal Yet." *The Nation*. 27 Mar. 2018.

Vanderspoel, J. Lactantius. *In the Manner, which the Persecutors Died*. Department of Greek, Latin and Ancient History, University of Calgary.

van Dijk, Meintje. Edward Kleemans and Veroni Eichelsheim. "Children of Organized Crime Offenders: Like Father, Like Child? An Explorative and Qualitative Study into Mechanisms of Interdependent (Dis)Continuity in Organized Crime Families." Eur J Crim Policy Res (2019) 25:345–363.

Vernon, W. H. D., MD *"Hitler, the man – notes for a case history" (PDF-Datei; 2.8 MB)*. In: *The Journal of Abnormal and Social Psychology*, Volume 37, Issue 3, July 1942, P. 295–308; compare Medicus: "A Psychiatrist Looks at Hitler." In: *The New Republic*, April 26th, 1939, P. 326–327.

Viereck, George Sylvester. *Kaiser on Trial*. The Greystone Press. Virginia. 1937.

Viereck, George Sylvester. "Speech at Madison Square Garden." 17 May 1934. RG 59, Box 4729, Folder 3, *National Archives and Records Administration*.

Vogel, P. Kenneth, Jim Rutenberg, and Lisa Lerer. "The Quiet Hand of Conservative Groups in the Anti-Lockdown Protests." *The New York Times*. 21 Ar. 2020.

Vujacic, Veljko. "Gennady Zyuganov and the "Third Road." *Post-Soviet Affairs*. May 2013.

Volk, Evgueni Ph.D. "Who Are You, Comrade Zyuganov?" *The Heritage Foundation*. No. 108 June 6, 1996. The Heritage Foundation Moscow Office.

Völkisch movement. The völkisch movement (German: Völkische Bewegung, "folkish movement") was a German ethnic and nationalist movement from the late 19th century until the Nazi era. Erected on the idea of " blood and soil, "characterized by the one-body-metaphor (Volkskörper) and the idea of naturally grown communities in unity, it was an organicist, racialist, populist, agrarian, romantic nationalist and, from the 1900s onward, an antisemitic movement. -Wikipedia.

Volkova, Elena. "Communist Christianity as Russian Political Religion: Does Putin's Dystopia look like Trump's Dream?" *Journal of the European Society of Women in Theological Research* 27 (2019) 279-298.

Vygotsky, Lev Semyonovich (a Bolshevik rose in authority as a Communist after transforming his Jewish sounding name). His presentations discussed learning, psychology, and internalization in Soviet-Russia: Vygotsky studied child development and the significant roles of cultural mediation and interpersonal communication. He observed how higher mental functions developed through these interactions and represented a culture's shared knowledge. This process is known as internalization. *Internalization* may be understood in one respect as "knowing how." New World Encyclopedia.

Wagener, Volker. "How Germany got the Russian Revolution off the ground." *Deutsche Welle DW News Europe*. 07 November 2017.

Wald, James. "Lenin's Willing Industrialist: The Saga of Armand Hammer." *Occidental Observer*. White Identity, Interests, and Culture. 18 Nov. 2017.

Walsh, Joan. *What's the Matter with White People: Why We Long for a Golden Age That Never Was?* Wiley; 1 edition (August 1, 2012). ISBN-13: 978-1118141069.

Walsh, Savannah. "Melania Trump Was Secretly Recorded Addressing Trump's Child Separation Policy, White House Holiday Décor." ELLE. 2 Oct. 2020.

Wamsley, Laurel. "'They Just Started Waling on Me': Violence in Portland As U.S. Agents Clamp Down." *National Public Radio*.20 Jul. 2020.

Weber, Thomas. "Hitler Created a Fictional Persona to Recast Himself as Germany's Savior." *Smithsonian Magazine*. 10 Jan. 2018.

Weisbord, Albert. "Bolshevism, Fraudulent Practice of Democratic Centralism." "*La Parola del Popolo*" November/December 1976.

Wentworth, Mary L. "Guest column Mary Wentworth: Is the Mueller report a hoax?" *Daily Hampshire Gazette*. 01 July 2019.

Westphalian sovereignty, or state sovereignty, is a principle in international law that each state has exclusive authority over its territory. The principle underlies the modern international system of sovereign states. It is enshrined in the United Nations Charter, which states that "nothing should authorize intervention in matters essentially within the domestic jurisdiction of any state."

White, M. H. II, & Crandall, C. S. (2017). Freedom of racist speech: Ego and expressive threats. *Journal of Personality and Social Psychology, 113*(3), 413-429.

White, Thomas. "The hollow men: moral evil as privatized self." The Free Library. 2015 *Association for Religion and Intellectual Life* 19 Jun. 2019.

Whylie, Christopher. *Mindf*ck: Cambridge Analytica and the Plot to Break America.* Random House (October 8, 2019). ISBN-13: 978-1984854636.

Wilkie, Christina. "Trump Held Fundraiser for Pam Bondi At His Palm Beach Mansion After She Passed On Lawsuit." *Huffington Post*. 09 Jun 2016.

Woodward, Bob. *Fear: Trump in the White House.* Simon & Schuster Audio; Unabridged edition (September 11, 2018). ISBN-13: 978-1508240099.

Wood, Daniel. Modern Language Studies. Melbourne University. Undated paper.

Wolff, Michael. *Fire and Fury* Henry Holt and Co.; 1st Edition (January 5, 2018). ISBN-10: 1250158060.

Wunderlich, Sophie. "We See into the Distant Future Because We Know What It Will Be" Destiny, Utopia, and Apocalypse in National Socialism." *Williams College*. Williamstown, Massachusetts. 16 Apr. 2018. Thomas Kohut, Advisor A thesis submitted in partial fulfillment of the requirements for the Degree of Bachelor of Arts with

Honors in History. Yates Memorandum. Copyright © 2018 Gideon Mark. Associate Professor of Business Law, University of Maryland Robert H. Smith School of Business. Professor Mark holds degrees from Brandeis University, Columbia University, Harvard University, New York University, and the University of California. Thanks to Brandon L. Garrett for very helpful comments on an early draft of this manuscript. "One of the harshest and most common critiques of the federal government's response to the Great Recession of 2007-09 has been that the Department of Justice ("DOJ") pursued enforcement actions against financial institutions but failed to prosecute any senior officers employed by those organizations."

Yates, Sally Quillian. Deputy Att'y Gen., U.S. Dep't of Justice, Memorandum to Assistant Att'y Gen., Antitrust Div. et al. (Sept. 9, 2015), Also Hiding in Plain Sight: The Spiraling Cost of White-Collar Crime, Comprehensive Fin. Investigative Solution (Aug. 19, 2015).

Yeadon, Glenn. White Rose. *The Nazi Hydra in America: Suppressed History of a Century*. Progressive Press; First Regular Edition. 31 Oct. 2008). ISBN-10: 0930852435.

Yen, Hope. "Fact Check: Trump Wrongly Says His Father Was Born in Germany." *Bloomberg. Associated Press*. 02 Apr. 2019.

Young, James E. "The Terrible Beauty of Nazi Aesthetics," in The Stages of Memory: Reflections on Memorial Art, Loss, and the Spaces Between (University of Massachusetts Press, 2016), 127.

Yourman, Julius. "Propaganda Techniques Within Nazi Germany." *Journal of Educational Sociology*, Vol. 13, No. 3, Education Under Nazism (Nov. 1939), pp. 148-163.

Zerofsky, Elisabeth. "Viktor Orbán's Far-Right Vision for Europe." *The New Yorker*. 14 Jan. 2019.

26 Stat. 209 (1890), 15 U.S.C. §1 (1958): "Every contract, combination in the form of trust or otherwise, or conspiracy, in restraint of trade or commerce among the several states, or with foreign nations, is declared to be illegal."

INDEX